MEXICO UNDER FIRE

Samuel Ryan Curtis (Massachusetts Commandery of the Loyal Legion and the U.S. Army Military Institute).

MEXICO UNDER FIRE

Being the Diary of
Samuel Ryan Curtis
3rd Ohio Volunteer Regiment
During the American
Military Occupation
of Northern Mexico
1846 ~ 1847

Edited and Annotated by Joseph E. Chance

Texas Christian University Press: Fort Worth

Library of Congress Cataloging-in-Publication Data

Curtis, Samuel Ryan, 1805–1866
    Mexico under fire : being the diary of Samuel Ryan Curtis, 3rd
Ohio Volunteer Regiment, during the American military occupation
of northern Mexico, 1846–1847 / edited and annotated by Joseph E.
Chance.
        p.   cm.
    Includes bibliographical references (p.) and index.
    ISBN 0-87565-127-5
    1. Curtis, Samuel Ryan, 1805–1866—Diaries.   2. Mexican War,
1846–1848—Personal narratives, American.   3. United States.
Army.   Ohio Infantry Regiment, 3rd (1846–1847)   4. Mexican
War, 1846–1848—Campaigns—Mexico.   5. Soldiers—Ohio—
Diaries.   I. Chance, Joseph E., 1940–   .   II. Title.
E411.C87   1994
973.6′2—dc20   94-5666
                                                                            CIP

To the memory of
Robert E. Greenwood
this book is respectfully dedicated.
May Math-e-magic live
forever.

Contents

Acknowledgements

Tʜᴀɴᴋs are due to many people who aided me in the preparation of this work. The Bancroft Library, University of California, Berkeley (which owns the Curtis diary), kindly granted me permission to publish this edited version. Special thanks are due to Dr. Bonnie Hardwick, Head of the Manuscripts Division of that library.

The interlibrary loan staff at the University of Texas – Pan American is due my special thanks for the efficient handling of hundreds of requests for peripheral materials. Nicole McKelvy, Virgie Waller, Dian Cook, and Ruben Coronado are a credit to their institution.

Dr. Sarah Neitzel, former chair of the Department of History and Philosophy, facilitated the preparation of this text by the loan of a microfilm reader from her department. This kindness made my labors much easier.

The Mississippi Department of Archives and History was very helpful in locating information on Jesse Edwards.

Several individuals supplied information which aided the successful completion of this manuscript: Charles Spurlin of Victoria College; Laurier McDonald of Edinburg, Texas; Caleb Coker of Jacksonville, Florida; Tom Fort of the Hidalgo County Historical Museum; and Dr. Jeffrey Mauck of New Albany, Indiana. Sincere thanks are due to each.

The maps and several of the illustrations herein were drawn by Dr. Will Martin of the Art Department, University of Texas—Pan American. Thanks are due for his keen eye and steady hand.

Eva Martinez was ever helpful and cooperative in leading me

through the maze of incompatibility created by my use of two different word processing systems.

Finally, I wish to thank the Texas Christian University Press for agreeing to publish this book, and especially Tracy Row of the press for his direction in editing the manuscript into a form suitable for publication.

Introduction

AMUEL RYAN CURTIS, son of a revolutionary war veteran, was born on February 3, 1805, near Champlain, New York.[1] The family soon moved to Licking County, Ohio, where Curtis spent the days of his childhood "in sugar camps." He was accepted as a cadet at the United States Military Academy and graduated from the institution in 1831. The young second lieutenant tarried at home only long enough to marry his childhood sweetheart, Belinda Buckingham, on November 3, 1831, before reporting for duty with the 7th Infantry at Fort Gibson, Indian Territory. His new wife accompanied him on this assignment.

Curtis resigned his military commission in the summer of 1832, and returned to Ohio to apply his West Point-acquired engineering talents to several projects of internal improvement for the nation. He was employed as an engineer on the National Road and by 1837 was the chief engineer of an improvement project for the Muskingum River in eastern Ohio. While administering this project he studied law, and for several years afterward he maintained a law office at Wooster, Ohio.

With the Declaration of War by the United States against the Republic of Mexico on May 13, 1846, Curtis was appointed adjutant general for the State of Ohio. He quickly set about organizing three regiments of volunteer infantry that were to serve with General Zachary Taylor in northern Mexico. Curtis assumed command of the 3rd Ohio Regiment. His diary begins with his embarkation at Cincinnati on July 3, 1846, for a one-year tour of duty.

The troops of Curtis' command, however, were not taken forward on the advance into Mexico. The strict military bearing and discipline of the regiment had impressed observers, and consequently it was ordered to remain in garrison at Matamoros to maintain peace and tranquillity in that city. The editor of the Matamoros *American Flag* reported with a deep feeling of relief on August 12, 1846, that "The third regiment are stationed at this place. They are very neat in their appearance, and conduct themselves in a very becoming manner. . . . The 3rd is commanded by Col. Curtis, a gallant and worthy officer." Matamoros at that time was a virtual powder keg, needing only a tiny spark for ignition. American regular troops and volunteers along with rowdy camp followers, whiskey merchants, and prostitutes mingled freely on the streets with Mexican civilians, merchants, and an unhealthy cadre of *ladrónes* and *rancheros*. This explosive collection of humankind could erupt into violence with the slightest provocation.

The need for laws and statutes for the military occupation and governance of conquered foreign territories had never been anticipated by the U.S. Congress. Furthermore, the military code of justice of the period made no provision for the trial and punishment of soldiers committing crimes against civilians of a conquered territory. But Curtis and others in authority managed to avoid total anarchy by using common sense, diplomacy, and expressions of good will toward the people of Matamoros and their existing civil government. This was the model of governance applied almost universally by the military as they strove to manage occupied northern Mexico.

By February, 1847, the 3rd Ohio had been moved upriver to Camargo. This little village, located on the Rio San Juan about three miles above its juncture with the Rio Grande, had become a vast warehouse of supplies for American soldiers at Monterrey and Saltillo. From this observation post, Curtis described the great suspense felt along the Rio Grande as General Santa Anna's forces encircled Taylor's army early in 1847. From Camargo, Curtis wrote a now-famous letter dated March 2, to President James K. Polk warning the president of the grave danger faced by Taylor:

> Communication with the army in advance of this place has been cut off for several days. . . . [F]rom the reports of

Mexicans and circumstances surrounding this place I am convinced that General Taylor is attacked in front by a large force and circumvented by a very large force of Cavalry which has cut off all communication. Should General Taylor repel the force of Santa Anna in front, still it will as I believe require a large force to scatter the Cavalry on this side of the mountains and to render his victory available the enemy should be followed to the City of Mexico. [I] therefore respectfully solicit a [force] sufficient not only to make success available, but also to provide for any disaster that may arise. . . . Under every view of the subject, I therefore estimate the force required at 50,000 men. . . .[2]

President Polk received this communication on the evening of March 23 and confided in his diary that, ". . . Col. Curtis must have been greatly and unnecessarily alarmed, for he asked for a reinforcement of fifty thousand men." After a long discussion with the bearer of Curtis' letter, Polk expressed the opinion that, ". . . the rumors of the perilous condition of the army on the line of the Rio Grande were greatly exaggerated."[3]

Thus, even the authorities in Washington were unaware of the perilous position of Taylor's army in northern Mexico and the potential for a major American defeat that could have been a turning point in the war with Mexico.

The news of Curtis' request for 50,000 troops was reported to the public in the March 23rd issue of the *National Intelligencer*[4] of Washington, D.C. This news, however, was followed quickly by published rumors of Taylor's stunning victory at Buena Vista; official reports of victory arrived in Washington on April 1. As accounts of the American victory at Buena Vista echoed across the nation, newsmen challenged the credibility of Curtis' assessment of the military situation along the Rio Grande and in northern Mexico. Editors far from the scene of danger were quick to ridicule Curtis in print. An agonized Curtis wrote to his brother, in response to these accusations that ". . . I have been falsely and villainously assailed by a corrupt and political press . . . but I hope to get to live long enough to disarm the cowardly vultures who seek to feast themselves on my reputation."[5]

By June, 1847, the one-year enlistment period for the men of the 3rd Ohio had expired and the regiment was ordered from Saltillo to Cincinnati to be mustered out of service. Curtis remained in Saltillo at the request of General John Ellis Wool to serve as military governor of that city. He took the assignment largely because he hoped to be part of an offensive launched from Saltillo into central Mexico. When it became apparent that the American thrust against Mexico City would be directed by General Winfield Scott, Curtis resigned his appointment and returned to his Ohio home. Curtis moved to Keokuk, Iowa, shortly after his return where he worked as chief engineer on a Des Moines River improvement project.

The activities of the 3rd Ohio Regiment in Mexico, however, would not leave him alone. They were to surface again in the politics of Zachary Taylor's bid for the office of president in 1848. The enormously popular Taylor was nominated for president by the Whig Party and opposed by Lewis Cass, the choice of the Democratic Party. The Democrats were in a quandary as to how to oppose Taylor, who had rarely expressed public opinions about politics during his many years of service in the army, and indeed, had not even bothered to vote in presidential elections. Taylor had, however, supplied Democrats in the states of Indiana, Texas, and even Ohio with political ammunition by his disparaging statements concerning the behavior of volunteer soldiers from those states. In official reports of the battle of Buena Vista, Taylor reported that, "the 2d Indiana regiment, which had fallen back, could not be rallied, and took no further part in the action. . . ."[6] "The mounted men of Texas," reported Taylor in official correspondence, "have scarcely made an expedition without unwarrantably killing a Mexican."[7] Some historians believe that Taylor's candid report on the Indiana volunteers cost him that state's popular vote in the election of 1848.

An article appearing in the *Louisville Journal*[8] in early summer, 1848, attacked the 3rd Ohio Regiment for alleged excesses that occurred on their march from Camargo to Monterrey in March, 1847, to reopen lines of communication and supply between Taylor's army and the Rio Grande. The regiment's march, according to an anonymous observer, was "everywhere marked by wanton violence and cruelty," including shooting cattle in "wantonness," larceny of private goods, and the burning of ranchos and private dwellings. Colonel Curtis, formerly a leading Whig of Ohio, came under harsh scrutiny again, this time for his leadership abilities. Taylor characterized the men of the 3rd Ohio (in Curtis' words) as a "set of thieves and a set of cowards." These words were hardened by election's eve to a statement reported in the *Dayton Empire*:

> [Taylor's] first salutation to an Ohio Company of Volunteers at Marin was 'You are all a G_d d____d set of thieves and cowards; you never came here to fight, but to rob and plunder, and will run at the first sight of the enemy.

Curtis, in a letter of September 11, 1848, to one of the captains of his old regiment, wrote in rebuttal: "Kentuckians charging my regiment with disorderly conduct!! There is more arrogance and self conceit in 'Southern Chivalry' than fleas in Mexico. . . . I'd like to have the 'Great Western' [see Chapter 5, note 22] give her account of Kentucky chivalry during the battle of Buena Vista."[9] Curtis did not deny the purported statements by Taylor, however, reluctantly admitting that his men had been "apprehended by the General in the act of hooking chickens," and that he had given the men "some license to forage." Taylor's comments were circulated in Democratic handbills throughout Ohio and in neighboring states where his statements were said to have been directed not only at Ohio troops, but at all volunteer soldiers in Mexico. Democratic mudslinging failed to derail Taylor's successful bid for the presidency, however.

In spite of the feud, Curtis remained in the political arena. He was elected mayor of Keokuk, Iowa, in the spring of 1856 and he served as a Republican representative from the First Congressional District of Iowa in 1856, 1858, and 1860.

With the outbreak of the Civil War, Curtis commanded Union troops in 1862 in the victorious battle at Pea Ridge, Arkansas. He was promoted to the rank of major general in recognition of this victory and given command of the Department of the Missouri. In this position, he clashed repeatedly with the Missouri governor, H. R. Gamble. Removed from his position by President Lincoln, Curtis later commanded the Department of Kansas. By the end of the war, he was in charge of the Department of the Northwest.

After the war, Curtis became involved in building the trans-continential railroad. He died at Council Bluffs, Iowa, on December 26, 1866, while engaged in the project.

With his diary, Samuel Ryan Curtis kept an almost daily record of activities and events associated with his year of service in the 3rd Ohio Regiment. "I wrote for future reference and for the gratification of my own family," he said. "I hope to leave on these pages of this book the evidence of my 'daily walk and conversation.'"

Curtis, in fact, documents the initial attempts by the United States government and the American military to oversee a conquered territory during a time of war, and, in the process, provides scholars with deeper understanding of the campaign in northern Mexico and its lasting effects on the the two countries. American military governors had no firm legal authority with which to administer justice, and authorities in Washington feared enacting new legislation to extend the judicial powers of the military. The result of this impasse was a climate of lawlessness and injustice that encouraged many ordinarily peaceful Mexican citizens to take up arms against the Yankee invaders.

Guerrilla warfare, which could often be confused with banditry, continued throughout the war in northern Mexico with no quarter offered or given by either side. Curtis documents the so-called Marin wagon train massacre attributed in part to the guerrilla bands of Canales and Romero. These forces united with the Mexican light cavalry under General José Urrea on February 22, 1847, to destroy a train of more than 110 wagons bound to resupply Taylor at Saltillo. The captured teamsters were horribly tortured and murdered. Accounts of this "irregular war" fought in northern Mexico seldom appeared in the American newspapers of that time or in official reports.

Curtis was a good observer and an articulate writer. He had a keen interest in the flora and fauna of the Rio Grande Valley, for example, and his detailed observations remind us of what this region must have been like almost a century and a half ago, before intensive agricultural practices denuded the valley of its semi-tropical native brush. His sightings of the whooping crane (now nearly extinct), the roseate spoonbill, and the immense flocks of migratory birds traversing the Central Flyway serve to warn mankind that we must be better stewards of the bounty of nature.

The Mexican people and their culture were of prime interest to Curtis. He lacked the extreme cultural bias found so often in the contemporary diaries and letters of American soldiers stationed in this area. His wide range of Mexican friends extended from the powerful Señor Agustín Menchaca and his family to a humble orphan boy. Of this boy, Curtis recorded, "I had proposed to take him home with me, and he said he would live here but not go so far." Curtis was invited into Mexican homes and ranchos, and reported on Mexican family life, schools, and the "peculiar institution" of peonage — a euphemism for slavery.

The Curtis diary is relatively unknown to most historians of the Mexican War. With the exception of a few minor quotes in one published source and one dissertation, no other use of this body of material has been found. Purchased in 1949 by the Bancroft Library, University of California, Berkeley, the original is contained in three copy books, with the first entry dated July 3rd, 1846, prior to embarcation for Mexico, and the last entry August 3rd, 1847, where he recorded that he ". . . arrived safe at home. . . ." There are twenty-two pages of prefatory material, ninety-two pages of text, and thirteen pages of end material. Entries are handwritten though additional materials — newspaper clippings and copies of pertinent letters — are attached to the entry pages. The end material consists of orders, letter copies, speech transcripts, sketches, and newspaper clippings.

Entries were transcribed from microfilm copies of the original diary supplied by the Bancroft Library; when completed, the manuscript filled almost 300 single-spaced pages. For the sake of brevity, some entries and paragraphs dealing with Curtis's personal life as well as those detailing the tedium of garrison duty have been omitted. Variations in punctuation and spelling have been left exactly as Curtis recorded them.

Joseph E. Chance
Summer 1993

N

OHIO

ILLINOIS

INDIANA

Cincinnati

MISSOURI

St. Louis

Ohio River

KENTUCKY

Fort Smith

TENNESSEE

Mississippi River

ARKANSAS

MISS.

ALABAMA

Fort Jessup

TEXAS

LOUISIANA

New Orleans

Port La Vaca

Padre Island

Fort Brown

Mouth of the Rio Grande

GULF OF MEXICO

Matamoros

MEX

0   100   200   300   400
miles

ONE

From the State of Ohio
To the State of
Tamaulipas

THE Declaration of War against the Republic of Mexico, approved by Congress on May 13, 1846, found the United States army unprepared to wage a "war of conquest." Troop strength was at the lowest level since 1808: about 5,300 regulars were distributed among eight regiments of infantry, two of dragoons, and four of artillery.

To augment this force, Congress authorized President James K. Polk to requisition volunteer units from the states. Not to exceed 50,000 men, they were to be mustered into federal service for a one-year tour of duty. The State of Ohio was asked to supply three regiments of infantry as its part of the requisition. Samuel Ryan Curtis, adjutant general of Ohio, immediately set to work to fill the required ranks. Newspaper advertisements and bulletins requesting volunteer soldiers were published throughout the state. Camp Washington, in the suburbs of Cincinnati near the Ohio River, was designated the point of rendezvous. The ranks were quickly filled from farms and schools by young men eager "to see the elephant" — or so they thought at the time.

In the democratic tradition of the American militia, the men of each regiment elected their officers, and Samuel Curtis stood for and was elected colonel of the 3rd Ohio Volunteer Regiment. Curtis, a West Pointer from the class of 1831, immediately set about trying to knock his recruits into some semblance of military order. After about a month of field instruction, the 3rd Ohio was marched to Cincinnati to be transported to South Texas. There, the Ohioans were to become a part of General Zachary Taylor's American Army of Occupation. Taylor's command was fresh from two victories over Mexican troops at Palo Alto, on May 8, and Resaca de la Palma on May 9, 1846. American forces occupied Matamoros, across the Rio Grande from present-day Brownsville, as Taylor prepared for the upcoming campaign to conquer northeastern Mexico.

The steamboat passage of Curtis and his regiment along the Ohio and Mississippi rivers from Cincinnati to New Orleans underscored the development by mid-nineteenth century of a superior river transportation system. The 3rd Ohio covered about 900 river miles in seven days — about 130 miles per day.

The major river cities along this passage teemed with military activity as volunteers from other states awaited transportation to South Texas. At the Falls of the Ohio near Louisville, Kentucky, troops of the First Kentucky Cavalry, led by Colonel Humphrey Marshall, waited orders to march to Texas. The requisition for Kentucky volunteers was to include one regiment of horse and two regiments of infantry. Across the Ohio River, near the town of New Albany, three regiments of Indiana volunteer infantry awaited steamboats for transportation to Texas. At Memphis, Tennessee, the 2nd Tennessee Volunteer Regiment, led by Colonel William T. Haskill, and the 1st Tennessee Cavalry, under Colonel Jonas E. Thomas, were being mustered into federal service by General John Ellis Wool. The 1st Tennessee Volunteer Infantry, which would come to be known as the "Bloody First" for its participation in the attack on Monterrey, had been transported to South Texas the previous month. At Vicksburg, Mississippi, the 1st Mississippi Volunteer Infantry, Jefferson Davis commanding, had left for New Orleans only hours previous to the passage of that city by the Ohio volunteers.

Troops by the thousands converged on New Orleans to take passage on ships bound for Brazos Santiago off the South Texas coast. Privately owned vessels, hastily converted to transport troops, were chartered by the army quartermaster corps for the Gulf voyage and troops were packed on board. Without adequate sanitary or cooking facilities, many a young soldier faced as much as a week of seasickness on the open decks or in the dark, stinking holds of a ship before being unloaded onto the beaches of Brazos Island. It is no small wonder that the mortality rates from waterborne and communicable diseases were high. Before the cessation of hostilities with Mexico, the beaches and river banks of southern Texas and northern Mexico were dotted with the unmarked graves of American soldiers who had been felled by disease.

July 3, 1846

Left Camp Washington[1] soon after steam raised. The right wing under my command went on steam boat Tuskaloosa.[2] The left wing under Lieut Col. McCook[3] assisted by Major Love[4] shipped aboard the New Era.[5] — My boat left the landing about 1 Oclock amid the cheers and loud hurras of thousands. The New Era followed soon after.

July 4

On the morning of this day found navigators at Louisville. — Col. McCook came on board and reported the loss of one man by drowning a member of the Coshocton Company,[6] who fell over in drawing water from the side of the boat. — Passed the Kentucky Dragoon[7] who were striking their tents at Camp Marshall[8] and taking up their line of march. Col. Marshall[9] and Major Gaines[10] came on board. Great rejoicing on the boat and on the shore as we passed the Kentucky troops. — This has been a glorious 4th July. Soon after leaving the locks[11] we passed the Indiana encampment at New Albany.[12] Neither of these encampments was large; not half the size of ours at Camp Washington.

July 5 Sunday

A very warm day. Many of our men complaining some of them quite sick. Passed several towns. — stopped a moment at Smithland[13] on the Kentucky shore at the mouth of the Cumberland. — On approaching encampments and towns I generally

Cincinnati in 1848 — point of departure for the 3rd Ohio (from the collection of the Public Library of Cincinnati and Hamilton County).

dress my Regiment up in uniforms. — They make a fine appearance and attract great attention and loud cheers from the shore which are heartily responded to by our men on the boat. — It escalates the pride and antimates the spirits of our men. As I am now writing we have passed by a cut off into the mouth of the Tennessee and the drum is beating on our approach to the village of Metropolis.[14] — 10 Oclock at night passed the mouth of the Ohio and entered the great Mississippi River.

July 6th

Passing down the muddy waters of the great river. — At 2 Oclock PM came to the 1st Chickasaw Bluffs[15] which is a red sand bank approximately some 60 or 100 feet high. — The country on both sides wild and generally uncultivated. — This day is very warm but the health of the sick appears to improve.

Captain Kell[16] is quite sick. — Ford[17] who joined the volunteers very feeble with the dyspepsia appears more healthy and mischievous than any one. — Capt Patterson[18] rather ill to day. — Stopped at Memphis for the purpose of calling on Gen Wool.[19] Saw some of the scattering Tennessee volunteers[20] Genl Wool came on board and visited our companies. Great anxiety prevailed among the men to get on shore, and they appeared riotous and rather disorderly after we came away from the landing. — It was dreadfully warm at Memphis though it was near 6 Oclock when we landed. All generally carried umbrellas to shield them from the intense heat of the suns rays.

July 7

We landed this morning on the Mississippi side. Our men were very much amused and disgusted with the Negro quarters. An old Negro woman half naked, with a little baby half clad was a great object of sympathy. She received a great many dimes. The cotton was in bloom and for the first time a great many of our men saw it growing, The flower very much resembles the holly hock. Some dark people and some light yellow almost white. A tree called the sweet gum,[21] new to me, also grows here. — The bark is a little like the oak.

We took a fine bath in the Mississippi and all the men appear in fine spirits. The sick are generally getting better, but the heat is dreadful. — Passed Montgomeries Point without noticing it. Would like to have seen it for no reason only that in 1832 on my way up to Fort Gibson[22] I and my wife were detained here some 2 weeks. — It is at the mouth of the White River and tis said "it holds its own well". —

About 20 miles below passed the mouth of the Arkansas. The water showed its peculiar red tinge. The town of Napoleon[23] at the mouth of this river is a poor looking village. Had a fine shower and hard storm about 4 and [or] 5 P.M. The atmosphere much cooler. The plantations on either side begin to show a fine degree of cultivation. — Generally a common cottage frame house, and near some 8 or 10 small hewed log houses with little porticos, all white washed. These are the Negro quarters. They generally have a very neat appearance.

July 8

Naches [Natchez] is a dull looking place. We see on arriving a line of buildings ware houses generally[24] — near the waters edge. They are rather plain buildings and every thing looked dull. The town on the hill is quite out of sight of the river and we did not stop to visit it. —

In the evening we stopped to wood at a Plantation belonging to a widow I think of the name Edwards.[25] She has I was told three plantations and some 500 Negroes. She was not at home but every thing appears to be under the direction of a very able overseer. The buildings were very neat and the Negro quarters were fit for any one to live in. I went out to the cotton field where a drove of some 50 were harvesting the cotton. They were under the supervision of a very black fine looking Negro who had a most villanous weapon — a large braided whip about four feet long 1 inch thick at the butt and tapering to the end. — Of course this weapon was not a mere ornament though I saw no effectual use made of it during the few minutes I remained. The working party was principally women of all ages from 10 years old up to 50. — They had bare feet and legs up to the knees, and a kind of loose fitting linen frock was suspended about the waist and thrown over one shoulder. They had no covering on their heads and every way appeared ignorant and stupid. —

ONE

July 10

Found ourselves at the New Orleans landing — a very sultry morning and the sun powering down the severest rays I ever experienced. Went to the quarters of Col. Hunt,[26] quartermaster when after waiting some time I found my quarters for encamping upon the Battle ground below the city. I hurried off and had my tents pitched on the very ground where the Battle of New Orleans had been fought. The ground is low and rather pleasantly situated about 5 miles below the city. A fresh breeze which came from the sea helped to cool scorching atmosphere and our men during the evening was generally quite cheerful. At night the mosquitos nearly eat us up (in common parlance) and all became anxious to leave the ground immediately. In the mean time I had been forwarding our arrangements for moving forward.

July 11

The ship Gen Vera commanded by Capt Fairfield of Bangor Maine a vessel of 400 tons. The Charlotte of about the same tonnage and the Brig Orleans were chartered to carry my Regiment to Point Isabelle or to Brazos Santiago[27] — the bar opposite the Point. Twenty days rations of provisions and water were hurried aboard and the Gen Vera and Charlotte came down from the city and we went on board — 4 companies under my command on the Gen Vera and 4 companies on the Charlotte under Lt. Col. McCook. The other two companies under Major Love were to start the next day.

I should have given some idea of my impression of New Orleans, but I could hardly spare time enough to get an impression. A low city — streets generally narrow and very rough. Hot as fire every where one night at the St Charles hotel[28] one of the most splendid lofty buildings I ever saw. I also passed by the St. Patricks Church or cathedral[29] which has an immense tower attached to it.

The Mint and several other buildings were pointed out to me. They are all fine modern specimens of modern architecture but all the rest have a kind of french, spanish, or foreign aspect very unfavorable to ventilation and very different from the gay and splendid picture I had formed of the city. During the evening of my stay in the city, I visited at the house of Capt. Belger[30] Asst quartermaster a very clever man too. He married a daughter of D. Bailes formerly of the army. I saw his mother in law Mrs. Bailes with which I had an old acquaintance at Fort Gibson. I met there also the distinguished Mexican prisoners Gen. la Vega and his aid Mons. Martinez [Mejia]. They spoke no English but had an excellent interpreter. They were very social in their way and very gentlemanly in their manners. The General told me he had a fine band in the Regiment which he commanded; and at the first fire by Gen. Taylor were almost every man cut down. The General has leave to visit Ohio and Kentucky and for that purpose designs to leave for the North in a few days. He complains of the heat of New Orleans and considers it as hard for him as for me.[31]

We stopped and took a social ice cream at a fine store near the St. Charles and farther opposite the Hotel. The General would not go in he is so much an object of remark but prefers to go to quarters a private house in the city. I was very sorry to leave Dr. Jenkins,[32] Capt. Patterson, and Capt. Kell all too sick to persue the journey.

July 13

We were towed out of the river by a steam boat which left the two ships at 6 Oclock this morning. The entrance which we made into the Gulf was through the South West Pass where we found ourselves left at the mercy of the waves and the wind. — We had very little of either, but the broken motion of the ship soon shook up our stomachs and very few at 8 Oclock were able to attend the breakfast call. For myself I was sick as death, and would have given a months pay for a moments rest on dry land. —

July 16

By an observation just taken we are in Latitude 26 degrees 56 minutes and Longitude 93 degrees and 6 minutes so that we are about 200 miles from Brazos Santiago. — Very dull progress and very wearisome. Such a number crowded on a ship with no accomodations for cooking or sleeping, it makes our volunteers feel that they undergo heavy privations and many of them begin to wish they had never volunteered. No doubt this wish will be often repeated in vain before the poor fellows can be permitted to visit their friends and home. — Being a little sea sick all the time a life at sea is to me very uninteresting. I never quite feel easy when I am tossing on the waves. I have never been three days out of sight of land, and the picture of the blue sea has become quite monotonous. A great sheet of blue water covered by a cloudy vault. The sky has rather a strange appearance it seems to be further off and vault of heaven therefore appears much larger than we find it at the North. A few fish jumping up and a few "Mother Currys' chickens"[33] are the only live things except one crow that present themselves. — Our Captain is a very pleasant man and gives every attention to his charges. — We have had several little squalls but no regular storm. —

July 18

I saw a line of low banks which only differs from the water because it is permanent. It is the shore of Texas. And then as I approach that shore I see the ships — some 20 sail lying at anchor[34] and beyond is the Lagoon and further I see the line of the Republic of Mexico. I have in these two months passed from all the endearing charms of social life and now having raised a little army in Ohio I find myself in command of a Regiment and on the shores of an enemies country. I have descended from the highest ground that divides the Mississippi and St. Lawrence and from Lat 40 to Lat 26 — and this too in the hottest season of the year. The men on the vessel look languid and rather sallow in their complexion. I can see that the climate and exposure have made their impression on all of us. Sea sickness especially is enough to reduce our [us]. The water on our vessel has become very disagreeable. The Captain of the boat says he never had water so poor on a boat. —

I have been examining the chart of the Gulf. — There is generally good anchorage for vessels some distance from shore; but vessels have to lay off at a great distance and their freight and passengers are carried in by "lighters". — I anticipate great difficulty in landing. The sea is rough and I do not see how a steam boat can come along side us. Cast anchor about 2 miles from shore. We can count a great number of vessels, tents, and other temporary settlement but there are no permanent buildings. The sea very rough. — Cant land.

July 19

The waves very high. The captain launched a small boat and I went with him to the steam boat which was laying along side a vessel of Kentucky troops.[35] Found them almost as miserable as we had been. On one vessel 3 deaths in the Ky Regt. —

July 20

Landed most of the Regiment and encamped on Brazos Island. On Brazos St. Iago. The best description I can give of this landing is as represented on the next page. It is the principal landing, where all poor suffering mortals traveling to post themselves in Gen. Taylors army have to stop. Every vessel exhibits the same picture. A large crowd of men in dirty underclothes, pale and haggard from several days sea sickness and Billious remittant rush on shore where they hope to find *some* trifling accomodations. But alas! They find a mixture of Mexicans, officers, mules, wagons, and sailors all and each paying no attention to them. No shelter for the sick No house or covering they are permitted even to shelter themselves for a few moments. The buildings of the quartermaster and sutler are here; but they are not adequate and though one of my men appeared to be dying, I was offered no accomodations but directly I got leave to lay him in the cabin of a steam boat and from there I had him transported to Point Isabel (some 4 or 5 miles across the bay or lagoon) where the poor sick man soon bade farewell to a soldiers life. He was a member of the Zanesville Company by the name of Cameron.[36]

July 21

Every day brings new vessels to anchor out in the Gulf but they cannot land their freight. The channel into the Lagoon admits small vessels and steam boats drawing about 10 feet [of] water if the sea is calm; but this appears very seldom . — The brig Orleans has been laying off shore 24 hours with two last companies of my Regiment and I cant yet get the steamer to go and receive them. Every vessel has to wait its time.

July 22

The wind is still strong. Cant land many troops. Capt. Patterson, who I left sick at New Orleans came into camp to day very

Thomas Bangs Thorpe's renditions of the south Texas coast: above, Brazos Santiago; below, Point Isabel (reproduced from Thomas B. Thorpe, "Our Army" on the Rio Grande [Philadelphia: Carey and Hart, 1846]).

much to my surprise. He brought with him a few volunteers who were sick at N Orleans. The vessel he came on was wrecked last night about 12 miles North of here; on the coast.[37] The crew all saved. I was extremely delighted to see the Captain. He was very sick when I left him but he has evinced a strange infatuation to follow on and I think his health is much improved. His company and all the Regiment are much rejoiced to see him. He reports that Capt Kell and Dr. Jenkins who was also left at N Orleans; are improving and will soon be able to come after us.

This sandy desolate place appearing to me like the poorest speciman of earth in North America. The sun has been intensely hot to day. — I was weighed and I draw 179 lbs. a falling off of some 11 lbs. since I left home. The sand dunes fly like snow and covers everything.[38] It is very unpleasant at night. — Hay! what is that cantering over my "sandy floor". Down on him stuck him with my sword point! Ah! it is a crab. Eli says he will be fine for breakfast. There is another crab or spider looking animal that we very often see making holes in the sand. This is a "fiddler" and gentle harmless. There are lizards but no snakes on this island. Fine bathing and a fine sea breeze are sufficient to make this rather a healthy though a very disagreeable location. A kind of saline grass growing in shocks and a kind of springy sea plant like clover bearing very pretty yellow flora is the only variety of growth. The rest is all sand sand! sand! The two companies which came on the Brig Capt Kells and Capt Allens[39] companies, under the command of Major Love arrived.

July 23

Heard yesterday that a new requisition of one additional regiment hs been made on Ohio.[40] Today the Louisiana volunteers,[41] called out by Gen Gaines[42] are on their return from the interior, marching home! They have been out but two or three months and are ordered home while others are being ordered forward. Col. Morgan of the 2nd Ohio[43] and Major Love of the Brig Orleans came on shore and called on me this evening. Col. Clay[44] my old school fellow and Major Fry[45] of the Ky Volunteers called also. All of our companies in misery and in the finest spirits in the world.

ONE

July 24

The Louisiana troops seem to have got dispirited because they were required to clean the ground of their encampments. It is said they gave their General (Genl Smith)[46] the cognomen of Genl Chaparrel had circulated. — The report that he had 5 cents an acre for clearing land.

July 27

After drill concluded I would cross the Lagoon and visit Point Isabella. This point receives its name from the bluff bank which is the head land of a ridge that is washed by the Lagoon which separates Brazos Island from the main land. It is a small field fortification.[47] In the enclosure is a very crowded mass of store-houses and old spanish sheds covered with a kind of sea grass. Dined with the commandant Major Gardiner [Gardner],[48] and and my old friend Capt Swartwout[49] of the regular army. Saw the strange accoutrements taken from the Mexicans on the 7th 8th and 9th May.

July 28

Lost a man who died in Capt Woodruffs company.[50] Charles Burr[51] who resided formerly at Mayesville Erie Cy Ohio. The diarrhea prevails generally in camps. Returned from Point Isabella and published an order to march off from this place on 30th at sun rise.

July 29

Private John Darns [Darne],[52] of Capt Merediths company[53] died this morning. He had been sick for several days. Was a young man of good habits from Coshocton or vicinity. Wrote a letter home.

July 30

Moved to the mouth of the Rio Grande. The march was a delightful one along the beach. We crossed a lagoon called the Boca Cheeka [Boca Chica],[54] which connects the lagoon with the gulf. The ground to our right is low and evidently overflowed when the wind is in that direction.

13

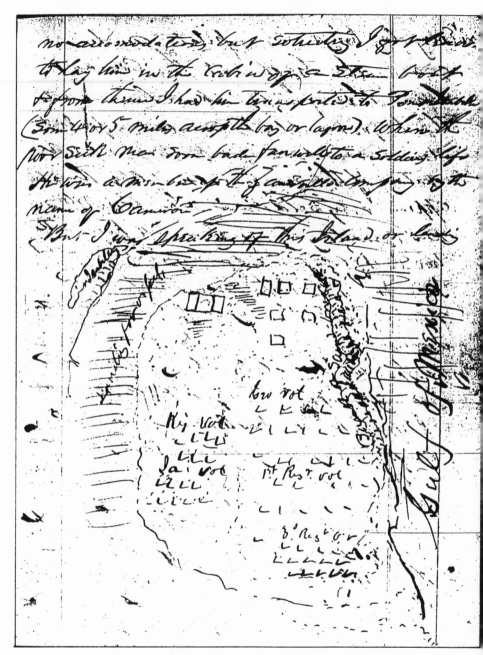

A page from the Curtis diary showing the location of Brazos Santiago camps (Bancroft Library, University of California).

July 31

The encampment is on the low ground near the mouth. The river is some four hundred feet wide. Very muddy and has a rapid current. My old friend E. A. Ogden[55] called on me. He is acting as quartermaster here. The land on both sides of the river is very low. On this side there are no buildings except two or three rough shantees made of planks and wrecks of steam boats which serve the officers as quarters. On the Mexican side are several Mexican houses.[56] I went over to see the people with Lieut Dawson[57] a very gentlemanly man of the regular army. We took a small boat in a few moments we arrived on the opposite side. A jump brought me on the hard clean sandy landing. — Walk up the slope and find ourselves on the unquestionable soil of Mexico. — Look around here and you see Mexican houses, Mexican men and Mexican women. They are all free to act as they please; but they see us on the other side the American flag and its broad folds now extend over this whole region. The houses are about 6 or 8 feet high with roof made of straw extending some ten feet higher. The first hut I entered was tenented by a middle aged woman sitting on the floor cross legged sewing. She had her frock laid loose around her waiste sleeves thrown off so that her waiste above was only covered with a chemise. She was a dark indian looking woman, black eyes black hair and dark skin. This is the character of the lower order of females as far as I have seen. I went into another of these lodges. The first door opened into a room some 10 feet square. The man of the house stood beside a bowl of beer which he sold at a "bit" (ten cents) a glass. I went into the gardens where I found nothing but a luxuriant growth of pumpkin vines and melon vines. Dogs and chickens and calves were the dominant animals. — I found one of the buildings better than the rest. It belonged to the pilot.[58] It was made as most of the rancho buildings were said to be. Wood and mud walls about 8 feet high and covered with a high thatched roof. — The house was about 40 feet square in one room with some four beds with clean furnishings. The floor was earth but clean swept and a servant offered us a glass of water as a testimony of a little kindness. We returned to the east side. I am satisfied with that visit to Mexico unless I can penetrate to the interior.

Aug 1

Marched off 5 companies under command of Lieut Col Mc-Cook with directions to encamp on the beach near the place where we are to make a more permanent encampment opposite Burrita.[59] Marched the remainder up the river. The route lay along the valley of the river, cutting off the bends. The river is the most serpentine stream I ever saw. The banks are very low and the plain is intersperced with lagoons. The day was excessively hot and we marched in column of platoons very slow but in good spirits along the river. — For the first five miles there is no sign of bush or tree. The ground is covered with a kind of rough grass or clover lookings weeds. Large birds of various kinds make their appearance and among the most numerous have been the white crain with black or brown wings.[60] Ducks and geese are also seen but not numerous. About 5 miles up the river we arrive at a sprinkle of woodland. It is composed of the muskeet tree[61] something like a small peach orchard over a few acres. This is the principle tree of this country. It grows from 6 feet to forty feet high and very much resembles in form a peach tree. The leaf however is more like the locust, and I suppose it belongs to that class. It is full of small thorns and makes a good hedge. I halted my command and rested for half an hour under these bushes. — We arrived at the encampment of the right wing in a hard rain. It was a miserable mud hole and I directed the tents to be pitched in a plain more filthy and muddy than most hog pens. I could see about ¾ of a mile back from the river a fine ridge[62] where we had been directed to make our permanent encampment; but our provisions and other baggage was to arrive by the river and it was too hard to pack every thing to the hill at such a time. By cutting weeds and brush we made ourselves places that were tenantable and with scanty supper located ourselves for the night.

Aug 3

Received orders to march forthwith to Matamoros[63] where I am informed that I am to be stationed to defend the place and sustain the laws of the country. This puts us ahead of all the 12 regts of volunteers but they are all to march past us in a few days to Comargo [Camargo].[64] Packed our things on boats and took passage ourselves for Matamoros.

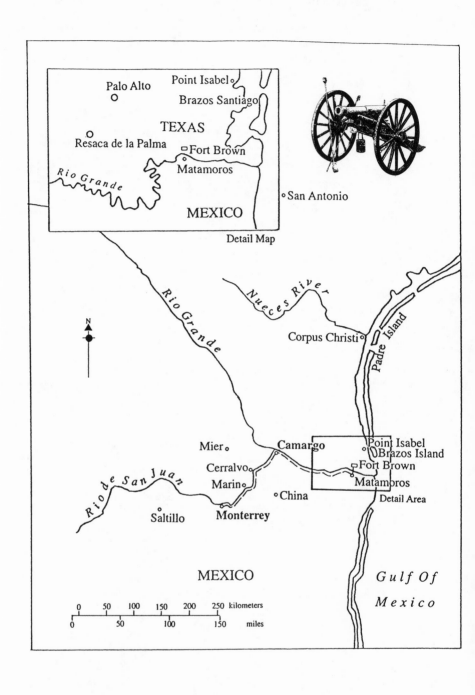

Detail Map

Palo Alto

Point Isabel
Brazos Santiago

TEXAS

Resaca de la Palma

Fort Brown

Matamoros

Rio Grande

San Antonio

MEXICO

N

Rio Grande

Nueces River

Corpus Christi

Padre Island

Mier
Cerralvo
Marin

Camargo

Point Isabel
Brazos Island
Fort Brown
Matamoros

Detail Area

China

Rio de San Juan

Saltillo

Monterrey

MEXICO

Gulf Of
Mexico

0	50	100	150	200	250 kilometers
0	50		100		150 miles

TWO

*American Military Rule
of Matamoros*

ATAMOROS was peacefully surrendered by the alcaldes to American forces under General Zachary Taylor on May 18, 1846. Taylor promised the civic leaders that Mexican civil laws and the rights of private property would be respected and that Mexican citizens living in peace would not be mistreated.

With no comprehensive laws about how Matamoros was to be governed during American occupation, however, city streets quickly descended into a state of anarchy. Camp followers from the earlier post at Corpus Christi descended on Matamoros, bringing gamblers, women of easy virtue, and floods of alcoholic beverages. American-style bars, "hotels," billiard rooms, and dance halls sprang up overnight. The literal dregs of American society were attracted to Matamoros with the prospect that "easy money" could be extracted from naive American soldiers or un-wary Mexicans. As the conflict dragged on the problem only worsened because the military did not have the authority to ban civilian immigration.

Daily acts of murder, robbery, theft, and rape were graphically documented in the bi-weekly Matamoros newspaper, *American*

Flag. Since many of these violent acts were fueled by an abundant supply of alcoholic beverages, Taylor issued "Order No. 94," on August 2, 1846:[1] "No spirituous liquors will be permitted to enter the river or the city of Matamoros. . . ." The law was impossible to enforce and liquor continued to be sold in Matamoros throughout the war.

Mexican citizens committing crimes against each other fell under the jurisdiction of the Mexican courts. For crimes committed by Americans against each other, however, or against Mexican citizens the question of jurisdiction was not as easy to resolve. American civilians accused of crimes were turned over to Mexican authorities but were generally released from custody after a few threats or a bribe. Mexican officials were afraid of recriminations and were quick to release those Americans charged with even the most brutal crimes. In desperation, the American military governor arrested the most flagrant perpetrators, but with no authority to try or punish the criminals, generally had them "transported" to New Orleans, where they were quickly released on *habeas corpus.*

Americans simply did not have judicial experience in governing conquered territory. American soldiers were governed by the articles of war, but the framers of these articles had not anticipated the American military on a mission of conquest in a foreign land. By these acts, soldiers charged with crimes were to be bound over to the civil magistrates with proper jurisdiction if the crimes were committed in the United States. But the articles did not address those charged with offenses in a foreign country. Thus many brutal crimes committed by the regular and volunteer soldiers in Mexico went unpunished. Colonel Curtis, a practicing attorney in civilian life, discussed this dilemma with his brother in a private letter dated of November 14, 1846:

Military law is poorly adapted even to the government of an army. Ours is a miserable code. It does no cognizance of an offense, even among the soldiers of an army neither does it extend to crimes unless you can show they are in someway connected with *mutiny.* Our army is governed by the officers, not by the "notes and articles of war." The laws of Mexico are insufficient and the Judges and Alcaldes would

not dare to condemn one of our citizens. Many criminals
have been sent to New Orleans, where no doubt the words
of Habeas Corpus has turned them loose on community. . . .
If General Taylor had the power of *proclatius dominium* in
issuing edicts perhaps under this we might find some portent
for punishing thieves and murderers: but General Taylor
always takes care to assert no such extraordinary powers . . .
I could not justify myself in ordering my command to execute a criminal unless he has violated our military code. . . .
Neither Mexican or American laws will prevail and justice
cannot be legally administered — the code of law known as
"Linch law" is not likely to be administered by the Ohio
Volunteers.[2]

General Winfield Scott, receiving reports "that the wild volunteers as soon as beyond the Rio Grande, committed, with
impunity, all sorts of atrocities on the persons and property of
Mexicans" courageously assumed the authority to try military
personnel for crimes committed against Mexicans or other
Americans while in Mexico.[3] His "Order 20," issued in Tampico
on February 19, 1847, had received neither the blessing of the
Polk administration nor Congress. "Order 20" established military courts to try Americans for crimes committed in Mexico
against the civilian populace. After several public whippings and
a hanging, such offenses by American soldiers abated in central
Mexico. But the military tribunal system was never very successful in northern Mexico, due no doubt in part to General Taylor's
reluctance to anger potential and future voters.

Aug 4
   The river is very crooked . . . as evening approaches we see the
out line of the city of Mattamorus but it is too late to define its
appearance. About 9 Oclock we land opposite the city. It is some
¾ of a mile from the river. — After seeing my guard properly
stationed accompanied with the captain of the boat and 2 others
I started by moon light for the city. The way is very muddy. A few
deserted Mexican huts are near the river and after that you come

to a canal which connects the river with a lagoon. This canal is covered with excellent brick culvert. Soon after passing this you come to the scattering buildings of the city. These homes are generally brick one story high with slate or brick roof all resembling a system of old forts. Every house seems to possess bars and bolts and the windows of the lower storeys are in some instances 14 feet high with iron bars on the inside. The streets are rather hollow in the center and very narrow. The sides are paved about 4 feet wide with brick. About the principle corners loiter groups of men of all colours and all countries are collected cursing swearing fighting gambling and presenting a most barbarous sight. Volunteers especially are conspicuous in these groups. — I hope in conscience the Ohio volunteers will avoid these scenes. Murder rapine and vice of all manner of form prevails and predominates here.[4] An order has been issued that in 15 days all liquor shall be excluded from the territory and among other duties expected of my Regiment is that of reducing this bedlam to a state of order and decency. I rank these services as honourable but extremely disagreeable. If I can do anything towards reducing this scene of confusion I shall regard it as worthy of all toil. It is a conquered city much the receptacle of all the dregs of the United States. — As it now stands, it is a disgrace to our country; for our own citizens are much worse than the Mexicans who are mixed up with them. Oh vice! how hideous are thy features!

We found it too far to walk back to the boat, so we went to several houses to find a sleeping place. Finally got leave to occupy a large room on the lower floor at the "American" a house kept by a large fleshy lady.[5] The room was at least 20 feet high and no doubt was regarded by its former occupant as of great value. It was a poor dirty looking place now, and did not appear to have been cleaned out for a month. I was given a cot, and a dirty sheet about 2 feet wide for my bed. I was very muddy and after stripping I had a very warm sleep with open doors. Two murders committed in town last night.[6]

Aug 6

After breakfast I returned to the boat and we passed up to Fort Paredes[7] where I stationed two companies A. and B. commanded by Captains McLaughlin[8] and Meradith [sic]. — In the evening I commenced landing and encamping the remainder of my Regiment on the east side of the river a little above Fort Brown.[9] — A Mexican was shot by a Texian a little above camp.

Aug 7

Busy arranging and completing our camp. Received special orders to draw a greater supply of ammunition and prepare my regiment as fast as possible for active duties. Called on Col Clark[10] Gov General who expressed some anxiety about his location. The Mexicans are all around him and he regards his post by no means safe. I have some fears that they may become exasperated at the treatment they receive from some of the volunteers and will rise and murder the American inhabitants in the city. There ought to be a strong police established in or near the city and martial law ought to be declared and executed. Every day produces new scenes of vice and disorder. —

I feel more mortified than indignant at the unnecessary desire manifested by the regular officers to put regulars forward and make them certain to be the authors of every acceptable movement. I admit that Gen. Taylor has had reason to rely on regulars and has had some reason to doubt the conduct of volunteers after the street brawls that have gone off in the city of Matamoros; but I fear there is that prejudice which will exist (and will manifest itself every day) enacted at the head of the army. In fact the *force* here is that of the volunteers, their commandants ought to have a full share in the operations of the army and should be, if competent, placed in commands suited to their rank. I am *honoured* with being selected to aid in the defenses at this place, but I am placed at a distance from the city where I could render no immediate aid if the city were attacked. *Lieut Col* Clark is commandant of the city. Capt Norman[11] with some 30 or 40 Regulars has command of Fort Paredes and I am directed to furnish two companies which is really his effective force. He has no guns that he can use and is busy repairing the fort.

On this side Capt. Lowd[12] an excellent officer has command of Fort Brown. He has few men, but his guns could effectively attack the city at any moment.

Aug 9

This is Sabbath. . . . The bell rang for matins in Matamoros this morning, but how can we expect religion in such a den of thieves robbers and assassins! I believe the place ought to be cleansed with *fire*.

We heard yesterday that the mail carried by express to and from Point Isabella had been chased by a party of Mexicans. This evening the boys came dashing past firing [their] his pistols and crying mail! mail! Our men took it as an alarm and the companies were ordered arms in five minutes. Capt Moore[13] Patterson — the grays under Adjutant Gen and Capt Allens Company of Riflemen were particularly active in coming into the line of battle. All the Regiment manifested much spirit and true courageous readiness and I can hardly believe they would any of them flinch in the event of attack. The alarm was false and so the companies were immediately dismissed.

Aug 12

Sent a party of 12 men under command of 1st Sergeant [John O. Derstine] Company C.[14] to Point Isabella to get letters, explore the country, and guard the Sutlers store as they return. Hicks Curtis sutler started for Point Isabella for his goods. The "flag" [*American Flag*, August 12, 1846] in Matamoros notices our position and, as this is the first notice of us in a *foreign* press I will attach the article.[15]

Sickness in camp appears to diminish generally, but those in the hospital tent continue to drop off or linger in rather dangerous form. I visited the tent this afternoon. Young Christmas[16] well known in several counties in the north of Ohio as a distinguished temperance lecturer has sunk so low his life is being despaired of. I called on him and he recognized me. His conversation was wild and incoherent. Poor fellow, he must die far from friends and kindred. His associates in the company, viz. Stark Rangers — Captain Allens Company — have been very attentive, but the malignant diseases of this climate appear unconquerable. Death makes fearful inroads in the ranks of my regiment. The measles have broken out in the two companies stationed in Fort Paredes.

Aug 13

Poor Christmas died last night about 12 Oclock. This makes about 12 men since we left Ohio besides many have been discharged because their health so enfeebled.

Visited Matamoros and Fort Paredes. The 1st and 2nd Regiment of Ohio Volunteers arrived and encamped on that side. — They are footing it to Comargo. Poor fellows they appeared almost overdone already. They started from Burrita yesterday. There were many reports about Mexicans being in force at Montaray [Monterrey];[17] but the reports are so contradictory one can make no certain estimate of the enemies forces. My own private opinion is that every precaution should be taken. The inhabitants appear very independent in their manners. The lenient conduct of General Taylor has given them the utmost assurance. They regard the war as a kind of visitation by foreigners who are to [be] fleeced by every possible means. Every species of property is much inflated in value since the war broke out so that in a commercial point of view the Mexicans are infinitely the gainors. They have their own laws and magistrates and war to them it seems to me can have no terrors conducted as it now is. *Subjugation* or *devastation* is my view of the matter. The people are semi savage and they must be made to acknowledge our sovereignty or this war will never end.

The funeral of young Christmas. After dress parade and after it was quite dark, accompanied by Lt. Colonel McCook I repaired to Captain Allens Company for the purpose of attending the funeral of young Christmas. The detail, a sergeant, escort, was turned out under arms. Two torches at the head of the procession cast a fluttering light on a plain coffin. The company of Captain Moore attended the funeral so that the procession consisted of two companies and several of the field and staff [officers]. The slow moving procession, with the low deep notes of the drum rendered the scene sad and gloomy. The grave yard selected is north of our encampment by a tree standing quite lonely on the plain. We have been here but a few days; but we have already erected several little mounds over the bodies of our companions. — One case of measles in camp to day. Thermometer about 96 in the shade.

The church at Matamoros as drawn by Thomas Thorpe (from Thorpe, "Our Army").

Aug 15

Visited Captain Webster[18] and Lieut. Donaldson.[19] They are encamped with a small part of their artillery company on our right. Mr. Webster is a very plain good man and Lieut Donaldson is rather a talented young man. They depreciate this war and dislike the character of the country. In fact I have yet to see the first officer who approves of matters generally as they are connected with this service. — Major Love has some fever and I fear he is going to be sick. Received orders to change position of my forces. Place two companies in Fort Brown and march the remaining companies over onto the Mexican side. Rode over to see Col Clark on the subject of location and appointed a meeting with him at the ferry[20] tomorrow at 7 Oclock.

Aug 16

Went over and selected ground on the south side. The river is very high and I see it is going to be difficult to get over to the ground. This is Sunday. In Matamoros it is a day of amusement. I for the purpose of seeing the mode of the people went with Col McCook to the show. It was in a yard. The seats were raised round the enclosure and full of men women and children when we went in. The performance consisted of some rope dancing and a clown singing all a very poor affair, but apparently quite amusing to the Mexicans.[21]

Aug 18

At 3 Oclock this morning I was visited by a messenger who came in breathless haste with an order that I move over forthwith and the messenger informed me that the people in the city were in great terror in fear of a band of Rancheros[22] that were expected to attack the city. The steam boat lay along side. It had drawn off the water from the boilers supposing we would not move till morning. — I was told it would take 2 hours to get steam up! This was terrible. However there was no way to expedite our movement. Steam was hastened forward with all possible haste and our companies (6) were ready to jump on board at day light. We formed on the opposite shore about a mile above Camp Curtis and marched in column to the center of the city and formed line on the plaza. The rancheros about 300 had

entered the city in the evening but fled before day. After reporting myself to Col Clark who said he had been up all night; I
marched to the north side of the city where I encamped calling
the encampment after my faithful Lt. Col Geo W. McCook. —
The move this morning was every where a military one. The
men were all in uniform and marched silently but with a firm
tread to the place where danger was threatened.

The same day "Order No. 13" from the commander of the city
gives me directions to make larger details of officers and men for
guards and patrols for the city. —

Aug 19

Our guards were very faithful and our patrols found the city
very quiet during the last night. Went to market, taking "Little
John" (Major Loves Negro) to carry marketing. The market
building is in the center of a square and is a high range of open
arches the roof of the whole covered with parapet walls. Round
this place are other high arched buildings which are used for
grocery stores confectionaries and etc. In the market every thing
had a very neat and city like appearence. Beef, mutton, eggs, and
many common article were in abundance. Eggs are 3 for a picayune, that is for a sixpence. Chickens two bits a piece and every
thing alike dear. I bought a leg of mutton 25 cents piece of liver
6 cents. Those larger birds of the snipe species already dressed for
three bits. Three little trifling apples 6/4 cents. One pumpkin 6/4
cents apples must be hard if these are a specimen. Perhaps cultivation would improve them.

Aug 20

Last night we were kept on the qui vive by the occasional
discharge of a gun in the city. The patrol was unable to apprehend the individuals who discharged them. They could never be
found. Capt. McCauslin[23] quartermaster appointed by the President arrived and received orders to do duty in this regiment.

Aug 21

Last night Mr. Hicks Curtis headed a patrol and caught two
prisoner. One fired a pistol and Hicks chased him with a revolver
in one hand and sergeants sword in the other till the man

stopped. He was a rather decent looking American, who said he was shooting a dog! The other was also an American, rather tipsy, who had been trifling with the patrol. There is something singular in the first that the pistol was fired at the same place where the disturbance initiated the night previous. I directed the men to be kept under guard till morning when I sent them to Col Clark to dispose of as he saw proper. The Colonel retained them a short time in prison where they expressed so much mortification that they were discharged.

Aug 22

Last night the patrol under Captain Noles[24] took a Mexican all arms and equipment. There were also 4 shots by sentinels at Mexicans but all appeared to have missed. A sentinel was snapped at by a Mexican first. — The Mexican prisoner lay in my tent all night and I gave him his pistols and sword in the morning directing him to journey to his rancho in the day time if he considered it necessary to go armed. He lives in Matamoros and has a rancho in the country. He seemed about as decent as the rest of the Mexican citizens and therefore is well entitled to liberty. They all possess great fear of surrounding robbers rancheros or militia and make this a reason or pretext for always going armed.

Aug 24

Last night a large number of pistols and guns were found in a spanish house. When will we ascertain all the secret mines that surround us?

Aug 25

Hicks Curtis with 5 privates made another tour of patrol duty and caught 4 thievish looking vagrants who were firing guns and pistols near a mean dogary [doggery or grogshop]. They had many Mexicans articles in their hands, no doubt the efforts of stealthy performance. I had them retained all night in the guard house and sent them this morning to Col Clark who discharged them I believe on the promise that they would leave the country. 3 other prisoners, two Mexican thieves and one drunken loafer were also apprehended. The thieves were turned over to the Mexican authority to deal with.

This is Sunday. It is very warm. A great number of the regiment have gone into the city to attend Catholic church. Father McElroy sent out by the President[25] is the only one I hear of who preaches in the English language. There is a kind of tempering whining policy in the position of our government in the matter of sending a Catholic priest into this barbarous Catholic Country. Does our government wish to Catholicise these Catholics, or is the government afraid of Catholicism and do they [do] this to flatter the church with our cause. The mode strikes me as pusillanimous and I place my private opinion here for future reference only. The idea of associating our government with any seat of the church especially one of the most despotic and monarchistic; I regard as encroaching on our Constitutional liberty. —

This evening called on Col Clark and Col. Taylor.[26] The news is in circulation that one of the steam boats above was blown up and some 30 or 40 men killed.[27] Another report has none killed. I called on Henry Clay. Poor fellow he is located in the heart of the city with Lieut Duncan.[28] He dislocated his elbow and has been very sick. I was vexed to see that his matras [matress] was stretched on the brick floor of a low rancho by the side of Lieut Duncan who was laboring under the influence of a severe fever. In a conquered city, where there are hundreds of high and commanding buildings it is outrageous that sick officers should find no better quarters than a shed.

Last night my standing complaint the diarrhea returned upon me with increased energy. I have now been almost constantly under its debilitating influence for a month. —

Aug 26

Feel better today. News reached town yesterday of the revolution in Mexico placing Santa Anna[29] in power and Paredes[30] out. From all appearances the news is true. Some seem to think this revolution will secure an early peace. I cannot see what this has to do with our war. Santa Anna is pledged to go for the war against the United States and if this be a mere pretense, yet he will not dare suddenly to disclose his treachery to his country.

Our daily duty grows rather monotonous. I sit here all day in my tent and sign passes for men, receive reports, and give orders.

Aug 27

A rainy day dark and drizzly. Our tents rainy wet and the ground all mud changes every thing into a dreary picture. Lt Col McCook, Clay, and myself took a long ride leisurely all over the city of Matamoros. In our part east we find an old military barrack quite battered into a ruin. Most of the buildings in that part of the city; show the effects of a terrible tornado that unroofed and destroyed a great part of the houses. This occurred some years since, and very few of the buildings are repaired. There is evidentally a great deal of mercantile business down in the city. Stores are very numerous and they all seem to do a good business.

Sept 1

Last evening I found myself unusually weak at muster and returned [to] camp early. In the fore part of the night I perspired very freely, but before day I awoke with a severe chill. It must have continued near an hour. After the chill I had some fever. During the day and while I write this I am oppressed with a severe head ache and unable to sit up. The doctor directs me to take quarters in the city where he wishes to give me regular treatment. Major Love and Hicks went to the city to purchase lodging. They found the public houses all full. They then went to the U.S. quartermaster who told them he had a fine room on the first floor of a building. — They found all the rooms filled with dead and dying. The association was too chilling, I would rather lay and die in my tent among my companions.

I directed Major Love and our own quartermaster of our own regiment to go up to town and find me quarters by force if necessary. The U. S. quartermaster expressed his want of right to furnish me quarters! Strange that all the lieutenants of the regular army who are stationed here find no difficulty in procuring spacious and commodious quarters. God forbid that I should say aught in [this] matter. I have always been proud of our regular army, but there are some small minds in all places and even good men do not all seem to regard with generous equality those who have volunteered to leave their homes and business to cooperate with them. —

Major Love returned without obtaining a room Col Clark said the orders of Col Taylor required all the property of peaceable Mexicans to be respected. All the property belongs to Mexicans and they all pretend to be peacible; so my quartermaster very properly under this order declaimed taking any for public use. As an officer of the State of Ohio I have often taken from the citizens of Ohio the most valuable property for public uses. It seems the rights of these Mexicans are better guaranteed than the rights of our citizens in the states would be, all of whom yield to the well established law that all the property of citizens may be sacrificed for public uses the state making compensation for the same. — Such a rule is inconsistent with reason and restricts the quarters of the sick so that 15 to 20 are crowded into one room and no doubt adds to the mortality that prevails.

The rule may be kind to Mexicans, but it creates extortion and injustice towards American citizens and adds much to the expense of our Government.

Capt Kell provided a room for me in the city a small one story building in a peaceful part of the town. It will be prepared for me this evening. Col McCook obtained leave of absence to go to Comargo.

Sept 2

I took a severe dose of medicine last night which operated well. I felt much better this morning. The terrible perspirations of last night seemed to reduce me very fast. I think of going into town to day. I have been some three months in the tented field and desire to recruit my health if possible.

After noon. Snugly fixed in a one story building made in american style. A little hall and doors open into two rooms. One north and one south. I have the north room which is well ventilated. I have my boarding house opposite a fine two story shaded brick. My little frame building is surrounded with trees and with a good cot and two soft pillows and fine clean linens.

Sept 3

I had some perspiration the fore part of the night but generally rested very well. I have had a fever from about 5 in the morning till 11 A.M. The doctor gave me 3 more doses of quinine which together with weakness keeps me on the broad of my back.

Col Clark Governor of the city and the American Consul J. P. Schatrell [Schatzell],[31] a very gentlemanly bachelor call on me and spent about an hour. — Col Clark is very much a gentleman and a good officer. He deserves great credit for having ordered this town to order and sobriety. Col Taylors order stopping the vending of liquor is easily evaded, but the system of guards and patrolls established by Col Clark cannot be evaded. Received a letter from my wife which is almost as good as a family conversation. — S. Presner a kind of translator clerk and factotum I should suppose of the Consul Mr. Schatrell bought me some variety of tamarinds out [of] which my landlady Mrs. Kidder[32] made me a delicious drink.

Sept 4

Took more quinine the last nights rest having been a painful mixture or oscillation of fever and perspiration. — To day I have no sign of fever except that my head gets too hot occasionally. Lieut. L. Chase[33] called and transacted business. Had received letters from several on the plane [plain] on the St. John [Rio San Juan],[34] where Gen Worth[35] has established a post [Cerralvo].[36] The account gives a gloomy picture of the country as we pass up the St. John and represents the post as located in a delightful country among "fountains of living waters" one of the dearest objects a country can possess.

Sept 6

Sunday. This is perhaps the hottest day we have had. A man marched off his post laid down to rest his weary brain, and died in ten minutes! Yet the doctor reports that our sick are rather improving though the list is still large say 150 in the whole Regiment. — It has been a very quiet day with me in the city. More like sunday than any day since I left home. Health evidentally improving. Read the Presidents offer of peace and the arrival of Santa Anna at Vera Cruz in the face of our blockading squadron! There is a coincidence![37]

Sept 7

News arrived from the interior reporting that 4 Mexican Generals have gone to Monterray, and that force of 7000 was already accumulated about that place. If this be true, we hope to get orders to march forward. Gen Taylor may find that he needs more rather than less numbers.

Sept 11

It rained last night and is much cooler and now pleasant. In the evening of the day I went out to camp. The walk was rather good for me, but I hope no relapse will grow out of it. The dress parade was a mere skeleton. Not more than ⅓ of the Regiment was out. — Camp looks like a hospital so many pale and sickly faces. The sun came out about noon and usurped again all his energies. When will the heat subside?

Sept 12

Sent letters home dated yesterday. Col. Baker of Illinois volunteers[38] call on me. He was recently badly wounded in attempting to quiet a mutiny between two companies of the Georgia Regiment. The news from the interior continues to bring reports of a gathering storm at Monterray. The flag [*American Flag*] of today again makes favourable mention of my regiment. These are hard earned but respected compliments. I do not know a man connected with the press here, and suppose therefore I must deserve some of it. I'll keep these little complements, they are the tracks we make in the sands of life; and these being far from friends and kindred they should be preserved. Various rumors come in all representing that Mexicans are gathering. They cannot forebear showing their delight at the least sign of revival of their cause.

Sept 13

Last night a party of Texian rangers on their way down from the army were fired on within about 20 or 30 miles of this place. Two men were badly wounded and the party, after returning the fire and driving the Mexicans; made their way to this place leaving one of the wounded men. To day a party headed by these rangers will go after the wounded man. Several of my Regiment go with them. This is sunday and we have a pretty strong breeze from the north. The sun continues intensely hot and I am informed by the hospital stewart that cases of sickness increase in camp. Both Dr. Robinson and Mulvany[39] are sick, the former here in my room and the latter at the house over the way. I am really terrified at this aspect of my regiment. There can hardly be found a well man in camp. Another death by the sun. A man laid down apparently well under his musquito bar, and soon after was found dead! It was one of company G. Capt Woodruffs Company.[40]

Sept 14

Feel rather thick headed and take a portion of salts. The party of Texians it seems killed 3 of the Mexicans.

As the steamboat *Corvette* was wooding yesterday, some volunteers who had walked out were attacked by a daring adventurer, one of Canales men. He was mounted and came up with his lasso making two throws at the volunteers. One of the party had a revolver and gave him two balls to carry off which it is believed proved fatal.[41]

Sept 15

A fine breeze but hot sun at 9 Oclock. News of the loss of the steam boat New York[42] came to town. Many of our men and among them Capt Ford[43] had leave to return home about that time. We fear they were on that vessel. If so they have escaped the Mexicans to find a watery grave. — No news from the army in the interior and no incident of importance occurred here.

Sept 16

Rose early this morning and walked to camp. Two men died yesterday; one was the brother of Capt Woodruff. A great number are sick, but they are generally "on the mend" as they say. Some are dangerous and no doubt many more will have to follow those who have gone before them. — My weight is 154/4 lbs. Received letters from home bearing good tidings dated the 28th of August. — A list of those lost on the New York shows that none of our officers or men were among them.

Sept 17

The river has been falling for the past week and has now got within its banks leaving considerable of ground exposed that has heretofore been covered. News by steamboat Corvette from above that General Taylor left Seralvo on the 13th with his force. The understanding was that some 10000 troops were assembled at Monterray and the Mexicans were fortifying a pass some 10 miles in front of the city with a design of fighting then and if necessary fall back on the entrenchments at Monterray. Gen Taylor will move cautiously no doubt, and move foreward or entrench himself as circumstances may seem to require.

Sept 18

Dr. Stone[44] and quartermaster, Major Arthur,[45] arrived this morning. They had been a long time on their way and bring now news from Ohio. I have been drawing a sketch of Mexico from a french map dated "Paris 1840" by M _____. A. H. Brue.

Sept 20

Sunday. This day always brings with it many dear associations. The *terrible* ringing of bells is always the announcement of sabbath in Mexico. A few attend mass, but all kinds of amusement sought by the large proportion of populace. No news worth rewarding with the miserable steel pen.

Sept 21

It seems the party that went out under Col Cook gave mortal offence to the Mexicans; I suppose he burned 60 or 80 of their huts and killed two men. To day one who acted as guide for Cook was shot dead in the street by a daring fellow on horse back, who came no doubt to avenge himself of the injury inflicted on him. The Mexican guide should be protected by our arms. Cook drew arms and saddles from the quartermasters and was therefore strictly under the protection of our Government. Col Clark no doubt gave no instructions to Cook to commit outrages, but if Cook exceeded justice and duty his guide should not the less deserve protection and his death should therefore in my opinion be avenged by our Arms. Col Clark however turned the matters over to the Mexican Alcalde where it is understood the matter will sleep! If Col Cook exceeded his instructions we should pun-ish him not the Mexicans and a *fortier* the same rule applies to those who were under the command of Cook. If Mexicans dare come to the center of the city in broad day light and kill a man I take it they may in the night find it an easy matter to kill any of us. I shall examine the caps on my pistols very carefully to-night.[46]

Dr. Robinson informs me that for the past two weeks the thermometer has generally reached from 96 to 98 at 12 Oclock! I thought the weather had become cooler. — No news from General Taylor.

Sept 22

I was directed by Col Clark to take the statement of one Harrison W. Davis of the origin of the fight between the Mex-icans and the Texian rangers. Davis is a large active man for-merly from Lexington Ky but now a citizen of Liberty Cy.

He had served three months with the Louisville volunteers when they were disbanded. Davis then joined Col Johnsons[47] Riflemen and served that Regiment till about the 4th day of September when he got his discharge and started from Comargo with six other Texians and one Mexican. After one days journey, one of the party took the measles and the party placed him at a ranch and established their own encampment about 7 miles from the ranch where there was water and feed for their horses. They remained several days trading with the inhabitants and carrying on this most friendly intercourse. — The sick being able to carry on their journey they all prepared to proceed for this place. — One of the neighbours proposed to conduct the party and did so until his conduct becoming suspicious the party determined to follow him no further. About the same time they discovered a party of some 25 Mexicans approaching them in front. — Davis and his party there turn back into the road and persue it for this place; and in order to ascertain whether they are persued they turn off from the road and conceal themselves behind the chap-eral. In a few minutes the Mexicans were in front of them. Davis's party demanded of them what they wanted, and the Mexicans immediately turned and retired at full speed. To avoid further pursuit Davis' party then took another way so as to pursue the middle route to this place. — After traveling some hours the party stopped and unsaddled their horses. They had laid down in the shade and their horses were feeding when they were fired on and immediately attacked hand to hand. A desperate fight ensued which lasted about 1 and ½ minutes when the Mexicans retreated. One of the Texians was mortally wounded and 7 of the Mexicans. All the wounded of the Mexicans were carried off but one. — The wounded Texian was taken some hundred yards off and hid in the underwood and left with water and provisions. The Texians then made their way as fast as possible to this place. — W. Davis gives references to Col. McKee,[48] Lt. Col Clay, Col Johnson, Gen Butler[49] and many others to prove his standing and character and also exhibited to me his discharge in due form signed by Gen Taylor. The above is the substance of Davis statement which he signed certified on honour and I handed to Col Clark commanding Matamoros.

Sept 23

Saw a letter from the chaplin in General Taylors camp dated 17th Inst. They were within 25 miles of Monterray and expecting to march up to that city on the 18th and to enter it on the 19th — The force there understood to be in the city was 7000 regular and irregulars. — General Taylor has 6000 and therefore more than a match for the Mexicans. The General has probably entered that city and he did this without firing a gun.

I have been engaged in taking the statement of John B. Williams[50] one of the Texians who corroborates the statement of Davis and gives an account of the second expedition which went out under Col Cook. He says they killed two Mexicans and burned some 30 or 40 houses.

Sept 24

More reports of accumulating forces. Col Clark has been advised that an expedition is fitting up to attack this place, and that the force is accumulating at San Fernando[51] a place of some 2000 population about 80 miles south west of this place. A messenger has been sent out to reconnoiter the premises and has been absent for five days. This evening Col. Bakers Regiment of Illinois troops (volunteers) came up from their encampment 8 or 10 miles below and arrived about 11 Oclock at night. We have had so many *reports* of attack that I feel quite certain this is a false alarm.

I commanded at dress parade this evening, the first time since my attack of fever. The regiment is improving a little in health. This parade was better attended than many have been. Still there is 135 on the sick report for the 8 companies located on this side. Several of the officers are better. Lt Col McCook and Major Love who are really too unwell to do duty but they will persist in doing it. Capt McLaughlin has been sick several days and Capt Woodruff is very sick and now laying under the influence of a high fever in the adjoining room. — Doctor Robinson has quite recovered and gone to camp today. —

Sept 25
The messenger came in last night from San Fernando reports no force in that region or within his hearing. The regiment of Illinois troops are directed to proceed on their way up to Comargo. They leave an additional number of sick. The number in the public hospitals, not including my sick who are in camp, are said to be 800! This is far from being the whole number of sick in the army. I am told there are great numbers.

Sept 29
The express from General Taylor has arrived at last. A hard battle of three days and a loss of some 500 of our forces!! The Mexicans permitted to march out with their small arms and battery of 6 six pounders. A cessation of hostilites for eight weeks. These terms are extremely favourable to the Mexicans. General Taylor cannot augment his forces while the Mexican General in two months ought to be able to triple his. Our army in fact daily dimninishing by sickness and death. To lay two months waiting is almost as bad as a defeat.

Sept 30
Attended to the inspection of my regiment. The sun was rather hot but I feel better than usual to day.

The great subject of conversation is the great victory we gained at Monterray and the little gains that may result from it.

All may be for the best. General Taylor must have had reasons for giving up the whole army which he had quite surrounded and might apparently have taken prisoners. I was surprised to find my weight just 150 lbs.

Oct 1

Well I ought to be thankful that for three of the hottest months ever known in this hottest of climates my life has been spared. One man died yesterday belonging to Captain Chapmans Company[52] which makes 24 deaths in my Regiment since I left Cincinnati. — Lt Col McCook has been suffering with a fever for two or three days and Major Love is quite feeble. I drew a months pay this morning 176.60 in full up to the first of September so that I have a month due me still. Daily pay rations all of 5.69.

News continues to augment the killed at the battle of Monterray. It is said now the Mexicans lost 1500. — If so more than two thousand must have been left dead on the field! I have felt better yesterday and to day than I have for 3 months past. It is warm to day but a fine breeze helps the matter very much.

About 8 Oclock P.M. Lt. Delong[53] came to inform me Col Clark was in great anxiety and alarm in consequence of the news of approaching Mexicans. I reported to the Colonel who desired me to send him three full companies to defend the plaza. Took cartridges to Col Bakers Regiment and hold myself in readiness to turn out at a moments warning. These orders were connected with prevailing rumors of approaching force. It was positively asserted a party of some 3000 Mexicans were within a few miles of the city. All that was enough to get up a great excitement. I came to camp forthwith and established my quarters.

Oct 3

Col Clark required but one company from my regiment to post themselves *near his person* the other two he obtained from Col Baker of the Illinois regiment which still remains stationed near Fort Paredes. A national salute was fired today at Forts Brown and Paredes in commemoration of the battle of Monterray.

My guard was fired on to day and a ball came very near Lt. Beaty[54] the officer of the guard and passed through camp. The person or party had been concealed behind a bunch of bushes and made their escape. A party of citizen rangers went out yesterday to reconnoiter the Mexican lines. The wind is from the south east again and the weather is quite sultry. In the mean time my health is much improved. Salutes were fired from Fort Brown and Fort Paredes in commemoration of the victory gained at Monterray by our army under General Taylor.

Oct 5

Went up to town and spent most of the day with Lt Col McCook who is still quite sick but much better than he was. — News arrived of the evacuation by the Mexican forces from Monterray and our continued possession of the City. — The most of the Mexican forces marched out on the 28th Ult. —This day was very warm. — A mexican prisoner taken with arms calls himself John Ramulons esq.

Oct 6

There was an express passed up the river last night in great haste to General Taylor.[55] Rumor says that Mexico has made a proposal which our government has accepted and that our troops are to be withdrawn from the West side of the Rio Grande. —

The steam boat Col Cross[56] brought Col Morgan, D. Trevitt,[57] Lt. Col Irwin[58] and Capt McLean[59] from the mouth where they have been spending a few days recruiting their health. They are all in fine spirits but all show the sad effects of distance. McLean and Trevitt are mere skeletons. Patrol party took arms a double bble pistol and knife from ranchero with ammunition enough (in a bag) for a siege.

Oct 7

Received a letter from H. Curtis dated 13th Ult. all well at home. This day has been warm with a fresh breeze from the South East. We had a serenade from the Indiana band Major Hunter and others.[60] We first met with these men at the Battle ground near N. Orleans. We met them again at Brasos and last night their music announced them to the sentinels lines where I met them and welcomed them into camp. — Their notes soon gathered the whole corps at my quarters. If we had good music every evening I think it would save the use of medicine.

Oct 8

I see by looking over my register that we have had no rain since the 25th Sept. The river has been falling for a month past and has not yet become low though it has fallen off 10 or 12 feet. The current is still rapid and the waters are very roily having all the appearances of a stream at the time of freshet. Steam boats continue to move up and down without the least difficulty and I am informed one has gone up the river above Comargo as far as Meir and is reported to have even ascended above that point. The object is to get a depot as near as possible to the line of General Wool.[61] He is proceeding from San Antonio de Bexar towards Chihuahua and will probably cross the Rio Grande at or near the lower presidio del norte.[62]

Oct 9

Still very warm. Hicks and I walked out to gather seeds. There is the greatest variety of shrubs in the chaperal of this country. One that I have supposed was an annual I found to be a kind of elder. It has branches of yellow flowers that change their hue according to their age. The branches are like the verbane [verbena?] leaf varying in all the shades from deep dark yellow to pale almost white. I have saved some of the seeds. The leaf of the shrub is rough and harsh about the size and form of catnip but not so dark a colour. The musqueete is a very green thorny shrub with leaves like the locust but much finer in texture. Then there is a kind of thorn very like our white thorn in the shape of tree; but the leaf is like the locust and very dark green with pods like the locust.[63] Then there are a thousand other small shrubs which resemble the lilac and snowball bush in form not in flower. It seem they all are inclined to grow small and stunted. The palmetto and musquite are the largest. The palmetto or cabbage tree[64] grows very straight and without a limb 18 or 25 feet high and at the top spreads out an umbrella shaped cluster of leaves such as they make fans and hats of. The body of the tree appears like a bundle of ears of corn. The musquite resembles the peach tree in form. Ebony also grows here but it so much resembles the

musquite and thorn that I cannot distinguish it. All the shrubbery is covered with vines resembling morning glories, and this
by the way, is a common vine among a great variety of them.[65]
The red pepper *kayenne*[66] is also common running up on bushes
as high as I can reach and full of peppers as hot as burning coals
of fire. The pepper is about the size of wild cherries and when ripe
it is red. It is used by the Mexicans when green and red in
cooking. Almost every dish is highly seasoned with it. The have
a kind of *hash* made by cutting up meat and pepper together. It
is very nice. — There is another shrub with a rich scarlet flower
on it.[67] It is a kind of box elder looking shrub and the flower
resembles in form the flower of the sweet scented shrub but it is
very nice and in the green chaperal attracts peculiar attention, I
design gathering some of these shrubs and try to cultivate them
at home.

The sensitive plant[68] is very common. Hicks and I amuse
ourselves by touching the leaves and branches and seeing them
close up their little leaves and branches. It is a very delicate vine
running close to the ground like camomil [camomile]. The leaves
are very delicate and compound like the locust but very small
and slender. Touch a bed of it ever so lightly with your hand and
you will see it shrink away instantly the leaves and little branches
all contract like close to the ground the leaves closing almost
entirely. The plant blooms all summer and has a pretty furry ball
flower a rich purple about the size of a potato ball. —

The report has arrived through the Mexicans that Gen Santa
Anna or some other commanding General is at Saltillo[69] and
that he rejects the armistice recently entered into by General
Taylor and General Ampudia.[70] As this is a mere *report* it will
not do to rely on. It seems to me improbable. The Mexicans have
nothing to lose by delay, but everything to gain. —

Oct 10
— Another nest of arms found in the city and taken. They
[are] new and excellent rifles. —

Oct 11
I rested well last night and feel perfectly well after breakfast. I
have just concluded to sent this book home by Mr. Abbot[71] who

waits, to carry it. May it have a safe and speedy passage. I will open a new book so fare well to this old companion of many hours.

Oct 12

To day I have been putting up a little box of seeds, shells and many other trifles which I have picked up in this country. I send them together with a letter to my wife by George Richards[72] of Company E a discharged soldier. —

The paymaster is paying off my regiment their first two months service. — This has been long delayed. It was due on the 1st of September and our men have needed their money very much especially when sick. — I hope they will purchase light food and thereby improve their health.

This book is composed of miserable paper and cost a dollar poor as it is — I do think I would be a little miss in composing this second epistle, but this soft springy coarse paper has disgusted me before finishing the first page. —

Well so it can be read, it will do to refer back to and may be useful if not interesting to me or mine in after days. This day is warm. I perspire freely writing in my tent with a fresh breeze which comes from the North. I was weighed yesterday and find my weight the same it was about the 1st of the month 150 lbs which shows a loss of flesh since I commenced campaigning of just 40 lbs.

I may as well state here in the first of this book the location of the military at Matamoros. It may be a matter of interest, our position as now posted was taken on the 18th August when Col Clark ordered my regiment onto this side of the Rio Grande. I had previous to that time been for some time differently located, eight companies had been stationed on the East side at Camp Curtis and two companies at Fort Paredes on the Mexican side. On the next page I have made a sketch showing the encampment. Companies are located thus A Capt. McLaughlin, B Capt Meredith, C Capt Patterson, stationed in Fort Brown, D Capt Ford in Fort Brown, E Capt Moon, F Capt Chapman, H Capt Noles [?], I Capt Kell, K Capt Allen. Companies C. and D. stationed in Fort Brown and on the south side of the fort. The fort has been almost inundated, and the companies have hardly found room to locate their tents. Capt Ford of Company D. is absent on sick leave. The plat will show sufficiently distinct. TTTT represents the places where dead have been deposited. The large grave yard on the S.W. adjoining the enclosed grave yard of the Mexicans; is the general deposit where all our soldiers who die in the hospitals have been placed. The other two little grave yards are those of the 3rd Regiment and it is to these we have often had to follow the slow hearse and muffled drum. It will be hard to leave these graves in possession of our foes, The places will no doubt soon be lost and forgotten, and mourning friends will find no trace of these graves. Fort Brown is commanded by Capt Lowd and Fort Paredes by Capt Norman. — There is a company of artillery in each of these forts under the command of Lieut Haskell [Haskin],[73] assisted by Lieuts Williams[74] and Johnson[75] stationed on the west side of the Plaza in the lower rooms of a large spacious Mexican barrack. It is over this, in rooms formerly occupied for court rooms, that Col Clark keeps his quarters. It will be seen by this, that the force here is as follows respectively

1 Company Artillery on Plaza
1 do in Ft. Paredes
3 do of my Reg. and 1, Art. at Ft. Brown
8 do Camp McCook under my command
13 Total thirteen companies.
All under command of Col. N. S. Clark U. S. A.

Oct 13

A rumor is going the rounds that Col Belknap[76] is coming down the river today, with full authority from Gen Taylor to change the disposition of the forces on the river. — Richards did not get off yesterday, so I did not send my box of seeds home. To day I made some further collections accompanied by Dr. Robinson, Adjutant Gray,[77] and Mr. Mete[78] our hospital Stewart.

Early this morning the wind was strong from the North, and it was cool enough to require woolen coats; but at two Oclock it was warm, though the wind continues all day from the North. Great numbers of wild geese, and ducks fly over camp in the mornings and evenings; some of them quite low, but none have yet been killed.

Oct 14

Last night was cold. Not cold enough for frost, but so cold I pulled my cloak and blanket both around me. My tent is large and does not come down to the ground close. The front curtains do not come together well, so that I get too much air for cold weather. My cot is too short, so that when I lay straight my feet project over about three inches! My whole bed consist of a cot small blanket and musquito bar. The musquitos "have just stepped out", but I keep the bar to protect me against other insects which flutter about our tents in great abundance.

Yesterday was the day of election in Ohio, I passed the day without thinking of it. How very difficult the matter would have been if I had been at home. My heart and hand would have been devoted to the strife.

Dined on wild ducks and geese with Lieut Crowley[79] of Company B. The day had been oppressive with heat. I find it so sitting in my tent with my coat off at 4 Oclock. The sick list to day is 61 showing a very favourable reduction within a few weeks, past. Several of my officers are still sick, but I think they are all improving. We have great reason to rejoice and be thankful that so many of us have escaped and that our health is being restored to us. —

Oct 15

Fine morning, but indication of another dry hot summer day. A steam boat came down, and Lieut Burket[80] took passage to the mouth of the river, to see young Richards, a discharged sick man, safely shipped to Ohio. I send home by this means two boxes, one with seeds and shells, and the other containing a "horned frog".[81] —

Col. Belknap came down on the boat. He is direct from Monterray with direction to make a new disposition of forces. What my destiny is to be I cannot learn, though I called on the Col and tryed to ascertain. He told me a great deal about the battle but nothing about moving me forward or back. His description of the country about Monterray is too glowing to imitate. — To one stationed here on this dry plain, where there is no hill, no tree, no mountain to relieve the eye, it is enough to make him mutinous! — River and rain water are the only means for quenching thirst. No springs, no clear running streams, or bounding cascades here. If we had ice it would answer every purpose; but that is not to be had in this country.

Oct 16

The wind blows strong from the south and the sun is too oppressive to be out[doors]. There must be a storm gathering, the motion in the atmosphere is unusual. I am exceedingly vexed that I have no instrument to make experiments with. Not even a thermometer. I supposed the surgeons of the army would all be furnished with such things but it seems the department for some reason has utterly refused. — No position of our army ever seemed to require surgical instruments so much and yet none have been furnished. I have had to send many of my men home because even a trep [trepan] could not be obtained in this country.

Capt. McCauslin, Hicks, and I started at three Oclock for a ride. We were all mounted on good Mexican mustang horses and armed with pistols. We rode out west of town. — The country is beautiful, covered with green vines and intersperced with scattering chaperal bushes not thick or hedge like but just low shade trees for sheep. The country is fenced in by ditching and hedging and has the appearance of old cultivation — soon after leaving the city herds of cattle sheep and horses present themselves in great numbers. They are much like our sheep in the North but a little more resembling goats — generally having horns, no wool under the belly, or on the leg, and more active in appearance. The wool on the back is very coarse but I think no more so than the common stock of the North. They are healthy, and I should think no country could be better adapted to sheep. Dry weather could not injure them, and the fine short grass that grows here on the prairie is the most suitable food in the world for them. Cows are very large and fine with immense horns like the oxen of the North. — Horses are all small but active and sure footed. —After going west two or three miles the country presented no variety. We stopped at a rancho and I bought a little species of dove for a bit and sent it into camp paying the Mexican boy another bit and directing him the place where to bring it "Americana-campo-colonel" which was about all the Spanish-English or En-

"Location of military force at Matamoros Mexico Oct 13, 1846 . . ."
(Curtis Diary, Bancroft Library).

glish-Spanish we could muster. The women laughed heartily at our spanish, but seemed to understand us which was all we cared for . . . so we return back to camp where I find the Mexican boy with the bird at my tent. — Our ride was very agreeable, and we all determined to take an early occasion to renew our adventures. I was too late for parade. Capt Allen took command just as we arrive. There is a great smoke rising from the prairie shown [sic]; that it is burning at no great distance south of us.

Oct 17

[W]e rallied the party of yesterday, and were joined by Captain Moore. — We stopped at a ranch, the best we saw in the route. The main building was a one story brick, with two rooms below; and back of these, a large shed or piaza [piazza]. We were invited into the south room which was about half full of corn in the husk. The other half was full of men women and children. —They were a little shy at first, but soon became assured, after they perceived our arms were not designed to operate against them. — We got corn to feed our horses, seated ourselves in the midst of them, and passed round segars to men and women who all participated in smoking as all good Mexicans always do. —The group is a fair sample of the inside of a Mexican house, and I may as well record it. — The fire place is occupied with a small fire, surrounded with skillets and small kettles. On the left on her hunkers (if there be such a word) is an old woman engaged in washing corn. On the right side of the chimney are two more women, in a similar posture; one is taking hominy or shelled corn from a mexican crock, and grinding it on a stone. — The stone is constructed from solid granite, and made to stand before her inclined, so the ground meal or "batter", runs down to the lower end of the stone. It is then taken up in her hands and passed over to the woman on the right; who rolls it out into a very thin pan cake, and puts it on a griddle to bake. After it remains a few moments on the iron plate it is taken up by the woman with her fingers and thrown onto the fire where it is smoked and dried a moment more. Then it is taken off and is the universal bread of this country. The cake is called a "tortillia [tortilla]" and is very good eating. — Nearer to us, on the right, is a very old man apparently ninety or one hundred years old, and on the left, opposite, is a dark mexican, who seems to oversee every thing; he is about 30 years old. All the intervals of this picture are filled up with little girls and boys of all sizes, who all seem delighted to see us. We infamous three, we all wanted dinners, and we were soon provided with what they, no doubt, regarded as something extra. — Our table was arranged in the back shed. It was about two feet by four, covered with a cotton cloth. — We were told to sit, and soon the center of the table was adorned with a plate of tortillias. — I was much embarrassed to know if we were to commence or wait for more. It was a moment of terrible suspense. —If we wait and no more is designed; it will indicate a dissatisfaction and mortify the family. — If we commence on this alone and more is coming; they will regard us as voracious boobies. I continue to pass a moment in adjusting my chair, and addressing a little black eyed girl that had crept up on a bench close on my left. — Our suspense however was soon relieved by the presentation to each of us with a saucer of egg and onion boiled and mixed together. Here was a fair foundation to start on, and we all "with one accord", took a tortillo, tore it in pieces with our hands, and commenced dipping the end of it into our egg. — Being very hungry, we found it an easy matter to dispense with knife and fork, even in eating soft eggs. — We had hardly commenced, when another saucer was presented with a kind of hashed meat and pepper; also semi fluid. I would have given a dollar for a spoon or knife; and really found myself quite fortunate in finding in my pocket a small pen knife. — It was interesting to see the means each of us contrived to convey provisions to our gaping mouths without interposing our fingers. — The Mexicans seemed much amused, and gathered around, as the crowd does at a caravan, to see the animals fed. We succeeded very well in satisfying our hungry appetites, and after paying two bits a piece, and presenting some of the children with trifles; we left them and returned to camp. — In passing through town I purchased at a shop for 21 dollars a very fine specimen of a Mexican blanket. —

Oct 19

I was roused this morning by the sound of guns and the squealing of wild geese. Flocks of them are constantly flying over and our men occasionally bring one down.

Captain McLaughlin, Captain Kell, and Hicks Curtis accompanied me on an excursion to the battle ground Resaca de la Palma[82] which lies about three miles North. We started about nine Oclock, and by some means took the wrong road. We traveled three or four hours, changing from road to road, till we found ourselves quite out of any road, and wandering in the paths which meandered through the chaperal.

Finally we came out at a prairie called the "Jackass prairie", which Hicks and Kell both recognized. — Here we were attracted by the *acres* of wild geese that were swimming near the shore. — We spent some time following game, and finally after spending many hours in fruitless search after the battle grounds, we turned towards camp, leaving the prairie to our left. — We fell in with a large drove of wild horses, and gave them chase for some distance through the Chaperal. Our way was very narrow, leading through thick chaperal, and admitting us only by single file. In this way we wandered through thorns and thickets, supposing we had got several miles from the prairie; when first at dark here we find ourselves at the same prairie and at the same place we had been at three hours before! We now perceived we were in for it, or rather *out* for the night, as it would be impossible to thread the chaperal in such a night. — Knowing the advantage of holding on to known places, we resolved to stick to the prairie, and therefore returned and rode through it. — The water was near to the girth of our horses, and our feet had been well soaked before in riding after the geese. We drove up droves of aquatic birds as we rode splashing through the water; among others found a nesting place of a kind of "water turkey". — It is a dark brown duck.[83] Their nests covered the bushes, and thousands of the birds were disturbed by our intrusion. — Finally, we found a path which lead to the road, and we persued the end which, as we supposed, lead us towards the river. After traveling some miles in the dark, we were suddenly brought in view of a fire and its reflection below indicating water. — We held a moment, counseled, and concluded we were at the camp of a ferryman who we knew to keep a ferry at the Lagoon on the road from Point Isabella to Matamoros. — This was the fact. We hailed the ferry man, and got the boat ready to cross, when we found on enquiry we were now on the right side, and that we had been travelling on the wrong end of the road! The night had now covered the world with utter darkness, and we being eight miles from the river, and weary from a days riding, and hungry from a days fasting; concluded to stop for the night. — The ferry man had a sheet tent covering about 12 feet of ground erected in a thicket of chaperal bushes. — Behind a hack berry tree spread its broad branches, and under its roof the fire was burning. Then we dried our feet and cheered our spirits by smoking, and taking a little good whiskey as a medicine. — Being very hungry we in-duced the ferry man to cook a pair of "wild chickens" that he had already dressed. — Our location in the thick chaperal on the bank of a clear sheet of water, far from all other settlements, in a country of savages; was rather wild and romantic. Our large fire lit up the dark green boughs of the chaperal just enough to show the gloom of the forrest. Owls, wolves, and aquatic birds kept a constant clammer; and opossums came and cracked the bones of the chickens within three feet of my head. All of the party was soon snoring round the fire except myself. . . .

Oct 20

At day break we had procured our coffee and I had the party mustered for marching. Our horses we had staked out; mine I found loose, but he was kind enough to stay with the others. — We returned towards camp, passing through a part of Jackass prairie and the battle ground of Resaca de la Palma. The battle ground has still many articles strewn over it that indicate a deadly conflict. There we find small mounds of earth which are rapidly settling and loosing their formation, places where the dead were interred. Old caps, coats, canteens, and human bones are mouldering together under the green boughs of the musqueets. The Resaca de la palma dry river, takes its name from the ground, It looks like the bed of a river which has become a pond. The Mexicans had retreated to the south side of this pond or lagoon, and no doubt thought they could prevent our army from passing. — Fatal delusion! The banks were not more than ten or 15 feet high, and there was little water in it. Besides the Lagoon is not over one hundred yards wide, and the two armies on opposite sides had equal advantages at point blank range for all arms. The Mexicans had cut and piled the brush a little, forming a trifling abbatis; but the North bank is well guarded by a thick growth of Chaperal, so that our army was as well provided with breast work as the Mexicans. Indeed all the defenses created by the lagoon, and abbatises; could not stay for a moment the enthusiasm of forces already victorious and driving their enemy. —

We stayed some half hour at the battle ground, which presents generally no natural curiosities, but is merely a chaperal forest, and arrived at camp about 8 Oclock where we found all well that were living but two had died the previous night. — One of the deaths was Lieut Francis,[84] of company G. and the other was a private in Captain Allens Company K. —

Captain Moores Company E furnished the detail and Companies G and F, attend the funeral together with most of the officers. — Lieut Francis was a very amiable and gentlemanly officer. He had been first taken with the measles and this was followed with the diarrhea and inflammation of the lungs, which finally reduced him to the grave. He was buried in the burying ground where most of the volunteers are buried, at the S. W. corner of the city, adjoining the Mexican grave yard. —

Captain Swift[85] with the Company of Pontoneers arrived yesterday. It is a fine looking Company, and they have pitched their tents east and near to us.

Oct 22

This day is quite warm; uncomfortably so. Another death occurred last night in Company E. I still regret to find many sick. Lt Col McCook appears better today. He is hardly able however to sit up. The mans name who died in Company E was Jacob Flicking Esq. [Flickinger],[86] and resides near Doylestown Wayne County.

Oct 23

A large party of us started at nine Oclock in the morning for the battle ground of the 8th May, "Palo Alto" (tall palm trees).[87] Our route was the road to Point Isabella, and therefore lead us over the battle ground of Resaca de la Palma. It is 12 miles to Palo Alto and we hurried forward without making any stop over a good road and chaperal country. One of our party shot a large rattle snake and another found another Mexican musket on the battle ground of the 9th.

The Asst. quartermaster Lieut L. Chase[88] has ordered a wagon to accompany us for the purpose of bringing in the body of Lieut Blake[89] who was accidentally killed on the 8th May, and buried on the battle ground.

Palo Alto is a large open prairie, several mile in diameter. It is quite level, and grown up with grass as high as the girths of our horses. There are ponds of clear water in many places, especially on that part of the field where the Mexican line rested. At the time of the battle it was all dry.

After disinterring the remains of poor Blake and starting the wagon homewards, we proceeded to explore the field. Lieut Chase had been in the battle and could point to the location of the two armies. They were both extended on this open prairie. The sights must have been beautiful and terrible. The Mexican line can just be traced by the skeletons that lie bleaching on the field. We followed it for a long distance. — Here you see a skull and there in proper position all the bones resting on the mother earth. It is strange they are not more skattered; but the water rising over the bodies probably protected them from the wolves till the flesh was all putrified. — We came to larger flocks of wild birds and I amused myself in shooting snipe. I killed some 20 in one plain. The flamingo is a pink coloured crane with a kind of spoon bill.[90] They are beautiful birds and rising up in large flocks before us presented a beautiful picture. We shot one and took it with a broken wing. I am sure it would be a great curiosity in the North but concluded to let it go after cutting off the broken wing — We fell in with Major Gardner, who was coming to Matamoros from Point Isabella and joining his party we returned to camp arriving about 8 Oclock P.M. I was beleagured and hungry; and therefore retired early to my cot.

Oct 24

Dined with Major Pool[91] formerly of the army and had a dinner most like home than any I have seen in Mexico. My regiment appears remarkably well at drill this evening. If my health continues I hope to make my regiment perfect in a few more weeks.

Oct 25

I dined today with Col Taylor (brother of the General), Major Denny,[92] Major Gaines, Lieut Chase, and two other gentlemen clerks in the paymasters department. — Col Taylor is a very decided and warm Whig and I would infer the same in reference to Major Denny. The origin of the war, and the end of it, were fruitful sources of conversation, and we indulged very freely in the review of the past, and in conjectures for the future. — We have fairly conquered all this region of country North and West of this place, since we have entire control over the avenues that lead through that region. The territory is immense, comprising New Mexico or Santa Fe, Tamaulipas, New Leon, Cohahuila [Coahuila], Chihuahua, and the Californias. —

The sooner a system of government is adopted for these states, the better it will be for all parties. —

Oct 26

Gentle showers sufficient to lay the dust and revive vegetation. The dry weather for the past month has materially affected the grass and other vegetables. Yet corn appears green and growing finely. — The inhabitants who pretend to cultivate the soil have every encouragement this year. I see in the gardens that cabbage and radish seeds have recently been sown and the young plants are just peeping out of the ground.

The abundance of vegetation for all kinds of stock is very apparent every where. My pony is a kind of pet and runs loose about the lines of camp. The grass is altogether sufficient to keep him in good condition here in the very edge of town. In the chaperal and on the prairies the grass in many places is three feet high but rather coarse. The grass most sought by cattle is a fine short grass that grows on open ground a little resembling our blue grass of the north.[93] A little dark Mexican boy brought me a bunch of flowers oleanders, red, white, and variegated and with princes feathers red and yellow. Jasamines and sweet basil, together with a lot of strangers to me. I offered the boy a piece of money but he said "non senor". — The little rogue would not take a penny.

Oct 28

There was so much rain this morning and during the past night, I dispensed with morning drill. The clouds disperse however, so as to admit of a four Oclock drill. I amused the boys by charging over a ditch and through a chaperal. The advantage of such a move is that it makes a drill change and looses the monotony which it otherwise acquires. — I always try to make my drill instruction seem to the privates, and as far as possible amusing. — For this reason I generally explain the reason of certain moves. The advantages of certain changes to repel an attack, and the mode of preparation for an attack. In this way the privates appear to learn the rationale and become as competent to criticise as officers themselves. The more I have to do with volunteers, the more I am satisfied of their entire fitness for any service. I try to treat men all of them as gentlemen. I never allow myself to use severe language or cruel punishments. — Obstinate and drunken men are often tied and kept in the guard house; but I see no use of treating men like slaves. I have all the distance and respect shown me that my rank and duties require without *forcing* it. It seems to increase daily as men acquire daily more the points and bearing of soldiers. I hope they will improve rather than depreciate in morals and manners. I am quite certain they would if we were removed from the demoralizing influences of this town."

Oct 29

This day has been noted for nothing. A regular succession of duty. Rise at 6 Oclock, and dress for breakfast. Perhaps read a little in Shakespeare or a drill book. Breakfast at seven on steak bacon and eggs, light bread and coffee. — Attend a little to the company drills, at 9 to 11; then sit here in my tent and receive reports and sign papers till ½ past 1 — Then dine on roast beef — generally; but today on turkey, light bread, and cold water.

Walked up town and called on the commandant and Col McCook — Returned to camp just in time for Battalion drill, which continues till dress parade. Take supper immediately after dress parade — tea, light bread, and cold meat. — After supper stood a little about camp and read in my tent till after ten Oclock when I retire to my cot. So goes a day in camp. — The guards are mounted by the adjutant, and the general supervision of camp is under the direction of the officer of the day. —

Oct 30

Dined with Captain Moore, Dr. Robinson, and Lieut Mc-Millan.[94] — I regret exceedingly that General Patterson[95] declines retaining Doctor Robinson. We have so far depended on his skill, and in his absence I really feel that we meet with a serious loss in the regiment. This day has been very warm. The perspiration rolls off a person sitting in the shade.

Nov 1

This month sets in like a *furnace* not like a lion. At 9 Oclock this morning it is oppressive. The perspiration rolls off me sitting and writing in my tent. It is Sunday — All Saints Day: And many are going up to church. The whole number of men and officers in my regiment is 678. Called on Colonel Clark and Col Belknap.

Col Belknap has just returned from Galveston Island, where the sick and hospital stores of that place have been broken up. Col Belknap told me that he supposed my regiment would be among the first to move forward; that the regulars coming on would be ordered to this place, and made the base of a line of operations towards Tampico.

There is a fine company of the 2nd Dragoons under command of Lieut Kearney[96] encamped in the Plaza. They all have iron gray horses, and appear remarkably well. A regiment of Tennessee horse[97] are some where between this plaza and Point Isabella.

A train of provisions goes out to meet them tomorrow, and I have just ordered a detail of one sergeant (Vantrees [Van Treese], of Co. G.)[98] and ten privates, to accompany and guard the train.

Nov 2

Sergeant Vantrees was not requested till near night. The quartermasters men always take their time. No doubt the Tennessee Regiment will think so before they get their provision. —

Nov 3

Capt Kauman[99] and his company of regulars moved up the river, and I placed Captain Allens Company in the Plaza. —

Nov 4

Col Clark sent for me this morning to inform me that he might want another company stationed in the City. That General Lanes Brigade of Indiana volunteers[100] was all ordered on, and my regiment would then be all the force stationed on this side the river.

A riot occurred on the steam boat "Exchange"[101] which induced me to take the Captain and his cook who appeared to be the principal actors, and place them in the guard house. At the same time I directed a Corporal of the guard to take Command of the boat. — So I would manage all drunken steam boat captains agents and engineers who act as common carriers. I am glad military law gives me power to prevent needless expense of human life.

Nov 5

Last night was quite cool, but this morning at 9 Oclock I find it very warm. I released two prisoners Captain and cook of steam boat "Exchange" and sent the boat off about its business.

Nov 6

I have spent this day calling on Col Clark, Col Belknap, Mr. Shattsell, and Father McElroy. — The officers and men of my regiment are becoming exceedingly uneasy and apprehensive that we are going to be left here and another expedition go forward without us. — It is understood Mr. McLean[102] has passed up with dispatches from Washington directing our army to remain East of the mountains. — I have written by Col Belknap requesting the Commanding General to move my regiment into a more active employment.

If an expedition is to be fitted out for Vera Cruz or some other places south of this I may stand a chance to go in that line. At least Col Belknap thinks so and assures me that he will use his utmost efforts to effect it. —

Major Love has just returned from Point Isabella where he has

been on an excursion partly of business and partly for pleasure. —

Nov 7

I applied for leave of absence to accompany Col Belknap to
Monterray, but Col Clark said he did not wish to spare me and
declined affording me perhaps the only opportunity that may
ever offer itself. Well I must stay when my duty calls me, but I am
tired of my duty tent here on the bank of the rio grande. — Col
Belknap appears to me to be an excellent officer. His duties as
inspector General are sufficiently arduous and he discharges
them to the satisfaction of all.

Nov 8

Sunday. I find the air a little cooler than it has been for the
past ten or 15 days. It is none too cool however for comfort. The
heat is the greatest evil. In the evening as I was crossing commercial street, I was surprised by several discharges of pistols
about fifty yards from me and near the Exchange,[103] a large
gambling house and tavern. Major Love and several more were
with me and we proceeded to the spot where we found a great
noise and excitement. Three or four persons, texians and gamblers had been shooting each other, and one man was mortally
wounded. The patrols came up and I directed three prisoners to
be taken, no doubt the men engaged in the fray. — The scene
was rather exciting. Several officers of the Tennessee Regiment
of horse were mixed up in the crowd and one a captain was
exceedingly boisterous being under the influence of liquor. Being
an officer I could not permit him to go to the guard house, but
found it very difficult preventing him from continuing the noise
and disturbance.

Nov 9

I went up to the quarters of the commanding officer, for the
purposes of directions as far as my influence might extend the
disposition of those men who had been engaged in the fight and
murder of the proceeding night. — I was too late; the Col had
sent them to New Orleans the Botney Bay [sic] for our arms.
There is no doubt they will relieve themselves by writ of habeus

corpus and apply their roguish talents to some profit among the good people of the states.

Nov 10

Last night I spent with Captain Patterson at Fort Brown. Companies C. and D. of my regiment have been stationed in that fort about three months. Their duties are light but the confinement must be very irksome. The weather continues very warm and many of the men are suffering with diarrhea and ague. The sick list in the whole regiment must be 110, that is including those sick in all of the ten companies. — The perspiration rolls off me, as I sit in my tent with my coat off writing this paragraph.

Nov 11

I have much anxiety and trouble to procure requisite clothing for my regiment. The clothing department I am informed by letter from the Qr.master Genls Office; cannot do any thing towards clothing the volunteers. That this law does not authorise the department to do so. Under this ruling, the pay of the volunteers is much less than that of the regulars, in this, that the United States runs all risques of contracting and expense also of transportation; while volunteers are obliged to buy at great disadvantage far from the place of manufacture. True the volunteers get *one* dollar per month more for clothing than the regulars; but this will not place them on any thing like a footing with the regulars. — A suit that the Government furnishes the regulars, for 6 dollars cannot be obtained for any price, and one costing 12 to the volunteers would not be equal to it. I have under all the vexatious negligence on the part of the department under whose supervision this should fall, determined to send some of my officers to New Orleans for the purpose of contracting them to the best possible advantage.

I have therefore ordered Col McCook to go to New Orleans, and to take such assistances as he may consider necessary to procure such clothing as the regiment needs.

Nov 12

Lt Col McCook, Capt Moore, Capt Kell, and Lieut Cable[104] took passage for New Orleans. I put up a box of baggage that has

accumulated on my hands and directed it to Rev. G. Buckingham Putnam. My cloak, a deck of Mexican cards taken at the
battle of Resaca de la Palma. — Some copper balls[105] taken at
the same place and no doubt once attached to the band of La
vegas regiment which was so woefully mangled in the battle — a
collection of seeds and a few trifling articles; make up the invoice
of the box. — Lieut Miles[106] of the 1st Regiment who was
wounded at the battle of Monterray is also returning to the
States. He spent the evening relating anecdotes of the battle
which no doubt our friends in Ohio will hear repeated with
thrilling interest. — All accounts prove that our Ohio volunteers
acted bravely in places of great exposure. —

Nov 13

Finished reading Waddy Thompsons Mexico.[107] I perceive the
country and people through the region Mr. Thompson travelled
are very like those we find here. As Mr. Thompson wrote from
memory he has made many mistakes. He has the advantage of
two years resided, but his notes are made some years after his
return home. — A daily journal, such as I have adopted would
have much more *certainty* in it, though it may contain too many
trifling incidents. — I wrote for future reference and for the gratification of my own family. — I hope to leave on the pages of this
book the evidence of my "daily walk and conversation".

Nov 14

Another hot summer day has rolled around without the oc-
currence of a single incident worthy of a place in history. A
private of Company K died today, another grave is erected on the
Rio Bravo. — Such is the daily reckoning and, if all the deaths of
volunteers were recorded in this book it would be a sad and
lengthy volume. — Sickness still continuous severe and cases of
ague, fever, diarrhea and disintary continue numerous. — The
climate is evidently unfavourable to the health of our men, even
in this month of November. — The river continues to recede
from the bank and the dry south east wind continues to parch the
surface of the earth. — Steam boats continue to navigate the
river up to Comargo without the least difficulty. —

Nov 15

Sabbath day and very warm. Called at Capt Kidders where I found the whole family very glad to see me. There was a Miss Bowen a lady from the united states who came out with some Eastern manufactors and for the purpose of teaching. She has resided at Saltillo and at this place and has acquired some knowledge of the language of this country. I mentioned to Capt Kidder that I was requested by Col Belknap to call on a Spanish attorney a Mr. Menchaca.

This lady at once asked me if I were Col Curtis? On my answer, she said she lived next door to the gentleman, and that she had translated a letter from Col Belknap introducing him to me! A strange coincidence. I had no knowledge of the letter, and never had before enquired after Menchaca!

This lady kindly offered to show me the house and I went with her, taking along our regular interpreter who I found on the way. —

The attorney resides on the South side of the City, in a brick building of one story high. He seemed glad to make my acquaintance especially because I was a member of the bar. The room was about twenty by 14 feet, and like most of the rooms in the city, parallel to the street. The floor was brick and good cane bottom chairs were distributed around the whole circumference. He seated me at the end opposite the fireplace where there was a rug for my feet and a full view of the whole room. The mantle was covered with china ware. Pitchers, cups, bowl, etc. In the center a vase and the imitation or the reality of a small gilt clock. The china ware and all the furniture were very clean. Small engravings, in old gilt frames were distributed and hung around the walls. A desk and dressing glass on the north side, and a dressing glass with drawers on the south side, made up the whole list of furniture. — I was not long seated before his wife a young woman with dark hair eyes and complexion, but rather pretty withal came and seated herself by me. — We all conversed as best we could through interpreters and very cheerfully too for some hours. — I was lead to speak of a beautiful cluster of flowers that I saw on the mantle when Mr. Menchaca prepared to show me the shrub it grew on. — This broke up the circle in the room where I have attempted to display Mexican manners and bidding

the ladies *adieu* I accompanied Mr. Menchaca with the interpreter to see his *vegetable* garden. — We walked to the south east
corner of the city where we arrived at an enclosure at the gate of
which we found one of these cane houses occupied by the gar-
dener his family and about a dozen cross dogs.

The garden is laid out in broad walks at right angles and all the
beds and borders laid out with much regularity. Onions, garlics,
beets, cabbages, turnips, tomatoes, and many other common articles, especially red pepper occupied a great part of the surface.
The garden must contain two or three acres. The beds are all
made *dishring* and the narrow walk between them is a little ridge
of earth. Lemon, orange, fig, Pa Pa [papaya],[108] and pomegranate
trees and shrubs are growing in rows and loaded with fruit. — I
had never seen the Pa Pa before, It resembles the castor bean
plant and the fruit hangs stringing along the stalk. The fruit
resembles our paw paw which grows wild in Ohio; the stem is
regularly inserted in the apple and the other end hangs down and
is largest. — The garden has a well and irrigating machinery.
The well is large, and above it there is a large wheel say six feet
in diameter with an endless rope strung with leather buckets
suspended over the top and extending down into the well. —
The water is raised in these leather buckets like the buckets in
a bolting machine of a mill. The water is raised about 7 feet
above the surface of the ground and falls in to a brick basin or
resevoir from which it is distributed onto the dishring beds in all
parts of the garden. The machinery is very rough, the leather
baskets loose water, and the whole affair exhibits a very rude
knowledge of mechanics.[109] — One of the gardeners boys got up
and showed us how it worked. It was moved by stepping on
treads, and seemed to go very easy. —

In this visiting and observing the garden, I spent all the time
I could command and returned to camp, promising myself the
pleasure of another visit at the attorneys. —

Nov 16
I was delighted to day with receiving three letters from my
wife, the last dated the 24th October. My wife was rejoicing at
my not being in the battle of Monterray. —
The "Col Cross" has just arrived with three or four hundred

recruits for the army. Our force is gradually increasing on the rio grande. — We have great need of accession. If we are to march forward successfully, we should have double the force we now have. A larger army would sooner decide matters and prevent a sacrifice of human life that is sure to be made when the Mexicans consider our numbers small.

Ten thousand troops at Monterray would have met with little or no fighting; but the six thousand forces of General Taylor affords grounds for the Mexican General to hope for success.

Nov 17

There was some disturbance in the city which originated among the regulars and Indianians. A Mexican was killed. I sent two patrols into the streets to quell the disturbance, and directed one of the regulars to be conducted to his camp. — The wind all day has been strong from the south and indications of rain are around the horizon.

Nov 19

Last night was uncomfortably cold, and the fleas were so annoying I could not sleep. — I obtained a new tent of the common wall pattern and have it pitched with great care so as to present a better defense against a "Norther". I received intelligence of the taking of Tampico by our Navy.[110] No resistance was offered and our marines marched in on [the 14th] day of [November]. All the military personnel and material had been removed to San Luis Potosi.[111]

Nov 20

Another cold and restless night last night. Our thin muslin tents are neither a protection against the sun or the wind. Something less penetrable should be adopted for this climate. At two Oclock the heat was so oppressive had to retreat from my tent. The new muslin is worse than the old canvas. —

Nov 21

The night was cold but the day is again warm. The wind has got round to the south again. I desire that this register should show the changes of climate and temperature as far as possible without the use of instruments. My neighbour the mexican *se-nora* who lives nearest the camp, sent me a plate of vegetables. — I carried the plato home this evening with segars, pins, and a pair of cotton stockings!

Hicks Curtis went with me to assist in talking Spanish. We know about three words a piece which we used to great advantages. The old woman was very glad to see us, but exhibited the natural politeness of good breeding by avoiding the examinations of the bundle (which she knew contained something) during the time we remained. All concur in testifying in favor of Mexican women. They have their own mode of dress; but they otherwise exhibit the same kind and decent deportment. We never see low and depraved beings, such as every city in the union exhibits. — They are all retiring and extremely polite. They have evinced the greatest degree of kindness towards the prisoners who have been taken in border wars and tales of heroic valour are numberless in the history of the country. We have a number of prisoners at Fort Brown who have been taken and retained in custody. Mexican women cross the river almost daily to give them little articles of provision which camp life in the fort does not furnish.

Nov 22

Sabbath brings with it a roaring of bells and barking of ten thousand dogs in Matamoros. I called on the Governor. I had written a severe note complaining of the medical department in general and the General Hospital in particular. The Governor informed me that my sick would hereafter be received.

I also called on Miss Bowen, the American lady who on a previous day accompanied me to the house of the attorney. I found her *tout suite* in her house consisting of a brick with three rooms. Miss Bowen is from New Hampshire. — She came to this country with an American family which resides in the interior, and she has all the desire for accumulation and enterprise peculiar to our New England adventurers. With all the sensibility and delicacy of a New England teacher, she has also the ambitions, fortitude, and courage of a good soldier. She has traveled more than eight hundred leagues through this country generally on horse back and for hundreds of miles with no company but hired servants. She can speak some spanish and has therefore formed profitable employment teaching and serving. She at one time set out from Saltillo for home, and her mode of travelling was sufficient to show how woman can endure danger and privation. Two Mexican servants were employed. — Men that she had never known, but who were recommended as faithful except like most Mexicans they would rob you for money. She therefore gave her servants to understand that she had but 5 dollars to buy provisions with, and the rest of her money was a check on the American consul at this place. She then procured horses and mounted herself on a mans saddle and thus accounted they traveled several hundred miles through a country infested with robbers and indians. She was annoyed by robbers and surrounded by many dangers, but arrived safely at Matamoros. — The incidents that occurred on her journey are fresh in her memory, and the narration of these gave vent to a profusion of tears. — She embarked twice from this place with the design of returning to the states; but was each time brought back sick once with yellow fever. — She still estimates the profit and loss of going home, and rather decides in favor of staying where she is. She says the Spaniards are very kind to her, and since she can speak their language, she begins to become attached here to the people. —

Miss Bowen accompanied me to the attorneys Mr. Menchaca. He had been ill, and his wife had the ague. He was very polite and I spent an hour or two very pleasantly. Some strange ladies, I think the family of the Alcalde came in. Two little children were very interesting and appeared to attract general attention. All these ladies and gentlemen imitated our fashions even to the wearing of bustles!

Nov 23

Yesterday the wind was from the North, to day it is from the south and too hot for comfort. Col Clark issued an order requiring the surgeon to receive the sick into General Hospital. Our sick prefer the regimental surgeons and dislike to go under the control of regulars and strangers. — I have urged the commanding officer to substitute a house for our hospital tent so that our own physicians could there as here attend to our own men. I have proposed the matter so warmly and so sensibly that Col

Clark has been fretting so much about it, I can press it no further. His cares are overwhelming, and I am resolved to submit to injustice rather than vex and harrass the Colonel who I regard as a good officer and well disposed as I believe toward my regiment. I wrote today a reply to the letter from the Quartermaster Generals department declining to furnish my regiment with clothing. — I insist that the volunteers are entitled to clothing in kind as the regulars receive it and informed the department that we expect to share in the "means and energy" of the clothing bureau. I suppose my letter will be no benefit to the volunteers because it will not influence the officers and besides arrive there too late. —

Every day I perceive something which developes a greater attention to those attached to the regular service. All the acting quartermasters and companies in this region are regulars and generally very active and competent men; but no more so and not so much so as some of the new officers. — The management of accounts may be better understood by regulars; but the management and value of boats, stores, wagons, horses, mules, and houses; would be better understood by men who have been more connected with the production manufacture use and sale of property.

My commisary has the rank of a Captain, and is well acquainted with property, and careful with accounts; yet a Lieutenant of the regular army is the principal comissary at this place and the new appointment is only required to do duty for my regiment. — I was directed by Col Clark to call to day and see who occupied the Ampudia house,[112] a larger building which I understand was in charge of the quartermasters department and which I had suggested as suitable for the sick of my regiment — I found that part of it was occupied by the sick of the Tennessee Volunteers, and the best part of it by a sergeant and ten men of the 2nd dragoons!! — The sergeant informed me that he had been there comfortably located for some time. — I did not express to the Commander my indignation at finding this accomodation awarded to a sergeant and ten healthy privates of the regular service, when I had been refused accomodations for myself, even when dangerously attacked with fever.

I write these facts down with mortification. I see that it is impossible for volunteers and regulars to come together on such terms of equality as should exist between them. The regular and volunteer force must be connected in peace and in war; or one of the classes must be abandoned. A republican government must depend on volunteers or militia: and when these forces come into the field they must be placed on terms of equality with equal grades and ranks with other classes of troops who are destined to act with them. — So far in the campaign, volunteers occupy a very insignificant position. — I am placed subordinate to a Colonel whose commission is dated subsequent to mine. General Lane of the Indiana Brigade is stationed at Camp Belknap below me, where there is no kind of responsibility; while my old friend and school fellow Captain Swartwert [Swarthout] is commander of Rinosa [Reynosa],[113] a town of some two thousand inhabitants.

The result of this matter will be that the volunteers will become the best soldiers. Left to rely on their own resources and sensible of their capacity to acquire knowledge they will soon be capable of performing all necessary movements, and will be better enured to privation, fatigues, and difficulties. These are the obstacles soldiers have to encounter, and the school is well organized to teach these things to the volunteers.

And the *final result?* What will that be? *It will be fatal to the regular army.* —

I do hope sincerely that this national jealousy which now exists may be removed during our term of service. — The least effort on the part of the regulars would satisfy the volunteers who came here only to do good service and then leave the matter again to the regulars whose experience all of us appreciate; but should a line of distinction continue, and the volunteers remain in the rear stations; there will not be many years roll round before they will be at "the head of the army". — A military revolution is needed in our organization and I apprehend it will be produced by the call for troops in the service. The only danger is that it may go too far. —

Nov 24

The attorney Mr. Menchaca called with an English interpreter and spent some time with me. — The day was actually sultry. My shirt collar was saturated with perspiration at two Oclock, and the inside of my tent was so warm I could not endure it. — At about four Oclock the wind changed from south to North and at six Oclock it was tearing our camp to shreds. My little tent stands it very well. It is now at tattoo, quite cool enough; and the Norther still continues to shake the canvas with fearful force. A few more such gales will deprive us of tents and drive us into the Mexican houses. — The news afloat is, that General Patterson is daily expected at this place on his way to Tampico. A regiment of the Illinois troops are arriving from Comargo.[114] They went up about a month since, and now they are countermarching. — It is not yet known what troops are to accompany General Patterson on the Tampico Expedition. As that place has been taken by our Navy, we see no great interest in the occupation of a place having the reputation for sickness which that place sustains. — I also understand that our Army is going to occupy a line of posts along the mountain ridge extruding from Monterray to Tampico. — This plan of operation will divide all our force and render further progress impossible without large reinforcements. At the same time Santa Anna is concentrating his forces at San Luis Potosi where he expects to check our forward progress. San Luis is beyond the mountain ridge which it is understood we are not to pass so that we stand a poor chance of seeing the Mexicans in force. —

Nov 26

The third regiment of Indiana Volunteers was received in the Plaza by the Governor. It is a good regiment and they tried hard to excel us; but there was a plain difference in our favour and I think all the spectators admitted our superior selirty [celerity] and accuracy of movement. — I attended a ball in the evening at the Tremont House.[115] It was very well got up. Americans, Mexicans, and French were singularly combined. There was also a glaring display of elegance contrasted with the rudeness of ignorance and barbarity. It is probably the first "Ball" ever announced in this City. — I was called out to visit Fort Paredes. One of Captain Allens Company, Private Malone, returning from the city to the fort about nine Oclock had been assaulted by two Mexicans with dirks and badly lacerated on the back and shoulders.[116] The perpetrators were secured and Captain Allen and his company deserve all praise for stifling the feeling of revenge which was sufficient to execute signal revenge on the cowardly villains. —

Nov 27

I sent the prisoners up to the guard house in town where they will await their trial. It is hard to find a competent court to try and determine their fate. Probably the court of the Alcalda [Alcalde] will have to be resorted to, and that is a very indifferent tribunal.

Nov 28

The weather is very fine. Rather warm at mid day. The wind from the south. The dry weather still continues. The river continues to fall but steam boats continue to make regular trips to Comargo. The "Flag" of this morning again takes notice of my regiment by alluding to this review by the Governor.

I called to day on the Alcalda to ascertain what species of trial and punishment could be inflicted on the villains who attempted to take the life of Private Malone of Company K. — The Alcalda seemed very willing to hear the cause; but his jurisdiction is singulary constituted. The first Alcalda can try, determine, and sentence; but the case must then go to a Superior Court at Victoria where it is to be again tried. — The testimony is required to be in secret. The accuser first produces his testimony in writing. The criminal then has the right to take rebutting testimony and the papers so prepared are submitted to the Alcalda who decides accordingly to the apparent weight of the testimony. — I am informed the Alcalda is very ignorant hardly understanding how to write his name. He appears like a clever old man, and when I pressed him as to the forms of a criminal trial, he informed me that in such matters he had recourse to an attorney learned in the law and regularly admitted to the practice.

He recommended me to Mr. Menchaca who he said understood such matters. — On such a blind path it is hardly to be expected truth will be ascertained; but I am inclined to bring the prisoners before the court.

On my way to the attorneys I called at a common day school where some half dozen boys were seated on wooden benches with sloping boards before them which they used as desks. The teacher was a young well dressed man, seated at a table surrounded with books. — There was a large black board erected on a tripod in front of him and the remainder of the room was occupied with benches and desks to write on or learn upon. The teacher was requiring the solution of problems in subtraction. The boys were required to put their work on the black board and the process displayed great ignorance on the part of the assistant teacher.

He had the sum written down on paper and could not perform the simplest subtraction without reference to it. — The teacher says his whole school comprises about 25 boys. They are required to attend six hours each day, but there were only five or 6 at school to day. Reading, writing, arithmetic, grammar, and geography are taught and the teacher gets two dollars per month for each scholar. — There was perfect equality between the teacher and the boys. They were all very polite and the boys all joined us in smoking segarrittos!! —

Nov 29

Sunday. This is the first sunday in Advent. I attended Catholic Church when Father McElroy explained the importance of this first day of the Eclesiastical year. After church I went to Don Augustine Menchacas to dine. This is the first dinner I ever attended at the house of a Mexican gentleman. The brother in law and a spanish young lady, Miss Bowen and myself were the guests. When dinner was announced I gave my arm to the Senora Menchaca and other Gentlemen accompanied their ladies to the dining room. — I was directed to a seat by the Senora and Mr. Menchaca did the honors of the table at the head. — The first dish was a kind of vermicelli without the soup. Plates were removed and a kind of hash containing onions tomatoes and like vegetables in a semmi fried form was handed us in clean plates. Next came a compound I believe of pork, turkey, and beef in soup plates — a kind of fricassee or stew (I am no conniseur in culinary sciences). Next a similar compound which differed in having a kind of red gravy and green gravy was also passed to us in a sauce dish. Next came another stew of kid which was cooked with the blood of the animal. After this came a plate of roast meat, I think kid. Next came a plate of beans *Frijoles*, then a saucer of custard. Next preserves and finally a cup of strong coffee with sugar but neither milk or cream. — During the repast claret wine was freely circulated and the whole party was in the gayest humor imaginable. — The servants were very alive and obedient, and I regard the difference of modes a very trifling matter which all countries seem foolishly addicted to. What can be the difference to a philosophical mind whether we commence with beans or end with them?

Nov 30

The paymaster Major Lloyd Bell[117] has finished paying my regiment. I attended a card party at the Tremont House in the evening. Ladies and gentlemen were invited. I met Colonels Foreman[118] of the Illinois In'f and Thomas[119] of the Tennessee Cavalry and spent the evening very pleasantly. Also made to day, the acquaintance of Captain Eaton[120] of the Army who is attached to the Comissary department. He is acquainted with my brother H. B. and appears like a very intelligent officer.

Decr. 2

Very warm at 10 Oclock; so hot I dispensed with the drill. I dined with Father McElroy by special invitation, in Company with Lieuts Chase and Simmons.[121] The Padre has comfortable quarters and keeps good wine as well as a good cook. He is a very agreeable and kind gentleman. — From the Fathers we went to Mr. Menchacas and to his gardens. Mrs. Menchaca amused all the party by teaching me my A. B. C. in spanish. — Took tea with Mr. Simmons and in the evening called on Mrs. Striker[122] with Hicks Curtis. — This lady has been left a widow with two or three children. She is from New York City, and has resided here fifteen or twenty years.

Decr. 4

General Patterson arrived on the Corvette. He is a large fine looking man. I called and informed the General that I would like to accompany him to Tampico. The General said he would like to have me with him for more than one reason, but that General

Taylor fixed the matter, and though he had twice requested that my regiment should be included in his command, he had received no intimation that it was to be with him. Col Mitchell[123] and Lieut Armstrong[124] of the Ohio regiment were also on their way home. Col Mitchell's wound is still painful, and confining him to his bed. Lieut Armstrong is quite well. His leg was amputated above the knee. — The Ohio volunteers were among the very furtherest in the attack on the left at Monterray. Col Mitchell says that his position was directed by General Taylor himself. Generals Butler and Hamer were also near him when he was wounded. — Officers and men all behaved in the most gallant manner. — I have received the same account from all those I have conversed with that were eye witnesses. —

Took dinner with Mr. Shatsell the American Consul. He was originally from Germany and after making and loosing a fortune in the States he removed to this place where he has accumulated another. — He is a bachelor of intelligence and good manners. His life is full of incident and his accounts are full of interest.

Dec 5

I have been uneasy about a challenge which I understand Hicks Curtis has received and accepted. If the matter were in relation to any other person in my regiment I would stop it at all hazzards; but Hicks is so nearly related that my interference would appear like a design of shielding him. — The seconds have agreed on rifles and now at nine Oclock I am informed that the matter is defered till tomorrow morning. Hicks Curtis awaited on the ground his antagonist who did not appear but by his friends requested a further delay till tomorrow morning.

Dec 6

Last night the friends of Mr. H. Curtis and Mr. Miller referred their matter to a board of honor who some way arranged a meeting and reconciliation. I am much relieved in my feelings. I would not for the world have had my nephew killed in a duel, but I regard the challenge in the light of a bullying operation that should be met. — As it turned out Mr. Miller who sent the challenge has gained nothing and Mr. H. Curtis lost nothing in any view that can be taken of the matter. Duelling is obnoxious to our morals and our laws; but Southern men must in some way be informed that we scorn their code of honor but do not *fear* their threats. —

Received orders to place two companies and one field officer at the plaza and relieve the two Indiana companies now stationed there. — Companies E. and F. were therefore ordered up and located in the building appropriate for the troops.

Dec 7

In pursuance of the orders of the Commanding officer I moved my quarters into the room occupied by him and now I am comfortably located in a room on the second story of a large brick building. Two doors and windows open onto an iron guarded piazza which fronts on the Grand Plaza. Col Clark expects to move out tomorrow and leave me alone in possession of this snug tenement. — Sent Lieut Lundsford and 18 men to Rinosa on the steam boat Aid[125] in charge of stores. A matter was reported to General Patterson this morning and I was ordered by him to have the perpetrators brought to justice. The steam boat Big Hatchee[126] conveying a detachment under command of Lt Col Haddon[127] of the 2nd Indiana volunteers was reported for shooting seven beeves the property of Mexicans near this vicinity. After some ten hours delay of the boat one man was identified by the witnesses and the Lt. Col and I went before the General for orders as to the further disposition of the matter. I was much pleased with the course pursued by General Patterson. He gave the Col a severe lesson on the subject of disorderly conduct of troops in good language and with great dignity. He ordered that the price of the cattle $35 or the man be placed in my charge, and that the boat proceed after this order was executed. — I thought the punishment was well adapted to the occasion, and well calculated to promote subordination in the service. —

Dec 8

Our guard room is full of prisoners taken in street broils. Lieut James McMillen is officer of the day and seems to display unusual activity in discharge of his duties. —

Dec 9

There was a heavy shower last night. At the general jail delivery this morning we had a miserable display of depravity. Mexicans and Americans all ragged and dirty formed in line and
made explanations. Generally they had "got a drop too much"
and therefore got up a street fight. Two of the Mexican prisoners
were taken at the Market Plaza in pursuit of an Indiana volunteer. They were endeavouring to stab him and were taken with
their weapons (knives) and prevented from their purpose of killing an *Americano*.

Dec 10

Major Arthur on his way to New Orleans called and gave me
intelligence of the death of Brig General Hamer.[128] — He died
at Monterray much regretted by officers and men who had made
his acquaintance. — He was a man of talents and agreeable as a
companion. — He was gaining the confidence of his associates in
arms, and at Monterray showed himself ready to perform his duty
in battle.

The death of General Hamer leaves a vacancy in the Brigade
which my seniority of rank would entitle me to fill. — How the
matter will be regarded in the volunteer service, it is difficult for
me to determine. By every rule of progression I ought to be
promoted. My conduct has met the approval of the commanding
General and the evidence of it has arrived the same day that I
have received the intelligence of General Hamers death. — The
following letter is such a distinguished testimonial in favor of my
regiment and myself: that I will endeavour to preserve it by
copying it below. [A large blank space in the diary indicates the
absence of a copy of the letter.]

Decr. 11

General Patterson reviewed all the troops in this vicinity. —
Being Senior Colonel I was directed to take command. I formed
the line in front of Col Foremans camp as follows. — The Tennessee horse commanded by Col Thomas on the right. My Regiment commanded by Major Love, then the third regiment Illinois commanded by Col Foreman and on the left the 4th
Regiment of Illinois commanded by Major Harris.[129] — The pa-

rade ended, the whole force escorted General Patterson to the Grand Plaza and was from there marched by regiments to quarters. — It was the most splendid military display I ever witnessed. My regiment received universal applause. It was decidedly the most distinguished without the least prejudice to the fine manly regiments from Illinois.

Dec 12

After discharging a lot of prisoners generally taken for street fights, I went over to the large chapel on the square where the Mexicans were collecting in great numbers. It is the saints day "Seniora Guadalupe" I believe they call the patron saint of Mexico. There are some two or three hundred, mostly females, all draped out in their best attire kneeling before the altar on the sand. — The Padre before a richly decorated altar was going through a long ceremony of crossing, kneeling, dressing, and rehearsing in Latin. — This was succeeded by music. A chant played on a violin, horn, and a large bass instrument accompanied by one or two voices. This piece of music and rehearsal lasted perhaps an hour. At certain periods the whole audience would go through the motions of crossing in the most rapid succession by bringing their hands across the forehead, eyes, nose, and mouths. At certain periods a little bell would ring and then the men all thumped their breasts with their tightly clenched hands. —

The picture was to me strange. The females were many of them richly clad and some at least very pretty. They all wore the rebosa over their heads giving them some the appearance of nuns. Some were almost black but these showed more of the indian than negro features. Men and women all showed the utmost devotion. — One very richly draped female, with large figured lace rebosa and splendid plain silk mantilla attracted my attention, and induced me to walk round to get a sight at the one eye the females always cast up on community. — After some edging round I got a full view of a most frightful indian squaw as black as the ace of spades. —

Dec 13

I obtained orders from Colonel Clark to bring my regiment into town, and have selected the buildings fronting westwardly on the old chapel plaza.[130] It is rainy and the streets present a muddy aspect for the first time for many months. I called on Col Taylor who is quite ill and has located himself in quarters for the purpose of recruiting his health. — The Colonel gave some flattering compliments to my regiment, and I know of no officer who has had a better opportunity of judging of the various regiments, one who is more capable. He said that my regiment was regarded as "the crack regiment" all along this line. —

Dec 14

Two Mexican prisoners were taken last night by the patrol for robbing an Illinois volunteer. I placed them with my other prisoners in the Mexican jail. One of the rascals was very nice as an old prisoner who had some time since escaped.

One company of the Tennessee Cavalry and the two regiments of Illinois volunteers took up the line of march towards Tampico under the command of General Pillow.[131] — They are ordered to encamp at Musquete 22 miles out, and there they are to wait the approach of General Patterson and the remainder of the Tennessee Cavalry who are expected to follow in a few days.

The rain of yesterday has started vegetation which had become parched with the drought. — Many of the trees have cast off their foliages, not from the effect of frost, but from old age. This is especially the case with the china trees and fig trees. —

Dec 15

A Captain Clay[132] had a deadly hatred for a Mexican, the brother in law of Mr. Menchaca. I could not blame Clay; he had been a prisoner here at Matamoros about the period of Gen'l Taylors arrival and had been treated very badly by the Mexicans. The latter was Captain of a company of Mexicans, and he came into the prison, drew his sword and made cuts at Clay grazing his body and cutting his clothes cursing him for a cowardly American and showing him how he could cut down the Americans. He displayed the bragadocious by violent postures, and told Clay that he was going to join in the massacre and share in the spoils of General Taylors army. — Clay had to bear his base insolence, but now that our arms prevail Clay is at liberty and the Mexican has received a severe pounding from Clay and fears further injury.

As a friend, Mr. Menchaca requested my interference and wished Clay to be reminded of kind acts that he and other Mexicans had bestowed on him for the purpose of restraining the violence. Clay readily acknowledged that one of the Alcaldas, Sen. Longoria[133] — a man of excellent character and Mr. Menchaca had both treated him with great kindness. — Menchaca had acted as his attorney without charging a cent, and the Alcalda had released him from chains and given him the best quarters in the prison; and finally offered him privately the means of escape. — Clay at first swore that he was not satisfied and would further chastise the Mexican; but putting the matter on his honour and at the insistence of the Alcalda — Mr. Menchaca, and myself; he agreed to take acknowledgements from the Mexican and give him his hand. — The matter was thus closed, with the pledge of honour on Clays part that he would hereafter cease to harm or molest the person or property of the Mexican; and treat him as a friend.

I relieved the poor Mexican and his family of the constant anxiety and fear and I rejoice in the satisfaction of having rendered a kind service to the family of my friend the attorney.

It is a very warm and pleasant day; the perspiration stands on my forehead while I sit writing in my room without fire, at seven Oclock in the evening. — News has been received that General Scott is *en route* for Mexico. This news will reanimate the whole army. However much we all admire the courage and success of General Taylor; we regard General Scott as the head of our army, and rejoice that he is about to assume command of our operations. — The five companies stationed on the bank of the river at "Camp McCook" marched up to town and took possession of the barrack on the old plaza. — Received by mail dates to the 22nd November from home. All were well.

Dec 16

Sergeant Babcock of the regulars attached to the general hospital was inhumanly murdered last night.[134] He received eight or nine stabs and was stripped perfectly naked except the shoes. — Robbers and assassins are the greatest curse in Mexico. They prowl about the country and sacrifice a mans life for a pocket handkerchief. — Years must roll round, before villiany can be properly punished. —

The officers of my regiment have drawn up and signed (all but Capt [William McLaughlin]) the following paper which is sent to its destination through Brinkerhoff, M.C.[135]

"To his excellency the President of the United States. The undersigned commissioned officers of the 3rd Regiment of Ohio Volunteers recommend Colonel Samuel R. Curtis commanding this Regiment to be appointed to the office of Brigadier General of the Ohio Brigade now vacated by the death of the much lamented Brig General Thomas L. Hamer.

Col Curtis has been favourably known for many years to the military of Ohio; having by repeated manifestations of his interest, and by his regular military education, contributed much to secure permanency and improvement in the volunteer system. Col Curtis has brought to Mexico a Regiment that in discipline and tactics, will compare creditably with any in the volunteer service. He is now the senior officer in rank in the Ohio Brigade, and by the rules of promotion adopted for the regular Army (which we think should be adopted also in the volunteer service) would now be entitled to that command. None will gainsay, that to the untiring energy practical military knowledge and indefatigable labors of Col Curtis, then Adjutant General of the State of Ohio, is mainly due the honor of the very prompt response of that state to the requisition of his Excellency the President of the U. States, and of overcoming the many difficulties incident to the organization and discipline of the whole Ohio quota now in the field. We most respectfully suggest that these considerations should not be entirely overlooked by the appointing power; and we know that such a token of the national esteem would assure to the Ohio Brigade an officer who would reflect honour on himself and the state, as well as credit on the service and the country.

Matamoros Mexico Dec. 13th 1846"

Dec 17

Captain Moore obtained leave to pass out to hunt and proceeded several miles south east. He had with him Corporal Barney of E Company a very quiet and dilligent soldier. They had got into a region of the country where the chaperal was scattered and full of paths dividing the ways and leading in various directions. Quietly persuing their search for game the Captain had separated from the Corporal, and as his path lead round a cluster of chaperal he was fired at by a Mexican who was concealed at the distance of 18 paces. The captain immediately raised his musket and fired his load of buck and ball into the Mexican who fell uttering most terrific lamentations. Corporal Barney hearing the cry came at full speed through the chaperal, and arriving within 30 paces of the captain was attacked by two mounted Mexicans with swords and carbines.

The Mexicans and Barney fired at each other without effect a ball passing through the cap of the latter. At the same instant Barney charged bayonet on them and one of the Mexicans received a severe wound from the bayonet. Barney was lassoed by the other Mexican and jerked to the ground with great violence and dragged a few feet in the chaperal when Captain Moore with four discharges from his revolver and blows with his musket assisted Corporal Barney in defeating the villains and putting them to flight. Fearing the horsemen might return with reinforcements, the captain and corporal made their way to quarters as fast as possible. The Corporal was unable to walk all the way and it was about sunset when they arrived. A party with Captain Moore started back immediately and Major Love at my suggestion followed on horse back. — It was so dark when they came in the region of this place, they could not ascertain the location. Major Love rode past the point and returned without uniting with them. They took two armed Mexicans with mules and horses who attempted [to] evade them after they were hailed and brought them in with their mules and horses.

Dec 18

At three Oclock, before day light, I again roused Captain Moore who was almost exhausted and organized a party and mounted them as best I could using the mules and horses taken in the evening. We arrived on the ground at day light and found the place where the Mexican had fallen. A fire had been made a few rods from this place, and there was a bed in the grass where a wounded man had lain. — Blood marked the place where he had fallen and the spot where he had lain; but he had been removed and beyond our search. We found a suspicious family residing not far distant, and searching the ranch found guns and sabers which we brought away. We also found the owner of one of the horses taken last evening and he accompanied us into the City where he found we had also two of his mules. I brought out the two Mexicans taken with these mules and horses. They pretended to have found them in possession of a strange Mexican who had fled leaving them the ownership. One of the knaves was nephew to the old man who claimed them and the latter told him in reply to his silly story that it was false and he knew his mules and horses as well as himself. I ordered the horse thieves to be turned over to the Alcalda and the horse and two mules to be returned to the honest claimant at the same time giving him the other two horses saddles and bridles taken from the robbers to indemnify him for other losses and reward him for his honest exposure of one of his own family who had turned out to rob.

Dec 19

Three or four Mexicans were taken concealing amunition and arms by some of Captain Allens company. They had not been long in prison when their friends appeared with a pass signed by General (now Col) P. F. Smith at Monterray authorising one of the men with nineteen others to pass from Monterray to this place with their arms. — I regarded the concealment and other conduct evidence of hostile designs and a breach of the pass which rendered them worthy of examination. Col Clark however directed their discharge and I gave them their liberty with reluctance believing that such armed bodies of men are always ready to act in conjunction with the bands of robbers that infest the whole country. — There was also found a lot of guns and pistols in a hacal [jacal] about two miles in the country which I have taken charge of. — We have taken about as many prisoners about this town as we have men in our regiment and arms enough to accomodate the same number.

Dec 20

Sunday morning always ushered in by a thousand clangs on the Matamoros bells, was also disturbed by the tumbling of boxes, loading of wagons and driving of mule teams preparatory to moving the columns of General Patterson which is ordered to march tomorrow morning. Dispatches arrived from Comargo they had been brought in 16 hours from that place by a Mexican. General Patterson received letters from General Taylor but does not disclose the purport. In the morning at the general jails delivery, two strolling actors were brought up for breaking into a house and stealing a trunk which the patrol caught them opening. Col Clark ordered them to be put in irons and sent to New Orleans after the officers of the day and myself had satisfied ourselves that they were guilty of burglary. They had advertised for a performance at the theatre this evening, and no doubt their sudden departure will surprise the audience.[136] Three Mexicans caught with arms were discharged by the commandant.

I called and took dinner with Mr. Menchaca. The health of his family is improved, and the Senora was able to take her place at the table and lecture me on my negligence of spanish during her illness. Mr. Menchaca has been elected one of the Alcaldas, and also a member of the Mexican Congress. — He is inclined to decline acting in both capacities: — and being asked my opinion as to his best course I told him he was in a delicate position and perhaps he had better suspend acting till he could ascertain what laws prevail. — He thinks that Santa Anna will dictate war measures on the congress and his opinions and measures would be over-crowded by the friends of one who has so many bayonets to sustain him.

Mr. Menchaca regards Santa Anna as a very base and deceitful man, and thinks that our president did his own country and Mexico a great injury by promoting him to return to Mexico. He says that war must confer on Santa Anna more power and more wealth; and whether it terminates well or ill for Mexico, Santa Anna will profit by the continuance of the war. — Both the countries are now in a condition to negotiate peace or prosecute the war, and on the government now rests a fearful responsibility. —

Dec 21

I called on Brig Gen Jessup[137] quartermaster general. He is a fine looking elderly man, of easy gentlemanly manners. He re-

turns to Point Isabella and from there takes his departure to
Tampico for the purpose of regulating the quartermasters department on the Rio Panuco.[138] — Rumors of assault on Saltillo and
ordering up troops to aid General Worth. It is said that General
Santa Anna marched on the seventh.

Dec 22

General Patterson marched about twelve Oclock. The train of
wagons was immense. They have been exiting out their long
lines for three days past. — What vast expense must attend the
prosecution of a war when all our supplies are brought so far. One
of the wagons had inscribed in large letters painted on the side of
the cover — "Tom Corwin."[139] — It was easy to understand
where that driver hailed from. — I have no doubt he has accompanied some of our political marches in Ohio where that name
has stood conspicuous on many a banner. It has been raining a
little this after noon, but the dry weather still prevails. Another
express arrived from Comargo, but I am not informed as to the
purport of the news.

Dec 23

A detachment, the last of the Tennessee Horse left town today
bringing up the rear guard of General Patterson's column. There
are many rumors afloat representing Santa Anna's army in motion and about to make an attack on our forces.

General Taylor must be at or near Victoria and it is said that
General Urrea[140] is there waiting his arrival with six thousand
cavalry.

Dec 24

This morning all the butchers had deserted the market so that
there was no beef. The butchers undertook to place their conduct
on the irregularities of the volunteers. I enquired into the matter
and believe it is owing to a usage in Catholic countries not to eat
meat till after twelve on the day previous to Christmas. Col
Clark at my request sent word to the Mexicans that if they did
not furnish the market with meat he would take the stalls from
the Mexicans and place them in the hands of Americans. — The

consequence was, that plenty of beef was found in market at three or four Oclock. —

Dec 25

Christmas day in Mexico. A bright sunshine, and warm summer day. Early in the morning, the plaza was decorated with a moving varying picture. Seniors and Senioras dressed in their gayest attire were going in lines to the Grand Chapel on the East side.[141] The guard was paraded in front of the chapel for guard mounting, and the old guard in front of my quarters. Soon after guard mounting I repaired to the church and took a seat quite solitary though hundreds of every complexion were sitting, kneeling, and standing around me. — A clarinet and trumpet accompanied a long chant that was being sung by the Padre and some other single voice. I tried to meditate on the sublimity of human worship, and especially on the event commemmorated by this day. I found however that my mind was constantly drawn off by the novelty of the service and the changes of the picture that surrounded me. — The devotion of some, and the mechanical drill of others was to me a matter of surprise. The music and center of performance was in the corner room where the altar and ceremonies were being performed. As the crowd dispersed a little, I pushed my way into this room. — I have before attempted to describe it. The Altar is in the east end, and on this occasion I had a close view of what before I had only seen at a distance. Above the altar was a cross, a looking glass, and on each side elevated about five feet, were two wax figures about half size representing the savior with crown of thorns and the Virgin Mary. Twelve lighted candles were burning, and the whole front view was decorated with pictures, trappings, and various objects of imagery. In front of the altar Father McElroy was seated draped in gay attire decorated with broad gilt lace bands crossing on the breast and displaying a beautiful white tunic or frock thrown over his shoulders. He was seated in a stooped position, holding on his lap was a wax baby about a foot long in state of nudity. — Ladies and Senioras were in succession approaching the altar and kneeling at the feet of the Holy father kissing this wax baby! — The performance was every way shocking to my nerves. I was immediately repelled, and left the scene mortified and disgusted.

Painful rumours of disaster to General Worth continue to multiply. Every day adds to the reputed strength of Mexican forces and a continued extension and expansion of our little army. — We look with the greatest anxiety for reinforcements, not only to reanimate our troops, but to blast the rising hopes of Mexican Generals.

Dec 26

Lieut Colonel McCook and Captain Kell are in good health and fine spirits. Several persons from Baltimore and Ohio came with them. — They report that Captain Ford came over with them and that he is at Point Isabella. After tattoo I went with the interpreter to a regular Mexican *"fandango"*. There were no Americans and I expected to find as I did, a dance after the fashion of the country. It was rather a remote corner of the city, and I took care to examine the caps on my pistol before entering on the excursion. — The house was a one story brick and closed up by shutting all the shutters. The tinkling of the guitar and shuffling of feet was the only evidence exhibited of living in-mates. After knocking for some time the door was cautiously opened and the inside picture was glaring before me. Some thirty or 40 in a small room, well lighted were engaged in dancing. Male and female were all cleanly and neatly disposed. The floor was earth and very smooth to dance on, and in this particular differs from other dancing rooms in the city which generally have rough brick floors. The women were generally dark and none of them pretty. They seemed to me to present an exception in favour of ill looks for there are a great many very pretty senioras in Matamoros. The dances consisted of quadrills and waltzes very much like those danced in the states. The deportment of all exhibited the utmost ease and politeness. I was treated constantly with distinguished attention. It was evidentaly only a medium class of the city, many of the men and women displayed the darkest outline of indian features. I stayed about an hour. Tried to waltz but could not get the step which varies a little from the the step my *distinguished* master *tried* to teach me. I did not find many to talk to and not being a good dancer, I could find no amusement and therefore bade them *Buenos noches*. —

Dec 27

News relating to Mexican force appears to become more fixed and positive. — I was present at the examination of an old and very sensible Mexican who appears friendly to us though he says he cannot oppose his own country. He reports that 6000 troops under command of Generals Urrea and Canales[142] now at Linares seven or eight days from here, and that the design is to attack this place within five or fifteen days. That General Santa Anna is marching to Saltillo with 27 thousand men and that Canales with about 300 Rancheros is at a ranch west of Rinosa and on the road leading to Monterray and some 20 to 30 leagues from Rinosa. — There can be no doubt the old man believes the reports. He says he is certain of the facts as though he had seen them with his own eyes. — Duplicity in the old man would place him in a very dangerous position here as he is an extensive property holder and an old and highly respected citizen. He did not volunteer his intelligence but gave it to a Texian with whom he has for fifteen or 20 years been on terms of friendship and intimacy. Col Clark, Col Taylor, and myself after taking down the statements believe there must be truth in the statement and dispatches and sent to General Scott at Brazos — where we are informed the General has just arrived. — Also to Genl Patterson now enroute to Victoria and to General Taylor who we think must have returned to Monterray.

I directed the officer of the day to exercise great diligence in watching the roads to ascertain who went from and who came into the City; and having so ordered matters, retired to sleep with the design of preparing my regiment to the best advantage for attack tomorrow.

Dec 28

No developments during the night increased the evidence except the following. A Mexican woman is said to have received a letter from her son, a quartermaster in the Mexican service directing her to leave this place and go to a ranch some 16 miles south east, that the Mexican forces were to attack this place in

a few days and she must seek safety in immediate flight. She told
this to an American boarding with her, and departed yesterday
morning. —

As my regiment and a small company in Fort Brown of regulars
is all the force here; our force is to the Mexicans as 1 to 10. I
proposed this morning to Col Clark that a counsel should be
called to take into consideration the best mode of posting our
little force in order to contend to the last extremity. He gave his
assent to the idea, but I expect he will exercise his own judgement and merely communicate orders, as I know he wishes to
originate his own plans, and as commander it is no doubt his
province to do so. — As I am really commander of all the effective force, I am deeply interested in the location of it. —

In compliance with previous arrangement, I rose at four
Oclock this morning for the purpose of making an excursion with
Mr. Menchaca to the Ranch of his mother in law twelve miles
south east of the city. I put on my small arms and walked over to
the house of Sent. Don Augustin Menchacas where I found a
carriage at the door. . . . The road is so perfectly level and clear,
you can go at full speed without the least anxiety about stumps
or other obstacles. Passing several large Ranchos, we arrived at
Santa Rosa about seven Oclock, before the inmates were
dressed. — Mrs. Menchaca (La Senora Dona Maria Rita
Chapa)[143] had gone out some days previous for the health of her
child and her brother Don Pedro Chapa and all the family appeared delighted to see us. The main building is constructed of
clay made into brick about twelve by fifteen inches and eight
inches thick sun dried and laid up in mortar. It is covered with
the palmetto leaf which is very generally used as covers to the
jacals (pronounced *hacal*). — In the vicinity of this main building and at various intervals with little or no regard to order, were
distributed houses (Jacals) of less sizes, some of them no larger
than tents for the servants. They ideally are generally made by
erecting the cane and thatching a roof in a very irregular amd
temporary style. There must be some twenty or thirty of these
grass houses on the Rancho giving it the appearance of a village.
We went round and visited all the families. They presented the
same simple, easy, indian style of living. Each family seems to
possess but a mere necessary out-fit — Something like a cot, a

cradle for the babe, a crock to hold water in, a rope to hang dried beef on, a pan to bake tortillos on, and a few piles of niblish [?] constitute the majority of the personal property of these peons. —

They all appeared very kind, polite, and glad to have us visit them. A beautiful lake which they call an *estary* is close to the houses. This sheet of water connects with the river and we had a delightful ride on it. — The Rio Bravo joins the hacienda on the North, and the whole plantation seems well watered and beautifully situated. It is indifferently cultivated, but affords the finest pasture I ever saw. — The greater part appears to be enclosed, but it is not half stocked. They could feed ten times the cattle. The grass was green and very heavy. A kind of coarse grass, but such as horses and cows thrive very well on. The day was very warm and leaving our coats in the rancho we found the perspiration rolling off our faces with the light covering afforded by our pants and shirts. Many of the children are entirely naked and appear to need no clothing to render them comfortable. — We saw great numbers of aquatic fowl in the water and many birds in the Chaperal. — I left the Rancho about four Oclock and arrived at my quarters about "candle lighting". — Some anxiety began to arise and arrangements were being made to hunt me out; but I arrived in time to allay all feeling of this kind and assure my friends that I had received the most hospitable entertainment and had a delightful excursion. —

Dec 30

The booming guns of Fort Brown announced the arrival of Major General Winfield Scott.[144] I called at the commanding officers to make my respects with my field and staff. The General seemed to recognise me, though I have never seen him since June 1831. He was President of the board of Visitors at West Point where I graduated, and after so many years I can hardly suppose he would recollect me. He insisted that he had some other link of recollection, but I could not give him a clue to it without touching on matters quite personal to myself and too much for my modesty. In political journals I have pressed the name of the Hero of Lundes [Lundy] Lane and Chippawa, and forwarded sheets from various quarters to his address. — These he does not now locate in his memory, and I am extremely glad of it for like all newspaper puffs they are trifling soap bubbles that I never wish to collect. The General is very frank and free, showing all my officers the utmost kindness and respect. — He stayed but a few hours and proceeded on the Corvette towards the supposed location of Gen'l Taylor. —

A company of the Tennesse Horse under Capt Haynes[145] returned to this place with a requisition for provisions. An express had been received by General Patterson from General Whitman [Quitman],[146] at Linares[147] dated the 21st Inst. General Taylor had returned to Monterray for the purpose of joining General Worth who it is supposed might be attacked.[148] General Whitman was pressing forward with three regiments of infantry towards Victorio. — General Whitman did not expect to find any force this side of the mountains. — Generals Patterson and Whitman will therefore form a junction at Victorio within a very few days, unless prevented by Urrea and Canales.

1837 [1847]

Janry. 1st

New Years day in Mexico is not kept as a day for any special amusement, In company with Lt. Col. McCook, Capt Allen and Hicks Curtis I rode up the river four or five miles. — Nothing of much interest has transpired. It is very different from the day in Ohio. The wind got round to the North, and the weather is therefore much cooler. News arrived from Saltillo bearing dates of the 22nd Ult. The reports had caused a general concentration of forces at Saltillo. — Gen Worth had written to Genls Wool, Taylor, and Butler who I believe all sent him reinforcements and General Butler leaving Monterray joined him in person.[149] All the reports proved false and matters there as here have settled back to a perfect calm.

News has been received from San Luis Potosi indicating a desire for peace on the part of the Mexican Congress and Santa Anna. — God grant that it may be true. War is the greatest evil that can come upon a nation and the news of peace should cause universal rejoicing —

I have directed new clothing to be issued to the men of my

regiment of the pattern obtained by Col McCook. It is a dark blue satinnet and a very good article. The round jacket and pants are very suitable for the service, and cost four dollars and twenty five cents *each.*[150]

Much excitement prevailed this evening among the volunteers in consequence of one of Company B. having been stabbed. Three or four Mexicans are taken and placed in the guard house, implicated in the matter. These criminal matters which deserve punishment, and find no adequate jurisdiction, are extremely troublesome to the officers. The vengance of the law is not felt and the villains every day go unpunished of justice.

Complaints of riotous and disorderly conduct among the volunteers have caused me much anxiety. I regret to find that parties of my men have committed excesses; entering shops and demanding liquor, carrying off bottles of wine and otherwise disturbing the public peace. — The foundation of trouble is the vending of ardent spirts. If the grog shops were closed matters would remain perfectly quiet.

Jan 4

More complaints. On visiting the Mexican houses where the riots occurred, I find that O'Sullivan,[151] a discharged regular, has been the leader in the difficulties. On bringing the Mexicans before the prisoners, they recognized him, and I had him put in irons and shipped out of this country.

Col. Drake[152] of the first regiment of Indiana volunteers arrived with his regiment ordered to relieve me. — At the same time orders came from General Scott for me to remain till he returns from Comargo. — I am inclined to think the General designs to take my regiment with him. — I have given orders for every thing to be in readiness for marching, and every one is therfore hoping to have the order to leave Matamoros. — It is now about five months since we arrived here, and I have formed many agreeable acquaintances not only with Americans, but also with the Mexicans. — I shall never expect to see them again after our separation; but I shall often think of their kindness and always cherish their memory. If I live till peace is restored to this unhappy country, it would afford me great pleasure to revisit this city. — Many who I am now obliged to meet would then no doubt give me kind looks where they now eye me with jealousy or mortification. The condition of a conquered people is no doubt painful but the condition conquerers are placed in is likewise delicate. To avoid arrogance and the appearance of ostentation should keep the Conquerers constantly on their guard. Any oppression, tyranny, or injustice to the disarmed citizens of this Country, I regard as dishonourable in us who hold the undisputed dominion of this region of the Country. — I have always exerted all my energy and influence towards the establishment of order and decorum.

I dislike to see my foes humbled and downtrodden after they have submitted. I regret that *laws* have not been established and exercised more successfully. On full consideration however of matters, I do not see how General Taylor could have acted more wisely. The half conquered condition of the country has rendered it impossible to establish a substantial code; and the mode adopted seems to be the only immediate remedy for the unsettled condition of things.

Jan 5

The exertions of my officers and guards last night reduced the town to the best possible discipline, every thing was perfectly quiet. On my rounds, I fell in with a man who speaks broken English, and seemed very desirous of making my acquaintance. He is an Italian who has resided in this place some ten years and no doubt accumulated a fortune. He amused me with various relations of incidents in the Mexican service, and taking me to his house, introduced me to his wife a very genteel looking lady who he married at Havana. He has evidentaly been an old soldier and sailor and I suspect his life would make a book of wonders and curosities; as no doubt the history of many of the citizens in this frontier would. —

I found at the store of the Spanish Consuls'[153] a watch and chain which I was informed was left in pledge by General Arista. Desirous of having it as a curiosity, I proposed to exchange mine for it. — In the frankness of Spanish etiquette, the Consul immediately handed it over retaining mine and refusing boot. I was not prepared to reply to such generosity and insisted on giving fifty dollars as a palpable difference in favour of his watch; but no, not a cent I had to hold onto my advantage. The Spanish Consul is a Spaniard by birth. He has accumulated a large fortune by commercial persuits at this place, and he continues to carry on a very heavy business. I would recommend him as one who appears rather friendly to our cause and an agreeable gentleman. His name is [space left blank].

Jan 6

General Scott arrived on his return from Comargo. He called me into his state room and gave me a long talk on the subject of the abominations committed by our troops. The General seems to think matters have been conducted in a disorderly way, and that outrages have been committed which disgrace this country. — I told the General that he had heard the worst side of the matter. That brigands had no doubt attached themselves to the service who were felons at home. But that in all countries and communities disorder and crime would always to some extent prevail. That every criminal court ascertained and often furnished specimens of depravity that would make any man of high moral character shudder at the contemplation. That in accumulating a large multitude of all classes to act as soldiers on the Rio Grande; they brought with them their vices and their virtues and with all their faults and follies they were still capable of the best feelings and noblest actions. — I am surprised at the character and direction given to conscience. The faults of the few will attach to the entire corps. If ten men in my regiment would take ten bottles of whiskey and start through the streets in a regular *stampede*: this town would be in the greatest terror. The Mexicans would scatter to the four winds, and all the Americans in town would cry out in horror, "look at the d _____ d volunteers, they are unfit for the service".

General Scott was pleased to say he had always heard my regiment highly spoken of. — That he had countermanded my order to march to Comargo, for the purpose of taking me with him. That in due time I would receive orders and they would be to follow him! That he wished me to prepare my regiment for action and dangerous service and be ready to march at any time within ten days or two weeks. —

The General did not come off the steam boat. Col Hitchcock

Curtis' headquarters during the latter part of his stay at Matamoros (from Thorpe, "Our Army").

(Commandant of the Corps of Cadets during the last two years of my sojourn at that school) came with me up into the City.[154] I have not seen him since I graduated in 1831. Time has made some impression on the Colonel, but he has gained very high standing in the army, and in all probability some day reach the head. — Captain Swartout my old friend and class mate also rode through town with me; and I ought also to mention Major Smith of the Engineering Corps and the Staff of the Commander in Chief.[155] The General and Smith passed down in the Corvette.

The weather has been very hot, and the wind has been from the south for a few days past. This evening about seven Oclock we were suddenly surprised by a roaring rushing wind that came driving a cloud of dust from the North. It is now blowing a tremendous gale. The whole town is covered with *thick* darkness. — It is a dreadful night for those who reside in ships or live in the tented field. I am very thankful that my lot is cast this night in a good room. May heaven preserve and spare those who are on the flood or in the field. —

Jan 7

There was ice this morning about half an inch thick. The wind is still from the north and very cold and chilling. A Mexican was shot near town and reports that two men with dark clothes and muskets met him on the road and demanded his blanket. That he gave them his blanket and started on his way. A few moments after, giving ten or twenty steps he received the contents of one of the muskets in the small of his back evidentaly a mortal wound.[156] The companies of my regiment were just turning out for drill so that I had an opportunity of calling the rolls and ascertaining the absentees. — I also had a good opportunity to examine their quarters and taking the brother of the wounded man, we searched every bunk and box for the blanket. Four men being found absent with muskets, when they came in they were taken before the wounded man who said they were neither of them guilty.

Jan 8

The wounded Mexican died at 11 Oclock last night. — I have been with his brother all day searching for the perpetrators of the

dastardly act. The wounded man before dying made a more distinct statement in regard to the men. He said one was dressed in
a gray frock and gray pants and the other in blue. After two days
careful examination I can find no reasonable ground of establishing suspicion on any of my regiment.

There are a great many straggling adventurers who have left
the army or follow it and commit deeds of villany shielding
themselves under the cover of our volunteers.

Jan 10

A paper signed John H. Wilson[157] was received by Col Clark
stating that some volunteers dressed in blue had entered the jacal
of a Mexican woman and murdered five or six of her children.
The Col met me in the morning and directed me to turn out a
company and the squad of convalescent Tennessee men was
ordered to prepare to go on horseback. I told the Col it must be
a hoax. That no men would commit so base an act of cruelty. I
insisted however in going myself to ascertain the facts and therefore mustered a party consisting of the Alcalda, Sen. Don Augustin Menchaca, several of my officers, an interpreter, and several Mexican police men. We enquired at every house on our way
for robbers and murderers and they reported that all was quiet.
Some parties of Indiana volunteers had been passing to the
mouth of the river, but had committed no offenses worth noting.
One party had taken passage on some Mexican ponies and another in a frolic had taken a jack up from a Mexican and rode
him some miles then turned him loose. After going some twelve
miles we enquired at a jacal for murderers, when we were informed by the good woman that she had two officers snugly
ensconced asleep in her quarters. — We found one of them to be
the veritable "John H. Wilson" a captain of the Indiana volunteers with whom I recollect to have had some acquaintance. I
asked if he had written a note to Col Clark giving the sad story
of a base murder by the volunteers. He said that he had, and
would conduct me to the unfortunate mother who was yet weep-
ing over her dreadful bereavement. We all followed the Captain
with fearful apprehension of a scene of woe and lamentation. On
entering the jacal I was accosted with "Senior Colonel" by a
little boy who I recollected to have met [at] Santa Rosa. The day

was very cold and two or three children were clustering round a fire in the center of the hut. The little boys eyes sparkled with delight. He is a very sprightly pretty orphan boy who I had especially noticed at Santa Rosa. I had there proposed to take him home with me, and he said he would live here but could not go so far. Meeting me again he hung around me though he had found his father, and I was almost as much pleased to see him.

The story of the murder was soon explained. The woman was sister to the woman in town whose husband had been shot. She was mourning the death of her brother in law and spoke of the sad condition of her sister who was left with five or six helpless children!

Capt Wilson expressed much regret that he should have given circulation to a report so entirely false.

We made a short stay and hurried home. The day was cold and towards evening it set in to rain and freeze. The ice formed on our clothes and every way we felt that winter was down on us with much severity.

Jan 12

Pay day brings money and money brings a spree and a spree in camp is abominable. We have a terrible confusion of language in the guard house. — Nothing transpired to day worth notice here at Matamoros. It has moderated a little, but I find a fire very comfortable this evening. —

This town is becoming a fragment of New Orleans. The French are seen at every corner with their smooth hats, cains, and faces. — Every eating house is called a "restorat" — and you generally find a Frenchman at the head of the concern.[158] There is one exception. The best coffe house is kept by a French *woman* two squares north of the Plaza. — It seems to me strange that a good looking female should have wandered from Paris to this place and have set up an establishment solitary and alone. — She says she arrived here four months ago, so that she must have come in midsummer with all the terrors of war, sickness and death staring her in the face. Women are strange beings capable of any thing and no doubt this woman has borne fatigues and privation with more fortitude than some of our soldiers.[159] —

Jan 13

Col Drake with his 1st Regt Indiana volunteers marched into the Plaza. The regiment makes a very good appearance for service. It is not any thing like as well drilled as my regiment but they show strong hands and strong heart ready and capable of doing good service. I marched down to their encampment with my regiment and altogether we displayed a pretty strong force.

My friend, Miss Bowen, the Yankee girl of whom I have before spoken, and who acts as interpreter for the Alcalda was very unfortunate this evening. She stepped out to visit a neighbor and returned about 8 Oclock in the evening, when to her surprise she found her door had been opened with false keys, her trunk taken, and her clothing and most of her effects. All her money was in her trunk, so that her hard earned gains have been suddenly stripped from her. — The Alcalda and myself, with Mexican and American patrols searched many of the adjacent jacals without success. —

Jan 14

The wind has changed so as to blow strong from the south, and the weather has again become warm. —

A legal matter pending before the Alcaldas between Bertrand Comb and Bacon has been accidentally or by some cunning devise slipped into the hands of Col Clark who has taken upon him self the power of deciding it. I have advised the Colonel that his duties are entirely executive and that he cannot interfere with the adjudication of the matter. The Alcaldas very naturally and properly insist that their functions must not be interfered with and consider the attempt to decide a matter under their cognizance as subversion of all their authority. I have recommended the Col to withdraw his note, and thus rescind his judgement, otherwise in my opinion he lays himself personally liable.[160] —

Poor Miss Bowen found her trunk this morning at the skirts of the town; broken open and robbed of every cent of her money and all her valuable articles of clothing. No evidence as yet is had of its location. She continues to bear up bravely under her misfortunes and sustains as she has in her long marches through the country; the character of a good soldier. —

Jan 15

Col Hitchcock came up from the mouth of the river. He says that General Scott is busy arranging matters for his expedition. That Brazos St. Iago is undergoing a general change and organization. If the General will reduce that place to order and system, he can regulate all Mexico; for I regard that as the most intricate labyrinth that ignorance and negligence could create.

Col Clark withdrew his note sent recently to the Alcaldas deciding the matter between Comb and Bacon. — This leaves the Alcladas jurisdiction to proceed as it may and as it should to investigate the truth of the matters in litigation.

I dined to day with commercial mess — Messrs Asher, Hepburn, Taylor, Belden,[161] and others, all very intelligent and sensible merchants pressing their fortunes in this new field of enterprise. Col Fitzpatrick[162] formerly aid to Gen Bolivar and notorious in the Florida War for having introduced the Bloodhounds from the West Indies, is one of this mess. He was also at the Battle of Monterray with the Texians and seen in some way allied to the service. —

Jan 18

Called on Col Drake at the Indiana camp. They are very anxious to go with General Scott on his contemplated journey southward. News from Brazos St. Iago is of no interest. General Scott is located on the Brazos Island in a building recently erected by the Quartermasters department. His officers, I am told, are very busy drawing maps and charts preparing to the departure of the troops.

I regret to hear that no building or shed has been provided to accomodate the sick. — I shall never forget the total negligence displayed at that place so far as quarters for the sick are concerned. Great efforts were made to build sheds and spread tarpolions to protect the pork, whiskey, and hard bread; but in August when boats loaded with sick soldiers were being landed, there was not a yard of canvas or the slightest covering to accomodate a sick volunteer. Is it possible that another accession of troops will find the same inhospitable reception in Mexico?

The wind has been from the south all day and it is quite uncomfortably warm in the sun.

Jan 19

At day light this morning I found myself cold under two blankets. The wind was rattling the windows and on examination I perceived it had again changed to the North and we are again chilled through with a cold rainy day. I am informed that orders have gone up the river directing all cavalry moving towards General Scotts head quarters at Brazos; to stop and wait further orders. — The horses of the mounted rifle regiment coming from New Orleans, have been most of them lost on their passage. The vessel tossing and tumbling on the waves made it impossible to keep the horses tied and breaking loose they were pitched overboard into the Gulf. — This is a bad time for moving troops on the water, and I fear disaster may befall some of those required to venture the hazzard. I would much rather march to Vera Cruz by land, and believe the chances are that we could start from here and arrive as soon by land as by water. There are so many difficulties and delays on the coast. —

Jan 20

A company of Dragoons commanded by Lieut Kearney arrived in town this evening direct from Saltillo. General Worth with other troops is between this place and Comargo, also on the way to join General Scott.[163] These movements take us by surprise. It is the first movement of troops that has not been previously anticipated by every volunteer, and in most cases talked of for weeks before hand. Verily General Scott is going to make a new display of our arms. The horses of this company are considerably jaded. They passed up through this place about the first of November. Their march and countermarch has been a needless movement and no doubt toilsome. I am delighted with my prospect of meeting General Worth. He was instructor of Tactics and commander of the corps of cadets when I entered the Academy. At the end of the first year he gave me the appointment of first corporal of the first company in the corps. I have since held many stations much more significant. — In fact, at the end of the second year I was promoted by him to the office of 1st Sergeant of the same company and at the end of the third year I was appointed by Col Hitchcock (then Capt Hitchcock and successor to Major Worth in this command) to the office of first Captain.

But I have never received any appointment that so much flattered my vanity and satisfied my aspirations as that of 1st Corporal in the Corps of Cadet. I had gone to West Point with much unfavorable qualifications. I had received a very indifferent western common school education, and had never devoted myself to any regular course of studies. I was exceedingly backward and ignorant of reading, writing, and arithmetic: and when I found my class mostly composed of regular students and many of them graduates of colleges; I saw my prospects were poor indeed. Military distinctions did not so much depend on previous studies, for we all had to begin at the school of the soldier. I found myself therefore on equal footing in matters purely military and I did not fail to exert myself when I saw a prospect of distinction. In other studies I would only expect to retain a respectable standing, and I found often that I could not at all succeed; but in the matter of drill and science of war, I seldom if ever missed any part of my lesson. General Worth (then Major Worth) was set up as a model for all of us to imitate. The whole army regarded him as the most accomplished soldier, and I almost idolised him. Next to General Scott, Major Worth stood preeminent, and any attention manifested by either was regarded as just ground for congratulation. My advancement was one of the most conspicuous in my class and in a military point of view gave me a distinction which I succeed in holding during my long course of four years. — When I look back at the period and remember the ties of affection and friendship that I separated from on leaving Ohio: I am surprised at my patience and endurance. Four years without writing my friends and my home. — And during that time engaged and fondly attached to my wife! — Oh! I can well remember the dreary months and days that dragged along; and I can remember too the emotions of my aching bosom tossed daily monthly and for years, with hope and fear. — The incidents of my life have been varied. The dark and light have alternated in my path. — In 1817 I was a boy playing in my fathers sugar camp. In 1827 I went to West Point. In 1837 I was appointed principal Engineer on the Muskingam[164] improvement, a most difficult and extraordinary *experiment* in civil engineering. In 1847 I find myself Col of the 3rd Regiment of Ohio Volunteers stationed in the Republic of Mexico! All these changes have been unsought and unexpected events in my life.

Jan 21

Cold windy weather. The air appears to [be] impregnated with watery vapor and looking out at my window every thing has the aspect of a drizzling snow storm. It is certainly cold enough for snow; but for some reason snow does not form. Sleet and rain seem to occupy its place. — Yet there is not rain enough to lay the dust. The ground has not been saturated with moisture for several months. —

Captain Johnson came down with the body of General Hamer. — I marched my regiment down to the landing and forming line fronting the boat presented arms in honour of the sad remains of our commanding General. It was a long cold march but willingly performed by the Third Regiment. — We have paid a sad tribute to the only officer I could expect to stand by and defend the rights of Ohio Volunteers. — All other Generals have their own state troops or old associates to contend for. Our Ohio volunteers have no Ohio General in the field and the regiments are separated. One in Monterray, one divided at Comargo, Seralvo, and elsewhere; and mine in this place.[165]

Troops are gathering here from all directions. Col Childs with his Artillery[166] — Col Hearney [Harney],[167] with "Duncans Battery"[168] and many other corps are pitching tents in all directions. We are quite surrounded. A detachment of the Tennessee troops arrived from Victoria with dispatches.

Generals Taylor and Patterson were at Victorio and about leaving, one for the gulf and General Taylor for Monterray. These movements surprise us here, and surely must have their influence on General Santa Anna. —

Jan 22

General Worth[169] arrived by steam boat on his way to join General Scott. I called on him with Col McCook and some other of my officers. The General has changed very considerably since I last saw him at West Point. Eighteen years make a deep impression on any man. When he commanded us a West Point he had black hair dark complexion and black eyes. Now he has gray hair, pale sickly complexion, and the clear black eye still remains perfect. — There was a great crowd of officers on the boat, but I had no time to form their acquaintance. I was glad to meet my old friend and class mate Capt. Charles B. Larned.[170] There are but few very few of my class in the army. — Capts Ogden and Larned are all that I have met with during the campaign. General Worth has moved his troops down the river, the Cavalry and Artillery are to encamp near Palo Alto where they will remain till orders are given for embarking.

Some of the officers think General Scott has done injustice to General Taylor in ordering matters forward without consultation. — I know that General Scott did design an interview with General Taylor and went to Comargo after he had assurances that General Taylor had turned back from marching toward Victoria. When General Scott arrived at Comargo, he learned that General Taylor had again started to Victoria, and so we all supposed to Tampico via of the region of the mountains. General Scott arrived here on the 6th Inst. returning from Comargo. If he had gone directly from this place to Victoria there was then no certainty of meeting General Taylor. He would however have met him then. If he had gone, it would not have been possible for him to have reached him before the 12th. Such then would have been the delay that General Scotts orders could not have gone out from Victoria before the 14th. That place not on the general line, it would have been a delay equal to defering here till the 18th. So that General Scott has gained about two weeks time by dispensing with the needless search after General Taylor who undoubtedly deserved the utmost respect. I regard every *day* and *hour* as a matter of vital importance to our movements. Any delay may prove fatal to our success. The Mexicans are increasing their forces daily, and likewise look forward to the period when the black vomito will garrison Tampico and Vera Cruz. — It often breaks out there as early as April, and we certainly therefore have little enough time to move to Vera Cruz where I suppose the expedition is destined. Surely matters of etiquette should not interfere with such considerations. — General Worth expressed anxiety for the line here on the left, and supposed it infested with those who were carrying on a guerrilla warfare. He mentions in illustration or in evidence of it, the circumstances of several persons having been murdered near Mear [Mier].[171] I do not apprehend any danger in that quarter. I do not believe there are any forces this side of Sierra Madre except the bands of robbers under command of Canales. No doubt it was some of his men who committed these murders. The only possible danger to this line is to be apprehended from a movement by Santa Anna. — He is not going to march against General Taylor at Saltillo if he hears of General Scotts movement towards Vera Cruz. But if he does march towards Saltillo, General Taylor will give him battle at several points before any serious impression can be made on this line.

In the mean time, this division will favour the movement of General Scott, who can take Vera Cruz leave that place with a small garrison, march to San Luis Potosi and attack Santa Anna in the rear. — All we want now is *forces*. We have too small an army for these combined movements; but such is the consideration we have acquired in our former battles, that our Generals will not hesitate with such force as they have. —

Jan 23

Several companies of the 2nd Dragoons under the command of Major Bell (brother of the paymaster) are ordered to remain here until further orders. — I see many of the men hanging about the grog shops, and feel as much disposed to riot and disorder as any volunteers I have seen in the field. My officers inform me that the conduct of the Dragoon officers is not calculated to improve the discipline of the men.

Jan 24

I visited Major Bell of the 2nd Dragoons at his camp. He is pitched about one mile below town on the bank of the river. — The horses and men appear some the worse of long marches. They have been in General Wools line, and therefore constantly marching for months past. The Major is a little bald, with rather a red face and agreeable ways. — There appeared to be no guard around the camp and matters appeared rather scattering. I invited the Major to visit my inspection at four Oclock; but he forgot his promises to attend.

I had a general inspection of all the Companies of my regiment on the Plaza at 4 Oclock. Colonel Clark went around with me. The regiment appeared very strong and able to perform duty.

There are very few on the sick list, but those that are sick are said to be dangerous —

The Dragoon band cheered us with the best of martial music this evening. It has been too warm for comfort to day, but this is a delightful moon light night and while I write this loud rich notes of the bugle, trumpet, and drum are filling my room with the richest harmony.

Jan 25

Among the prisoners taken last night was a Mexican in the act of robbing one of the principal hotels. I took him before the Alcalda and directed an examination as to his conduct and accomplices. He would give no intelligence of his companions and the Alcalda ordered him back to prison. In a few moments the Alcalda requested me to accompany him to the prison to see what confessions the criminal made. I was curious to know what appliances the Alcalda had used to ascertain the truth, and readily followed him to the prison. I found the prisoner in a most painful machine undergoing a torture that drew the cold sweat from every one. I never before conceived of torture. The criminal was a large, bold, dark, and good looking Mexican. He was seated astride of a long bar about 14 inches wide and four thick. This bar was made of two pieces and came together like bullet molds leaving holes of various sizes to suit the legs of the victims. The ankles of the criminal were crossed through these holes so that his legs were twisted and his body drawn down in a most painful condition. I was tortured myself to see the man in misery and begged the Alcalda to release him immediately. After asking him a few questions the Alcalda consented. His admissions did not amount to much. He is evidentaly a hardened villain and well deserves punishment; but the idea of *torture* was so revolting to my senses, I could not permit the Alcalda to persue it a moment longer. It is a disgrace to the age and humanity requires its immediate disuse. I shall never forget the picture of horror and hope never to write the like again. —

News comes from below stating that a party of Dragoons had stopped at the ranchos of St. John and Santa Rosa and frightened women and men by firing their pistols and by other acts of violence.[172] That they had robbed many of the jacals and tried to violate the women. That in one instance they had torn the clothes all off a young girl. Such villanous outrages, if they had been committed by volunteers would be heralded all over the country — We would never hear the last of it.

Jan 26

The wind is shifting and I therefore expect another Norther. Reports come to the Alcalda and through him to the commanding officer representing that certain outrages had been committed at San John (pronounced San Whan) by troops wearing the uniform of the United States Army. —

Jan 27

I was directed by the commanding officer to go down to the neighbourhood of St. John and there ascertain the facts relating to the matters reported to the Alcaldas. I was furnished with a party of seven of the Tennessee mounted men as an escort. [Senator] Don Augustin Menchaca being ill, I procured a wagon of the quartermaster and at nine Oclock we were en route. Our party in the wagon consisted of my interpreter Oscar, Hicks Curtis, the Alcalda and myself and a driver Rose. The interpreter took his guitar, Hicks his flute, and I my sword and pistols. Thus "armed and equipped" we were rolling down the smooth and level road towards San John.

We stopped at the Hacienda Longorano and got a description of the troops that had passed on Sunday the 24th the same day the offences were said to be committed. The owner of the ranch stated very clearly the character of those supposed to have been guilty of the offences.

Lieut Deas[173] and two other officers had stayed some hours at this ranch and permitted the party of men to proceed in detached parties under the sergeants and corporals. They did no damage at this ranch, but got up a street fight among themselves. — We stayed here but a few moments and proceeded to the Rancho which is San John. Here we were informed the soldiers had committed many acts of folly and extravagance, firing their guns in the houses, menacing the inhabitants, stealing blankets and other articles. The next rancho is Santa Rosa of which I have before spoken. The owner Senora Dona Anna Domingo Chapa and all her family were absent and matters had been for some days in charge of the Major Domo who received us very gladly, and gave us the charge of our own accomodations. We ordered our dinners and sent for the peasantry who had been injured by the soldiers. They gathered by the dozen from San John, Santa Rosa, and the next Rancho called "Rancheeta". After eating our "tortillos" and refreshing ourselves a little we entered on the examination of witnesses. Some had been robbed of blankets, some of handkerchiefs, some of chickens, one exhibited a trunk which had been broken and the money jewelry and valuable articles had all been pilfered from it. One woman had been rudely and brutally attacked in an attempt to violate her chastity. She bore on her person the marks of cruelty and exhibited her chimese torn in shreds. Her father had entered the jacal to relieve her, and the soldier had brutally turned to him and attempted to shoot him with his musket. Lieut Deas and the other officers had arrived in time to prevent further violence but did not stop to ascertain the enormities of his men. At the next ranch below "Rancheeta" they had cut up a saddle and one man had rode into a jacal and committed like foolish and wanton extravagances. —

The Alcalda and I heard all their just complaints, promised to persue the culprits with the rigors of the law, and then advised them to cheer up and dance off their sorrows. They all readily consented and proposed to meet at our quarters and hold a Fandango. . . . [T]he dance having terminated, the senors and seniorettas took leave thanking us kindly for the priviledges granted them of showing their regard for us, and for an occasion of amusement. — I felt that we were the ones that ought make acknowledgements, but I had neither English nor Spanish words to express a full reply to the *"Millo Gracias"* of the kind hearted peasantry as they each in departing gave me their hands. —

Jan 28

We drove home after breakfast. It was a cold ride and I find matters here in Matamoros in *status quo*. I made a written report to Col Clark of my investigation, and he forwarded it to General Worth who commands the encampment at Palo Alto. — The officers and men ought to be severely punished who so wantonly permitted and engaged in such barbarity. I have seen no instance among the volunteers that equalled these outrages, and none of my regiment has been guilty of anything like the same improprieties. It shows the folly of speaking of outrages as though they attached to the *volunteers* alone. I have no doubt the regulars are generally under better discipline than the volunteers; but crimes and misdemeanors are committed by all classes of men in all countries and it is folly to expect *perfection* among troops of any kind stationed in an enemies country, where crime and ignorance predominate and where no system of laws prevails. Whenever the regular officers wish to indulge in wholesale denunciations of the volunteers, they should pause and consider well and remember the stationary positions occupied by the volunteers, their greater numbers and the constant movement and honourable position always granted to the regulars. — If they are still inclined to persist in general denunciations; I ask them to go to the Ranchos of Longorania, San John, Santa Rosa, and Rancheeta; and they will hide their faces as I have done with grief and mortification at the relation of crime, and the inhumanity of my countrymen. —

Jan 29

My old friend and classmate in the Military Academy, Capt Wm Chapman[174] of the 5 In'f called on me before I was dressed this morning. I was glad to see another of my companions at West Point. Chapman was one our best soldiers at the Academy and he is one of the best in the Army. He is on his way to join Genl Scotts expedition now encamped at Palo Alto.

General Worth arrived this evening on a steam boat. I called on [him] with Lt Col McCook and others. He said that I would receive orders in a very few days to join him, that he had a conversation with the Genl on the subject. —

Jan 30

This morning Col Clark called and informed me that he had received a letter from General Scott directing him to advise me that the General could not take my regiment and that he left me to perform my orders given me previous to his arrival in Mexico. This of course throws me back on my order to go to Comargo. My disappointment and indignation I cannot express. I had reported to my friends that I was now sure of going into the field, that the word of General Scott was pledged to it and I could not doubt it. I determined to go immediately to General Scott at Brasos before Col Clark could make out any order relating to the matter. I therefore mounted my horse and started full speed. I designed to say to General Scott that I could not satisfy my regiment. That I had again and again directed the men to the distinct risks and dangerous service they were to enter upon, and that they should regard our labor or expense necessary to prepare for it. They have under this prospect entered heartily in my design put themselves in the most perfect order.

I have gone with Lt. Col McCook some two or three miles beyond Fort Brown, when I was taken by a kind of stitch in my back near my right shoulder which was so painful that I could hardly sit on my horse. I was obliged to return and I did so with pain. I succeeded in getting to my cot where after undergoing cupping I feel myself more comfortable. On my return here to my quarters I found a copy of a letter sent by General Scott explaining the reason why he General Scott had changed his design of taking my regiment. It seems Generals Butler and Taylor had objected to his taking these volunteers and placing new ones in our places and *therefore* General Scott could not comply with the expectations he had held out to me. — If I had received the letter of General Scott in explanation at the same time I received the intelligence of his design, I would not have been so much displeased and should not have used expressions so severe. But I feel yet that General Scott has done me and all the volunteers on the rio grande injustice. My regiment especially have reason to feel it. To pass by us and select *regulars* from Saltillo and even from General Wools column is saying plainly you are inferior and General Scotts letter does not avoid this plain and palpable prefference for troops that have the *stamp* of regulars on them. — I *know* that these regulars are so misused up with recruits they are in no respects worthy of this prefference. I have sent word to General Scott that if he has any regiment that he regards superior to mine I dare the commander to the test. I am near enough to the camp of the regulars to make this proposition a fair one, and no vain boast, I have no fears of a fair test. My regiment I know cannot be excelled by [any] regulars in this army, and General Scott should not have sent seven or eight hundred miles for regulars without even looking at my regiment or sending an officer to inspect it.

Col Clark called and informed me that he had to leave for Brasos Sant Iago where he had been ordered on a court martial. I told him to tell Generals Worth and Scott that I had always been their friend, but I considered they had insulted and disgraced me. That I should obey my orders and serve out my time as a resignation would only make my position that of the defensive. I would then have to explain why I had left the field. —

My old friend and class mate Capt Chapman drilled my regiment this evening. I care not who drills them if they only get the right words of command they will always execute the movement. In consequence of Col Clarks leaving for Brasos, I published an order assuming command. Before doing so I had an interview with Col Clark informing him that I had served under him as a matter of courtesy and not of rights. That I had no doubt of my seniority of rank as it was admitted my commission bore date previous to his. That the law under which I served expressly placed the volunteers "on the same footing with other troops in the United States service" but that I did not desire any rupture or difficulty during my term of service and was determined to submit to any and every thing rather than trouble the commanding General who had placed him in command over me. Col Clark admitted that I had served faithfully and he had so represented the matter, that I had a good regiment and he would much prefer if he stayed to have me remain with him. —

Jan 31

Many officers and friends have called to see me this morning. — I have enjoined on my officers to keep down every feeling of indignation that prevails, and show our superiors that *we understand the dutys of soldiers* and while in the service will continue to perform them. — There was a universal murmur and universal feeling in the corps, but so far I have prevented the least act of disorder. —

I defy the world to show me a corps that could be placed at such a place as this and exhibit such a state of discipline under

such repeated and mortifying disappointments. — Col Cook returned with intelligence that General Scott had treated him with
great respect and kindness, but the matter of our destiny is fixed.
We are to stay and execute former orders. — My fate I consider
sealed.

General Scott will go forward with his regulars and new wol-
unteers and will carry every thing before him as I trust and hope.
All the honour will be heaped upon his command, and we will
return to find humble graves. The General has made many ex-
cuses for not carrying out the promise held out to me, that I "had
remained faithful in the rear and should now go forward to the
front", perhaps more than I ought to ask or expect. Still the
painful and humiliating *fact* remains that for some reason I am
left and others of the stamp *regulars* are almost all taken from this
river.

Jan 31 [duplicate date]

Many trouble some matters are pressing themselves upon me,
and I am like Sancho Panza; already tired of the office of Governor. There being no steam boats that can be obtained, I have
directed the march to commence on Tuesday morning the 2nd
February, as early as teams can be provided.

THREE

Suspense in Camargo

L ATE in 1846, U.S. forces faced a two-pronged attack from the Mexicans. First, Santa Anna had gathered more than 25,000 troops at San Luis Potosi with the intention of making an offensive thrust against Americans occupying the states of Tamaulipas, Coahuila, and Nuevo Leon. The second and more immediate threat to Colonel Curtis' command came from General José Urrea's light cavalry division which entered northeastern Mexico through Tula Pass, southwest of Victoria in December of 1846. Urrea's movement was detected early by American forces, but his objective remained a mystery. Colonel Clarke, commanding at Matamoros, had information that an assault on his garrison was imminent.[1] Clarke suggested that the river towns of Matamoros and Reynosa be reinforced to counter any possible threat.

Allied with Urrea's cavalry were ranchero forces under the leadership of General Canales and Colonel Romero — an alliance that boosted the morale of the irregular Mexican forces. Their guerrilla activities against American lines of supply and communication were not only intimidating but effective. Colonel George Morgan, who led a force from Camargo against Mexican guerrillas which preyed on American supply trains around China, reported a large force of rancheros in that area.[2] An American officer riding with Morgan on the raid to China reported in his diary that in the Mexican villages along the way no men were present and Americans were greeted by an ominous silence from the villagers.[3] Canales' irregulars had become increasingly bold in their attacks on Americans; in the month of February, Canales reported that 161 Americans had been killed by his forces.[4]

By December Santa Anna's strategy was beginning to unfold. Urrea, Canales, and Romero were to unite in an effort to disrupt the lines of supply and communication from the Rio Grande to Taylor's forces at Saltillo and Monterrey. Santa Anna would march north from San Luis Potosi to attack the front of Taylor's army, now severely weakened by General Winfield Scott's competing plan to invade central Mexico. Scott had taken all of Taylor's regular forces to man the attack on Vera Cruz, leaving Taylor less than 6,000 volunteers around Saltillo and Monterrey and about 1,200 volunteers in garrison posts along the Rio Grande. The troops that remained with Taylor were nearly all one-year volunteers and had almost no battlefield experience.

Santa Anna knew of Scott's impending attack on Vera Cruz and could easily have moved from San Luis Potosi to counter but reckoned that he might finesse the Americans from Vera Cruz. Santa Anna could force Scott to divert his forces to save the American army on the Rio Grande by defeating Taylor's weakened garrisons along the Rio Grande and in northern Mexico. The growing weariness of the American public with the war in Mexico, coupled with a major defeat of Taylor's forces could have spelled an end to the war. A very perceptive strategy.

From Camargo, Colonel Curtis sensed that momentous events were quickly unfolding in northern Mexico, events that could effect the outcome of the war and the lives of many American volunteers. With a feeling of urgency, Curtis addressed his famous "50,000 troops" letter to President James K. Polk[5] explaining the perilous position of American forces in northern Mexico and requesting immediate aid. Letters of a similar tone were sent to General Scott in Tampico and to the governors of Texas and

Louisiana. The letter to Texas Governor James Pinckney Henderson beckoned for immediate action to avert disaster:

> All communication has for several days been cut off between this place and General Taylor's Head Quarters. Our last communication is dated the 21st. Ult., and the General was then threatened by a large army in front, and a very considerable force in his rear.
>
> Private communications inform us, that Santa Anna had demanded a surrender, and General Taylor had replied to him to come and take him. Since that date all is doubt — darkness — rumor. It is certain the General is besieged, and that too, by a large force of Cavalry in his rear.
>
> I believe the occasion requires a large force to raise the siege, and therefore request you to call out two thousand mounted men. As far as possible, they should procure arms and ammunition, and repair to this point as fast as companies can be organized and equipped. The call might be for four month's men —[6]

Curtis also summoned to Camargo the Texas Mounted Volunteer companies from Corpus Christi and the companies that had just been mustered into service in San Antonio. The company from Corpus Christi, led by Captain Mabry B. "Mustang" Gray, was a hardened set of men who would commit many crimes against Mexican civilians during the war. One of the San Antonio companies, led by Captain Walter P. Lane included the notorious John Glanton,[7] enlisted as a private. These "Texas Rangers" left a blackened trail of death and destruction among Mexican civilians wherever they went — crimes that often went unpunished.

One can almost feel the anxiety and tension in Curtis' diary as he anticipates his fate at Camargo.

Feb 2

I turned over the command to Col Clark who returned from the mouth this morning. — At ten Oclock I had my regiment under arms and enroute to Comargo. The very dry weather has made the road exceedingly dusty. The wind has got round to the north so that the dust arisen by the head of the column was driven with violence into the face of those in rear. We have traveled about eight miles to the ranch Guadaloupe[8] and are encamped on the bank of a pleasant lagoon. A few flowers were scattered through the chaperal, but the leaves have generally left the musquete and the forest therefore presents the leafless aspect of winter. Yet the day was uncomfortably hot till late in the evening. Now it is quite cold, and I expect to suffer with all my clothes and blankets round me.

Farewell to Matamoros and to all my friends I leave there. The Mexicans and Americans all expressed much regret at our leaving and especially our departure to Comargo a place every way forbidding. — Senor Don Augustin Menchaca and family all regretted my departure as they found me a friend and they had imagined all Americans quite *ferocious*. The *Madre* the real head of the family and owner of the property threw her arms around me and gave me a hearty hug! Right before her husband too!! I of course had to hug her a matter that embarrased me more than it entertained me. She sent me two cakes of Mexican sugar and a bottle of molasses manufactured by herself at Santa Rosa! She also gave me letters to her friends at Comargo, and they all promised to send forthwith for me if they got into difficulty with strangers.

Feb 3

Got my regiment under way about nine Oclock. The night had been very cold and the morning was uncomfortably so but we all started in good spirits. Our mules are the most unmanageable donkeys ever caught in the chaperal. They are generally quite wild never had harness on before and therefore quite unfit for service. The teams have each four mules, but one or two in each team pulls the whole load. Our march today was near the river. I took the road in preference to the one more direct for the purpose of getting water. Our road lead us through a thick chaperal and winding among the musquete trees it was difficult for the wagons to pass. I intended to make only about twelve miles but I have come from fifteen to twenty and encamped on a lagoon near the Rancho Campota [Capotilla?]. We are among the thorns in a thicket of rough under brush.

Wood and water are the matters most important to our en-campments. When these two luxuries are combined, we acco-modate ourselves to every thing else. We passed to day several very large and apparently well cultivated Ranchos and must have tried our traveling powers very well. The men stood the journey very well but it was hard exceedingly hard marching. The dust on the road is five or six inches deep and it is therefore like wading all day in the snow or sand. The mens feet are badly blistered and I fear I shall have to stop before I get to Comargo for the purpose of recruiting the feet of the men. In other respects they are now at tattoo in good health and fine spirits. —

The people here at the Rancho Campota were as much alarmed at our arrival as though we had been Comanches. They called, many of them, and explained the reason of their anxiety. They had been very badly treated by troops passing down some two months since on a steam boat and they feared a repetition of trouble. —

After a hard days march I am comfortably established here in the "wilds of Mexico" with my cot spread out for a table and a box for a chair. Major Love is reading a paper by my side and we enjoy a comfortable fire at our tent door. — To establish confi-dence in our stay here, Col McCook has gone up to one of the jacals to sleep. So passed my tented day in 1847.

Feby 4

We again moved in column of sections at about nine Oclock. I find the character of the soil and the trees of the forrest chang-ing gradually for the better. The ebony and musquete are larger but they are still small. When the underbrush is trimmed out the woods resembles an old neglected orchard. In some places we marched along the bank of *Esteros* and *lagoons* where the lands had the black colour of our rich bottoms of the north. One place soon after starting was very beautiful. A broad *Estero* of clear water, a low bank, and scattering undergrowth gave the prospect every attraction. I halted the column and laid down on a green herbage which resembles the Dandelion. I soon found I was covered with small wood ticks! millions were creeping over my

clothes, and I was obliged to strip and give my unmentionables
at least a hundred lashes. — We had the musquitos in camp and
the flees in the barracks; but here we have a new plague poured
out on us, the ticks are like the dust in the high way. —
We passed several fine ranchos. The Siliciana it is the most
considerable. It is quite a village well arranged in streets at right
angles. It is the property of two senoritas of Matamoros, I think
the prettiest and most distinguished young ladies I have seen in
Mexico. Whoever gets these fair daughters of the sunny south
will have pretty wives who play and sing beautifully and no doubt
become the owners of a large plantation abounding in Peons and
cattle and cotton. — The Alcalda sent me word that he was
anxious to afford me any and every accomodation and gave me
all the appearance of friendship he could manifest. We arrived at
the rancho of [left blank] where I encamped on the forrest on the
bank of a lagoon.

My tent is on the edge of the sloping bank under an ebony tree
which continues perfectly green all winter. — This and the lignum vita⁹ are the most clad with foliage. The lignum vita is a
light coloured wood with small twisted trunk and leaf resembling
the red seder [cedar]. The trees are all small none of them larger
than peach trees. — Several new forrest trees appeared in the
varieties exhibited along the road. The elm¹⁰ with trunk in some
instances fifteen inches diameter and forty or fifty feet high
loaded with spanish moss seemed to be the prevailing timber. —
Spanish moss is very plenty on most of the trees. — I was told
my horse would eat it, and I pulled some and handed it to him
with his corn before him. The horse prefered the moss. . . .

I have just been round through the camp. It is about eight
Oclock at night, and the men are generally out of their tents
grouped around their fires. On the fire you see a camp kettle
boiling full of salt pork. Here you see a man with a wooden
bucket soaking and rubbing his sore feet. There another rubbing
and greasing his blistered toes. They call it being "hoof bound".
It appears to be the only complaint. The sand working in the
shoes scours off the skin and the men suffer very much with sore
feet. I am glad to see however they are all in fine spirits. We
marched I supposed twelve or fourteen miles. It keeps us busy all
day to strike our tents, do our cooking, lift mules and drag wag-

ons; so that when our tents are pitched and supper over we find the only leasure to talk over the events of the day. —

The Mexicans appear perfectly friendly and gather round to sell us eggs, chickens, torillos, and *pain de dulce* (a kind of round cake made of flour and sugar). . . .

Feby 5

Our march during the forepart of this day was winding through low lands that appeared to have been overflowed. Our mules make poor progress in rough roads. Some of them have quite given out. Small swamps and swampy grounds appear, but no signs of living water. About two Oclock we found the first hill, and ascending by an easy grade we came up on an elevation some fifty or one hundred feet higher than the plane formerly traveled. I had designed to stop early and this high position offered a tempting inducement: but alas! there was no water. The ground had been cleared and there was the ruin of a deserted rancho but the entire absence of water was manifest for miles around. — Persuing our way we soon came into the common broad road that is usually traveled from Matamoros to Camargo.

Our encampment is on the side of a small lagoon under the hill. — It is not a very pretty place being in a thicket of *huidachas* [huisaches] a thorny unsightly bush very like the musqueete but growing on the edge of lagoons where the ground is occasionaly inundated. From the bark of this shrub Mexicans manufacture their ink. —

The most striking characteristic of all this region of the country is the absence of water. Though I adopted a new route for the four past days; I have found it difficult to find water at the proper distances for encamping. I have kept as near the river as its meanders permit. The country out from the river must be entirely destitute. Trails showing the approaches of the cattle to the water are constantly seen. — I am informed they come nine or ten miles to these lagoons and to the river. — Larger reservoirs in the interior may supply the absence of water; but I see no other way of supplying the country. Wells are not attempted. Where they have been dug about Matamoros they are all salt and the only water used is that which has been spread over the country during the high water in the river; or retained in systerns [cisterns] from the rains during the rainy season.

I mess during this march with Captain Patterson and Lieut Higgins[11] and Sergeants and Privates of D. Company. They are all clever fellows and have a way of getting up good meals in short notice. We had fried eggs, fried beef, hard bread and coffee for our supper and I paid *four rials* (fifty cents) for a fat kid which Baggs of our mess has already prepared for breakfast. Poor little white kid. How my children would have rejoiced to keep it as a pet. Its bleet was so pittiful I could not have killed it myself. —

Feby 6th

We marched at eight Oclock being determined as usual by the teamsters harnessing their mules. The road was hilly or rather we continually ascended to the upper plane some fifty or sixty feet and then again ascended. — There was not a breath of air during the whole day and water being very scarce the heat almost prostrated the regiment. I halted for the night on a clear grassy plane at a deserted rancho. A beautiful sheet of water skirts our camp in rear, and all together this is perhaps the prettiest camp we have seen since we started from Mattamoros. — Our men have many of them gone out to shoot. Turkeys and deer are seen in all directions around the camp. — Others amuse themselves bathing in the *estero*. — Care and responsibility constantly restrain the commanding officer. All the other officers have their duties and cares, but the *responsibility* and *severity of discipline* must be assumed by me. — I could here with wish myself relieved, at least for a time, so I too might run and revel in the "forrest wild". —

My comissary, Capt McCauslin, has just secured two good beeves at five dollars each. We can get plenty of meet in this country, and there is no need of starving while that can be secured in abundance.

Feby 7

Sunday. There is no way of avoiding the march today. Our provisions are already becoming short, and we have yet four or five days journey before us.

My lips are very sore from the burning sun, and many others are suffering from the same influences. We passed several indifferent ranchos. The people rely more on robbing than producing. — Last night there were some of our men who found an old rotten trunk sticking in the forks of a musqueet tree. It had been a hair trunk and was unlocked. It contained two old Mexican bags: one partly finished. One white silk hankerchief with blue border. Two calico sun bonnets, one for a child of eight or ten years old. A pink calico dress for a child, some table cloths and some other small clothing for children. Also two glass cupping glasses. — The trunk was found about one mile from the place of our encampment last night (the rancho Los Potreritos). — I have intelligence of bands of robbers about here, and I therefore have been watchful and curious to find their lairs. —

About three Oclock P.M. we came in sight of Reinosa [Reynosa] and encamped as near as I could to the river within half a mile of the town. Reinosa is situated on a beautiful emminence about sixty (perhaps less) feet above the river on a solid limestone ledge. The plane rises very gently to the Grand Plaza and the streets are at right angles following the direction of the cardinal points. The buildings are of white lime stone and therefore have a very substantial and beautiful appearance. It contains some ten or fifteen hundred inhabitants, a very large church partly finished and many other large buildings. —

I called on the Alcalda for the purpose of inquiring into the reason of so much robbing and outlaw [activity] in this region. The Senr. Alcalda is a young man very well dressed and apparently quite intelligent. He said that Canales men were in the habit of coming into Reynosa and that he could not do any thing to arrest them because he had not the force. He also said that he could not because it would be treason to his country. I told him his position was held under our dominion and if he held allegiences and aided Canales he acted treacherous to us, and I should regard him rather as a spy aiding and abetting our enemies. He evaded this dilemma by intimating that there was a middle course which natural law gave him the right to occupy. — I told him that I could see no advantage in a civil jurisprudence that did not protect the country against robbers. That I understood that it was peculiarly the province of his office to take cognizance of criminals and I regarded robbers as the worst of criminals that if he did not take and punish those who were prowling about this region that his functions would be suspended.

The Alcalda said *I should not be attacked while in his dominion!!* I told him I asked no favours. That if Canales dared to attack us the sooner he came on the better. I would like it. That if they are disposed to continue the war in this region, we were prepared for all emergencies without relying on his assistance.

I parted with the Alcalda very cavalierly satisfied that he is himself devoted to the Mexican cause and entirely hostile to us. I feel very much inclined to reduce him from power, and certainly would if I was commander of this place. There should be a garrison here by all means. There is not a point in all this region so much exposed as this. —

Feby 8

Started at seven Oclock and marched up onto the Grand Plaza when I halted for the purpose of again calling on the Alcalda. I found him rather more sensible this morning and he promised to advise me of any lurking band of robbers that might hereafter be found in the region of this place. — I also inspected a lot of arms that are deposited in the public buildings. They are entirely worthless. Some sixty guns of various patterns are rusting among other rubbish of a dirty room. The Alcalda also showed me the proceedings of the municipality by which it had been enjoined on the Alcaldas to arrest all suspicious persons.

After enjoining on the Alcalda that he would be expected to act in good faith towards the American Government, I again took up the line of march. The road leaves the valley of the river and leads over a succession of *molas* (hills) all very barren and almost white with ledges of white limestone that crops out near their summits. The shrubbery is generally white thorn and lignum vita growing from two to five feet high. — At the end of three leagues (nine miles) the valley of the Rio Grande again opened out before us and we descended by a rapid inclination towards the plain where we rejoiced in the prospect of finding water. On this North inclination the hill appeared to be composed of ledges of sand rock and lime rock as sub strata and the vallies were filled up with a mixture of clay and round smooth gravel. This was the first appearance of any thing like gravel and we rejoiced in the prospect of change in the natural products of the earth. The day has been excessively hot and the men rushed toward the river almost furious for water. Several of them fainted and fell exhausted from heat and some injured themselves by drinking water in spite of my endeavours to prevent it. — We encamped soon after arriving at the river bank at the Rancho [left blank] rather a poor destitute plain. The owner I found to be the Second Alcalda of Reinosa and a very sensible and agreeable man. I enquired of him in relation to the *ladrones* [robbers] who are known to infest this country, and I am convinced they have fled before us and all taken to the hills and mountains to secure themselves under the shelter of Santa Annas guns at Tula[12] or San Luis Potosi.

Feby 9

We again struck our tents at seven Oclock and after filling our canteens persued our march. I halted at an estero at the "Old Reinosa"[13] ranch, and stayed for some hours. — This is a large Rancho and we stopped for purpose of buying corn for our mules and horses. I called on the Alcalda and enquired into the particulars of certain haunts of Canales men in this region. The Alcalda seems well disposed and promised to give me secret and immediate intelligence of any of these parties. They have all fled before us, and as the Alcalda believes gone to Tula. — The remaining inhabitants appear devoted to their usual persuits, but I am satisfied a very considerable force has gone from this region to join Santa Anna. — I am encamped on a lagoon, about one league from Old Reynosa. The water is brackish, but I could do no better without going a long distance out of my way. We have traveled about twelve miles to day. The teams are unable to go to the next watering place which is some four leagues ahead. — The wind has got round to the North, but it is still very hot and perspiration pours off me while I write in my shirt sleeves. — The health of the men was never so good. I can hear of a few slight cases of ague, but no real sickness appears to attack them. The cases reported are merely the lingering cases that originated some time since. Many of the men however, are unable to march in consequence of blistered feet. — The sand and sun operate very severely on the feet of the men.

Feby 10

The wind from the North succeeded in reducing the temperature till we find it cold enough. Our march during the day has
been on the valley of the river and apparently from two to three
miles from it. The soil is so parched it appears entirely barren and
quite desolate. Large numbers of mules, horses, and cows are seen
wandering their ways to the river. Our encampment this evening
is on a lagoon or estero four leagues from Comargo near the
Rancho *Tepehuaje.*[14]

A large fire in front of my tent renders the camp warm and
cheerful. The march has been easy today though we came about
fifteen miles. I design to leave the regiment here in camp and go
on to Comargo for the purpose of seeking a place to encamp and
for the purpose of giving a little time to the men to recruit. The
dust is bad here, but it is said to be much worse in Comargo and
I hope to find a location out of the town where the dust will not
be so disagreeable.

Feby 11

I left the regiment encamped at Tepehuaje and accompanied
by Major Love and Doctor Stone I rode into the town of Comargo. — The country is a flat plane covered with low under
brush and offers no variety of landscape. You see the cupola of
the church[15] three or four miles before you reach the place, and
as you approach a dark rough line projecting a little above the
plane shows you the outline of Comargo. It is situated on the
bank of the San Whan[Juan] which here runs almost in a North
direction. There are three squares which lie nearly parallel to the
river and the Town is extended beyond all of them in a confused
and disordered condition. The streets appear to have been laid
out parallel and straight but the houses have not been erected on
the lines and therefore present a miserable display of awkward-
ness. The church is on a good plan and nearly finished, but the
other buildings are in a delapidated condition. — The water rose
last spring so as to cover the whole plane from six to ten feet
deep. Most of the houses having been constructed of sun dried
brick, they crumbled down and left the poor inhabitants in a
wretched condition. Some have repaired their huts and many
have moved up the river where a new town has been laid out

called new Comargo.[16] — I could hardly conceive of a more miserable or wretched place than this. — The dust is terrible. On arriving, I found Col Morgan of the 2nd Ohio in good health. I also met a merry hearted and generous old school fellow Lieut. F. Britton[17] of the Comissary department Doctor Truitt, Adjutant Joline,[18] Major Wall,[19] Capt. R. M. Sutton,[20] and many other officers of my acquaintance. I rode round the plaza for the purpose of determining on an encampment and crossed over to the opposite side of the river where the 2nd Ohio Regiment under Major Wall had constructed a very good field fortification[21] composed of [left blank] bastions. There is such a cloud of dust every where that I can scarcely breathe and am determined to locate my regiment out of this fort and out of the town.

Feby 12

I found lodgings at the comissaries and slept soundly after the fatigues of yesterday. — I have spent the day in walking about the town, climbing onto the buildings, viewing the surrounding country, and talking of the affairs of the post with Col Morgan who has had the temporary command since General Marshall[22] left here. — Col. Morgan has just returned from an excursion after some of Canales men.[23] — They came down on one of our trains and took some 60 mules. Col Morgan gave chase and followed them beyond China[24] burning some of the Ranchos and requiring contributions from others.

Yesterday some of the companies guarding a train set fire to some other ranchos on the route to Monterray and I regret to perceive that desolation and devastation are spread far and wide.

Col Morgan is making his arrangements to leave on Sunday and I have directed Major Love to ride out and direct my regiment to march in tomorrow — Saturday. — I have determined to encamp the regiment for the present on the bank of the river south west and therefore a little above the town. —

Feby 13

I assumed command of Comargo and appointed Lt. C. C. Gray adjutant of the post. My regiment marched into town, and are encamped a little above town on the bank of the river. — The arrival of steam boats from below brings up news from the mouth

The plaza at Camargo with troops drilling in the foreground. The etching appeared in The New York Herald, on January 30, 1847 (copy courtesy

and Matamoros of little importance. General Scott had not departed on the sixth and some further changes have been made in
the orders for marching troops. —

Feby 14

Sunday. In conformity with my mode of proceeding at Matamoros, I had a general jail delivery liberating some fifteen or
twenty Mexicans and some four or five Americans. There still
remain ten or dozen of all shades and hues.

The Alcaldas and municipality called on me, and I expressed
to them my views of their allegiance and they expressed to me
their fidelity. — The Senr. Alcada is an old man bending under
the weight of years and adversity. The people of this town have
indeed been afflicted. Their houses have been reduced by the
flood, their peace destroyed by war, and sickness has spread its
horror every where. Sad and sorrowful; the old Alcalda told me
he had received a letter from Mr. Menchaca the Senr. Alcalde of
Matamoros informing him of my character and speaking so favourable of me as to induce him to hope for better prospects. I
assured the old man that I would exert myself to the utmost to
establish peace and order, and that I expected his frank and
constant aid.

Feby 15

I moved to day into my quarters on the West side of the Grand
Plaza.[25] I have one large room on the first floor, and after having
a glass window placed in the front wall (the second luxury of the
kind known in the city) I feel quite comfortably located. The
plaza in front of me is quite crowded with long tarpoleon tents
full of quartermaster and comissary stores. So the plaza has nothing interesting in its appearance. —

I went to day to New Comargo. The town destined to super-
cede this place. It is on the opposite side of the river about one
mile above. Capt F. Britton of the Comissary department, and
Capt J. M. Love[26] together with my new interpreter Mr. Kidder[27]
accompanied me. — The people of the place told over their
grievances. Some of the volunteers of Col Morgans regiments, or
the wagoners on the opposite side — have been guilty of many
acts of folly; shooting chickens, hooking blankets, and terrifying

the women. — I did all I could to quiet the anxiety of the people by giving them every assurance of my desire to preserve peace and good order among those who desire to live in peace. The people appear quiet and inoffensive, but the families of some of the officers of Canales band reside in New Camargo and no doubt they must keep a private intercourse between each other.[28] — The Alcalda desired me to come again and dine with him, so I promised to do so on Sunday next. — I expect another succession of chopped meat, tortillos and frijoles. —

The day has been sultry and the wind strong from the south has kept up a cloud of dust almost smothering us.[29] — I feel very awkward in my present position. The public property is piled in every direction. The wagons mules and drivers are crossing and recrossing the river: the streets are irregular and the houses all tilting over; and I feel indeed like a cat in a strange garret. — The regular officers except Lieut Britton have kept a *respectful distance*. I called on Capt Crossman[30] who seems to be a very industrious assistant quartermaster on matters of business. He has not returned the call, although I believe he did visit my camp yesterday for the purpose of seeing me. There are several other officers, lieutenants and captains, who are stationed here. They could no doubt aid very much in the duties of this post if the dignity of their profession could induce them to call and make the acquaintance of the commanding officer. My old friend Capt Britton is an entirely devoted gentleman. He shows himself willing and ready to aid and assist me in every way possible. He commenced showing me his kind attention on the first day of my arrival and so far he has been constantly placing me under obligations to him. I always knew him to be a strange [man], generous, full of wit humour, sense and kindness. He is a man below medium stature, of a sandy complexion, sharp chin and long nose. He is so exceedingly fond of fun and eccentricity he is always turning every thing to account. — I knew him at West Point and he was then regarded as the leader of every dance or frolick. He dresses in an indian leather hunting shirt with a red Mexican sash round his waist. He seems to move along here like one of the natives. All the Mexicans appear to know him and no doubt he is the best man in the world to please them. — He has been so long mixing with the indians of Florida and Arkansas and with the people of all the extreme borders of our republic that he is adapted to any country and climate and his untiring wit and wagory [waggery] is enough to delight any audience. —

Feby 16

I have got myself so comfortably established in my quarters that I begin to feel at home in the exercise of my duties. — The regulation of civil matters connected with the government of the place and surrounding country occupies more time than my duties as commander of the military. — The civil jurisdiction is without authority or system, and therefore requires perplexing contraversies and tougher rules to be construed: but the military rules of the soldiers are sufficiently understood and readily decided. — I received a letter today from my friend the mother in law of the Senr. Alcalda at Matamoros Senora Donna Anna Domingo Garcia de Chapa. She has sent her servant to ketch a run away servant. Such are the laws of Mexico that the Alcalda of Matamoros gives a warrant which being received by the Alcalda here will carry back the peon to Matamoros if he does not pay his debt.

In this instant the peon was found but did not return to his mistress because he found a man to pay his debt and take him into his service. — I took no part in the matter, The Alcaldas have their old laws and customs to go by; and I should not meddle much when the matter lies between Mexicans.

There is one advantage in the servitude here over that in some of the United States. The peon can always pay his debt off by using economy, At least this is the case now that our war has made such a demand for labor.

Feby 17

General Butler and staff, (Major Thomas and others)[31] arrived from Monterray. They bring nothing important. Every thing is quiet at present in that direction. General Butler has leave of absence and goes home to recruit his health. He is a tall gray haired man of very intelligent appearance and easy manners. His hair is gray "a la General Jackson" which gives him a military air. The absence of General Butler of Kentucky, places me under the command of General Marshall of Kentucky. This line has been commanded by Gen Taylor, Gen Butler, and General Marshall all of Kentucky.

Since the death of General Hamer the Ohio Volunteers have no General in the field and are not Brigaded at all. We are required to report to head quarters of General Marshall. There is no injustice intended in this, no doubt it is done for the convenience of the service; but the result is that we of the Ohio Volunteers are constantly kept on garrison and train duty in rear of the main army. — General Butler thinks that General Taylor will move forward towards San Luis Potosi about the first of April. I saw the same statement in a letter from the quartermaster at Saltillo directed to the quartermaster Capt Crossman [Crosman] at this place.

As these statements are made without the slightest injunction of security, it will no doubt be published for the benefit of the Mexican Generals long before we are moved forward. General Taylor always has given timely notice of his movements; but he has never yet failed to accomplish his designs. Perhaps he would save the loss of men by moving more cautiously. —

Capt Thomas F. Marshall[32] commanding the escort of General Butler reports to me for duty. He is a tall fine looking man and all the world knows he is a man of extraordinary talents. —

Feby 18

I received a letter from home mailed on the 20th of January. By this means I perceive [I] am likely to receive letters in good season from home and elsewhere. I hope my dispatches will go as speedily. —

My room has been all day upside down. Workmen are engaged white washing my quarters. I am making a great improvement in the appearance of things with a free use of lime and mortar. —

Wrote a long letter to my brother in law Rev. G. Buckingham expressing my fears that Congress has taken erronious views of Mexico and the war and especially deprecating a letter I perceived having been published in the Intellegencer from Mr. Thompson. I see that divided counsels at home and a divided army in the field may jeopardise our position and strengthen our foes. — I regard any delay or draw back at this time as exceedingly unfavourable to the termination of difficulties. The idea suggested in Congress to withdraw our forces to the east side of the Rio Grande I regard as a monstrous proposition. Coming up in our Congress, it will encourage the Mexicans and should it prevail all this frontier region will be hunted down by Santa Annas soldiers who would follow our retiring army with a march of triumph. They would not stop at the Rio Grande, but scatter death and desolation through Texas. The member who introduced that proposition will earn for himself an immortal infamy. — The very introduction of such a doubting policy is calculated to do more injury than I can express. — It seems to me there is a strange fatality directing the counsels of the two nations, all tending to protract this unfortunate war. — An unfortunate jealousy, perhaps a positive misunderstanding exists between Generals Scott and Taylor which adds to our evil. These two Generals are organizing two different lines which must act entirely separate without the least concert because they will have the Mexican Army between them. — Each should therefore expect the combined forces of Santa Annas army. — If Santa Anna moves against one of these columns and proves successful, his success would so inspire his soldiers as to render the fate of the other column certain. — General Taylor has at Monterray and above that point only 6250 men, mostly volunteers. Between that point and the mouth of the Rio Grande there are stationed at different positions about 1600 so that his entire force may be set down at 7850. The new levies of volunteers will add to this if General Scott does not take all of them on the Vera Cruz expedition; but without a considerable accession, General Taylor will have no force which he can safely advance with. He has no more than enough to hold with safety the line already acquired. —

Feby 19

I had a call from the first and second Alcaldas this morning for the purpose, as they say, of again expressing their acknowledgements for my efforts and success in establishing peace and order.

The *Padre* my next door neighbor also called. He is rather a gentlemanly man and apparently intelligent. He was very polite in his way, and excused himself for not having called sooner. —

An old man by the name of Chapa, to whom I brought a letter

of introduction came in several miles immediately on the receipt
of my letter. He is a fine looking old man of probably more than
eighty years. He did not know himself, and I find most of the
common people are ignorant of their own age. He is one of "the
old inhabitants" and saluted me throwing his arms around me at
first sight. I was taken by surprise but gave the old man a corre-
sponding hug. — He pledged his entire devotion and seemed
disposed to display his best manners.

The town has been thrown into a great excitement in consequence of the reported approach of a woman who is represented
to be a new "Saint". — She was announced some hours before
dark as approaching from Reinosa on foot. Thousands went out
to meet her and such was the crowd about her that it required
some hours for her to travel the last mile. The Mexican women
children and men rushed onto her, throwing themselves at her
feet, kissing her hands and pressing her on sides. It is said to be
rather an elderly woman who walks with a black veil over her
head and an umbrella sustained by two other women. She is said
to have walked from Reinosa and some hundred women have
accompanied her. I directed the officer of the day to keep his
guard on the alert till I ascertained whether she comes as a
minister of peace or war.

I went at early candle light with Lieut Britton and called on
the Padre for the purpose of getting his views of the matter. —
We found the Padre in grave consultation with the Alcaldas and
other municipal officers of the City on the subject of the extraordinary visitation. The Padre told me he had not yet examined into the matter, but that he designed to do so, and that if
she was found to be a true saint he would then call and introduce
me to her. — Various wonderful stories are a foot concerning
her, but as I hope to get the true version through the Padre I will
delay the record for another day. —

Feby 20
The Padre and Alcaldas have been taking statements in writing relative to the "Saint" and I am not yet informed of the
result. Some of my staff called this evening — Adjutant Grey
and Dr. Stoner with an interpreter. She sits on the side of a bed,
draped in white with a rebosa on her head, a rosary in her hand,

and her feet on a cushioned stool. These officers represented themselves as American Catholics and on entering the room they assumed a grave countenance and made the sign of the cross. Her saint ship offers them first her foot to kiss, but our officers thought this stooping rather low, and satisfied themselves with kissing her hand — On being questioned she spoke through a companion to the interpreter and he translated the following brief account in reply to a few questions. She said she had been dead Eight days and was buried at San Jose near Reinosa. — That she had seen Jesus Christ three times. — They enquired of the appearance of the Saviour but this question was evaded. — To others she has said that this war would continue for seven years, and at the end of that time the Americans would have possession and that it would result in a benefit to the people of this Country. — All kinds of stories are afloat and the excitement continues unabated. Thousands have called, I am informed, and I could see a constant stream going and returning to and from the jacal where she is located. — Out of respect for my position I have avoided my inclination to go also, and wait patiently the result of the examination on the part of the Padre and Alcaldas. —

Two steam boats arrived this evening bringing news of General Scotts departure and General Worths having assumed command of the embarkation which is still going on at Brasos St. Iago — I suppose General Scott has gone to Tampico to attend to the movement at that place — News also arrived from Saltillo, by express in four days, every thing is quiet there. General Taylor has been for some time established about ten leagues in front of Saltillo at a place called Nuevo Agua [Agua Nueva].[33]

Feby 21

Sunday — According to promise I prepared to go to New Comargo to dine with the Senr. Don [left blank] 2nd Alcalda of this municipality. The Padre and Senr. Alcalda called to accompany me and with these men, Lieut Britton and my interpreter we rode up to that place. — Servants were ready in waiting to take our horses and we were repaired into the Jacal of the Alcaldas. Though it was only ten Oclock the table was already spread, and almost ready to serve up. — It was plain to see they had specially prepared for us, and very soon we were seated at the table. As usual at Mexican tables we had a succession of dishes and a little claret wine. — A well roasted pig came on for the third course and the carver cut it with a knife alone, not seeming to understand the use of a fork. Of course he had to take hold of the fat pieces of meat with his hands, as all Mexicans do usually in eating. They were all evidentaly desirous of showing their utmost regard and respect for me. — The Padres and Alcaldas had over and over again their expressions of *sentionientes* for the *Senr. Commandante* and I had to return complements as fast as possible without the least diminution of efforts on their part. I see they expect more of me than I can accomplish. They suppose I can regulate every American, which all of the world knows is absolutely impossible in places where good laws and good offices are the boast of community. I would like to be out of the scrape as soon as possible.

In returning home a Mexican called for redress. A man had stole his horse and taken him into "Fort Ohio"[34] — soon found the horse, but the man that had taken him in there — an Irishman — had "bamosed el Mucho". — I gave the horse to the claimant and left orders to take the knave if he came near the fort. He is not one of the troops, but one of the loafing *followers* of the army who had attempted to steal, and cast the odium on the volunteers.

We all stopped at the landing and went on board the "Col Cross"[35] where Captain Pratt showed his boat to the Mexicans and at the same time manifested his hospitality.

The steam boat is a great curiosity to the Mexicans and they could not fail to express their admiration. — The Senr. Alcalda tells me the river is lower than he has ever known it, and I infer therefore that boats drawing three feet of water can always navigate up to this place.

I saw to day a new species of *Quail*. It is a very little larger than one of the North, more slender and more of a bluish tinge. It has a slim neck with a small bluish "top knot" — on its head. It is a much prettier bird than our quail and having longer legs, it seems to move easier on the ground. It is said to have the same call "Bobwhite" and otherwise seems almost identical with the species of the North[36]. —

The simple woman who sets herself up for a saint has deferred her receptions and has not profaned the day I am told with her mummery. I know there is much ignorance and bigotry in all countries, and I have often lamented the inconsistencies of the church at home. But with all its dogmas and superstitions the great outline is still there. — The quiet peaceable enjoyment of a sabbath at home far surpasses the mode of passing the day here. I shall rejoice at my return to the land of puritanical customs and in the language of the psalms exclaimed — "Deliver us O Lord our God, and gather us from among the heathen; that we may give thanks unto thy holy name, and make our boast of thy praise."[37] —

Feby 22

Washington's birth day. — A day almost sacred and worthy of perpetual commemoration. No salute was fired as the guns of the post are not regularly manned and I feared a balk might be made of it. — The so called "Saint" has rather declined in public esteem. The multitude look for a miracle and no miracle is performed.

Feby 23

Two persons charged with stealing have been brought before me to day. One I have found guilty of stealing sixty or eighty dollars in money and I have placed him in irons and ordered him to be shipped out of the country. The other is charged with stealing horses and I have him in irons also. — Both these men are irish men who have been in some way brought out with the army. —

Feby 24

While employed at company provision returns with Lieut Britton at half past eleven oclock I received this note from Col Morgan: "Head Quarters Seralvo, Feby 23rd 1846 [?], Col Curtis Sir. I have this moment received orders from Head Quarters of Genl Taylor to stop all trains from Comargo to Monterray. You will please act in accordance with these orders. I march with my command at day light. The enemy are said to be in great force. I am sir" etc

Lt. Col McCook also wrote me a note but no more definite than the former. General Taylor would not issue such an order without good cause, and I send a letter by express to Matamoros; giving Col Drake notice to be on his guard. —

The letter from Col Morgan arrived about 11 Oclock and of course creates a little *stampede*. I have ordered Maj [John S.] Love with companies C, D, and E to reinforce Capt [James M.] Love and take command at that Fort. Companies F and K are ordered to take post within the plaza. — Thus arranged I shall wait patiently for the enemy. I have written to Col McCook that he can use his own discretion about falling back onto this post. — If he finds the enemy is approaching in considerable force, I recommend him to fall back, as he has neither cavalry or artillery.

I immediately ordered a cordon of pickets to surround this place, and guard every entrance. I did this to secure intelligence and to prevent the outlet of intelligence. In a few minutes I had Mexicans brought in from every point of the compass and I found some had come from some five and some twenty leagues. One from Monte morellos [Montemorelos],[38] in four days assures me there are no soldiers about that place. From all this, I infer that all the force is beyond the Sierra Madre as I have before asserted General Taylor must be pressed in front and has sent this order in relation to the train out of abundant caution, and also being devious of drawing forward all available force, he does not want any engaged in guarding the trains. Several persons arriving from Mear [Mier], direct from Saltillo also inform me that General Taylor still has his post at *Agua Nueva* about thirty miles in front of Saltillo. It is a mountainous country, and no doubt the General has a strong position or he would not remain at it. — From all the news I can get by taking every Mexican that approaches the city: I think there is no force this side of General Taylor, and I therefore hope he has all his enemies "in front". — Santa Anna will have to fight at several places before he drives us from our posts; and I think this place will stand him few days at least.

He must have a large army and very considerable artillery force to take such a place as the Black fort at Monterray or this "rough and ready" fort at Comargo.

Feby 25
I am informed by 10 Oclock that Gen Scott left Brasos on 15th and Genl Worth to assume command. — That when the

steam boats just arrived left the mouth of the river, there were still about sixteen hundred of the troops to embark.

An express arrived about ten Oclock from Monterray conveying an order, for me to march forward as soon as I am relieved by a new regiment. — Also for Col Drake at Matamoros to do likewise. The same order specified instructions to march no party forward less than a regiment and directing me to keep my force always on the alert. — In view of this order I direct Col. McCook to fall back from Meir as his force is less than a regiment I consider the order as imperative and direct Col McCook accordingly. — Soon after sending an express with this order to Col McCook received an express from him in reply to my note of yesterday, saying that his ammunition had arrived and he could defend himself against all the Mexican country. — My order for him to fall back will probably reach him by 8 Oclock this evening.

Another express arrived about 12 Oclock dated the 23rd at Monterray stating that the Mexican Cavalry was in Marin.[39] It will be seen that Col Morgan left Seralvo on the 24th at day light. He would reach Marin that night. i. e. last night. If the statement be true his way is intercepted and he must fight on arriving at Marin. There was also a large train about that place. It left here on the 17th and I fear must fall into the hands of General Urrea. — If it has they have taken upwards of 100 wagons and several hundred mules. — The express also stated that a detachment of the cavalry, some three or four thousand, was detached at China and marched about the 22nd for this place. They ought at this time to be near us, and I perceive we have seen no Mexicans from the region of the approach.

Every thing indicates a fearful contest above. The last express states that General Santa Anna had sent to General Taylor to surrender. General Taylor sent back word to Santa Anna to come and take him. — General Santa Anna sent word that he was coming with 20000 troops and would cut him to pieces if he did not surrender. The letter closed by saying that General Taylor was "giving the Mexicans hell". —

I feel much anxiety for Col. McCooks safety. If Urrea hears of his advanced and weak position, he will certainly attack him. — He and Col Morgan are both in hot places, but Col Morgan can defend himself against a large force of Cavalry because he has his whole Regiment with him.

Several steam boats arrived safely from below bringing nothing definite as to when the new volunteers can be expected. General Taylor evidentaly expects the new regiments to meet the order on its arrival at this place.

I received a reinforcement of a company of mule drivers from Texas with their mules. I have given directions to have the drivers armed. They come across the country with a company of Texian Rangers which are yet on the Texian side or about crossing.[40]

I have sent Captain Marshalls command out on this side of the river to occupy the road leading in from China and to also patrol across to the Matamoros road where he is likewise to establish a picket.

I have also a small armed force, some 20 men of the dragoons under command of a sergeant which I have ordered to the west side to patrol and watch the approaches from Monterray leading in on that side. — I have also to day placed the guns, 6 of various calibers in Fort Ohio and arranged all the remainder around the square. These guns now at 10 Oclock at night are all guarded by sentinels and have the ammunition lying close along side of them. — The gun squads are all detailed and will be ready to man the pieces at a moments warning. Capt Hunt[41] of the artillery and Lieuts Waynewright[42] and Benton[43] of the Ordnance Corps are ordered on duty with the guns. I also have the services of Lieut Britton and every other officer and soldier who is detained here on any occasion. —

I have designated to Captains McLaughlin, Allen, Chapman, and Hunter their several angles which they are directed to guard and shall myself keep a general supervision of the two forts. — It does seem to me I can give them a hard fight, and my force no doubt can resist two or three times its numbers at a moderate estimate.

Feby 26

Lt. Col McCook with his three companies and all his baggage except for a few days provision arrived safe this morning. No news has been received up to this hour 3 Oclock P.M. from above. Col Morgan must be near or at Marin today.

Capt Conners company of Texian Rangers arrived from the other side and encamped on the west side of the San Juan. — Some two hundred families have left the town. — My quarters have been crowded all day with Mexicans asking for "pasites" [passes] to move out their families. They are in great terror and I sincerely pity them. To see the old and young all fleeing from their homes in almost destitute circumstances, it is indeed piti-ful. — Oh the evils of war! How they harrass and ruin the Coun-try! —

I perceive by my reports and express arrivals that General Urreas Cavalry must have entered Marin the same day our train of 100 wagons arrived there and one or two days before Col Morgan could have reached that place. — I am fearful they have all fallen into the hands of the enemy. Col Morgan will fight hard, but he must be intercepted in his way by an overwhelming force, if the report from Monterray is correct.

Capt Reynolds[44] with forty men of the 2nd Ohio Regiment returned from Meir with Lt Col McCook. He was on the way with a train of mules, and under my orders the train was stopped. — I regret to learn that on leaving Meir last night, something like 111 mules were left and their packs are in the houses of the Mexicans. Col McCook informs me that he waited an hour for the muleteers and did not deem it proper under my orders and the circumstances to wait any longer. — The most of the stores were brought away and the Alcalda of Meir was di-rected by the Col to take charge of the remainder for the quarter masters department. It may be the Alcalda will be able to protect it. I am informed that Col Morgan burned his stores that he could not conveniently carry with him before leaving Se-ralvo. —

Feby 27

A mule driver arrived from the Rancho Ramas[45] about four Leagues from Marin. He states that the train was attacked by a large force of infantry and cavalry and taken. —

I issued orders, directed to the Captain of a Company at Cor-pus Christi, and to three companies at or near San Antonio to march forthwith to this place.[46] — 12 A.M. Just received a private note from Clay Davis[47] on the other side stating that he has private intelligence which he believed that General Urrea entered Meir yesterday at 1 Oclock. ½ Past 4 P.M. An irishman by the name of Hays[48] has just arrived from Meir. He left Meir this morning. He says that there were soldiers at Meir last night — an advance party of 50 or 100. That he saw and conversed with them, and they reported to him that they left some 2000 at Seralvo and 4000 at Marin. They also reported that the train was taken near Marin and all the men killed.

Four men of the 2nd Ohio who were attached to the escort of the train that stopped at Meir have just arrived. They had passed on, not knowing the rest of the escort had returned to this place, as far as Pont agooda [Puntiaguda],[49] which is with[in] 12 miles of Seralvo. Here they heard of the Mexican force at Seralvo and turned back. They traveled all night in by roads and down the Rio Grande in a canoe.

The people of Pontiagooda and Meir saved the lives of these men by cautioning them in that way and by telling them how to evade the Mexican soldiers. They lay by the road side when the Mexican soldiers passed there coming on the Meir. — Captain Marshall who has charge of the advance pickets on this side of the river brought us a muleteer who comes from the region of Marin. He reports nothing new but confirms our former intelligence as to numbers etc. — I sent a party of ten men mounted on the best horses I could procure, to accompany a train of mules which went up after the packs left in Meir. — I started this party before the intelligence of the arrival of Mexican soldiers in Meir, but cautioned them that I had rumors to that effect. The detachment is from Captain Conners Company of Texian Rangers and commanded by Lieut Jett.[50]

Feby 28

A bright morning after a long night. I have been so anxious to hear from General Taylor and our Army that I have counted hours and minutes, keeping a sentinel on the top of the church looking out for the express. — Far over the chaperal you can see the opening road, with Mexican carts carrying the poor Mexicans and their little property out of the reach of danger. But no express rider is seen. — Terrible silence! Not a word from the west since 12 Oclock of the 24th

10-Oclock A.M.

9 Oclock P.M. Nothing important has arrived today. My scouting party went to Meir and learned that the few Mexican soldiers who had come the previous night fell back to Seralvo where I was informed a considerable force is encamped. The party sent to Meir was advised not to attempt to bring away the mule packs as the Mexican force would no doubt persue and secure them. The party prudentially and no doubt properly hurried back without them. — One of the party stopped and slept at *Wardaw* [Guardado Abajo],[51] — a ranch some twelve miles out. He was told by the Mexicans that Col Morgan and Col Irwin was taken and that a party that came from Monterray to assist Col Irwin was also taken. This is not a probable story because it does too much; but that part of it may be true *Quien sava?* It seems like folly to lay down to sleep, when such fearful intelligence comes in from our front, yet such is the nature of constant toil and anxiety, it brings on the hour for refreshment and sleep and we obey the dictates of nature in all extremities. — All the Mexicans seem to have left the City. — A *jacal* was burned on the windward side of the city; but it did not effect — what was no doubt designed the distinction of the place and the lives of all of us [?]. — A kind providence has so far preserved us, and oh! may the Almighty ruler of the Armies of Heaven and Earth protect and defend our companions and all of us against the dangers that stand thick around.

I sent two copies of a report to General Taylor, sufficiently certain for him, and sufficiently vague for our foes. — One is designed for General Taylor and the other to alarm our adversaries. — See letter book.

Mar 1

Sent an express to Capt Lamar[52] for the purpose of enclosing orders which I find here, and also to direct his march via of this place, in conformity with my orders from head quarters not to send forward less than a regiment and to prevent the captain from throwing himself into the hands of our foes. — Two companies of the Virginia Regiment arrived this evening and four more are on their way up to this place. The officers report that this regiment is all the new troops destined for this place and half the regiment was at Old Point Comfort when last heard from. — General Worth was at the mouth of the river on the 25th, but all the troops had embarked except a few companies of Cavalry, those of which are destined for this region of Country; so that I may expect in a few days only 6 Companies of Infantry and three of Cavalry. — Beyond these resources I see nothing but doubt and delay. The order of General Taylor directs me to march when I can be relieved by a regiment of the new volunteers. Only half of a regiment is arrived. — When can I look for force to arrive in size. Under this wretched condition I have written the painful intelligence to the Commanding Officer at Monterray that I cannot hope for force within a short period and therefore they cannot look for aid of any importance. Shall I disobey my orders and march before a whole regiment arrives? Would it be safe to leave this place with a less garrison than that designated by the Commanding General? —

My letter is concealed in the shoe of a Mexican, who agrees to return an answer in four days from this evening.[53] — I directed some of the *jacals* to be removed that are close to our pickets. Capt Hunt set an unfortunate example by firing a small one. Capt Chapman who had some to remove followed the example, and in a few minutes a dozen were on fire. I gave immediate orders to have it stopped; but the devil seemed to possess the people, and more than a hundred of the huts have been burned to ashes. — This town is now, indeed a wide spread ruin. — The silly and wicked distinction of property must exasperate the Mexicans and induce suspicions to the Mexican homes.

Mar 2

I called a counsel of officers composed of Lt Col Fontelroy[54] USA, Lt. Col McCook 3rd Ohio, Lt. Col Randolph[55] Va. Vol's, Surgeon Jarvis,[56] Surgeon Turner,[57] Capts Crossman USA, Capt Hunt USA, Capt McCauslin asst. qm., Capt McLaughlin, Capt Allen, Capt. Chapman, Capt. Kyle 3rd Ohio Vols and several other officers — to take into consideration the situation of this division of our army and the propriety of sending for forces. —

I proposed calling on the president for 50000 men and I believe the proposal was unanimously agreed to. I send two officers, one to the United States [General Scott's army] and one to Washington — [the first officer] for the purpose of making a move [by Scott's Army at Tampico] in favour of General Taylors forces . . . and at the same time draw from the U States sufficient forces to terminate this war.

I believe that I will forward this book to my wife as it is now nearly full and in the event of any catastrophy to the army I may not find it in my power to carry it safely.

I will therefore trouble Surgeon N. S. Jarvis to carry this book and my watch to Washington to be forwarded there to Mrs. Curtis.

It is excessively hot to day, and the perspiration rolls off me as I sit here writing in the shade.

2 P.M. I have just received a letter from the Alcalda of Meir stating that a Mexican force entered that place at 2 Oclock last night (this morning) and took our stores and the goods of all the Americans who had resided there. —

Mar 2, 1847 [second entry on the same date]

I dispatched three officers to day. One to Governor Henderson by Captain Conner, one to the President of the United States — Surgeon N. S. Jarvis and one to General Scott via Tampico — Lieut and Adjutant S. N. Tidball.[58] — All these important messengers bear messages designed to extricate General Taylor and give a new impetus to our Arms. — The message to the President requests a call for 50000 six month volunteers and bears a letter to the Governor of Louisiana requesting him to call out ten thousand in anticipation of the call which is expected from the President.

I am under orders to march forward; but those orders from General Taylor direct me to march after being relieved by a regiment of new volunteers, and only a half regiment has as yet arrived. — I look for the other half daily, and I am arranging my affairs to march at the first instant after the whole regiment arrives, perhaps before. — In the mean time I am proceeding with defences and strengthening myself by all the artificial means that I can imagine. — knowing that in all probability I must push my way forward through many dangers. I sent my 2nd volume of my register home by Doctor Jarvis and I also gave him my gold watch with directions to leave articles with a friend of my wife in George Town D. C. who is requested to forward the register by mail and the watch by the first safe opportunity. —

Sent another express to General Taylor by a Mexican who has it put in his shoe for concealment. By this I apprised General Taylor of my extraordinary doings. — All the responsibility assumed by me is enough to kill any man. — If it aids General Taylor, and assists in terminating this unfortunate war; I shall thank God though it do destroy me.

I know that whenever officers have called for troops, they have been denounced from one side of the country to the other. — It is attributed to needless alarm and some times to ignorance of law. In making my report to the President and supporting my opinion as to the requisite force to carry on this war: I only publicly expressed an opinion that I have before privately expressed over and over again. — Being senr Officer on the river, I have to speak the voice of reason and the Army. Anything less would be pedantic cowardice, and any thing more would be arrogance and sinful. — Before sending these messages I called a board of officers many of whom have seen a life of hard service and I believe all assented to the propriety of acting boldly. Capt Crossman made this figurative expression, that "we have been pricking with needles till it was time to use some more formidable weapons". — I look upon the matter in this light. If General Taylor sustains himself, and really kills off half of Santa Annas army, still we have not sufficient force left after such a battle to carry forward the campaign and garrison the towns we conquer. — If General Taylor is indeed closed in, and unable to extricate himself with our present forces: nothing but a powerful effort can restrain the accumulating enthusiasm which is already gathering forces around Santa Anna. —

The moment the "long roll" calls the United States to arms, the morale will turn in our favor. Our forces will begin to augment, and before the call is half filled up the advancing columns may establish a peace between the two nations and the levy may then be checked. — The town is full of rumors that General Taylor has fought his way back to Monterray, and is now struggling at that place.

Mar 3

No tidings from General Taylor: this is the most terrible, and most universal exclamation. —

The irregularities of the lines of this enclosure, and the importance of holding onto the public stores, have induced me to direct all my force to the construction of entire new lines in many places, and adding to the strength of the old lines. I have ordered the entire force out except the men who were on guard yesterday, and are on guard to day. Col's Fontelroy and Randolph think the fort on the other side should be abandoned. I am inclined to favour this, because it will require less artillery to defend one than two forts, and I will have by this means more artillery to carry forward. I dislike however to abandon the work on the other side, because it has cost much labour, and as I suppose was made by General Taylors orders. —

I also sent out two scouting parties, one towards Meir, and one towards Chiny [China]. — The forces commanded by Captain Patterson and the latter by Captain Marshall. There never was a country so capable of concealing every thing. I have sought every possible means of obtaining intelligence. My interpreter, Mr. Kidder, has lived here among the Mexicans for twenty years, and I asked him if he could find one Mexican who would go and reconnoiter the enemies lines, and give me intelligence of the position and quantity of force. He could not find a man that I could rely on. —

The rumor came in yesterday, or rather Mexicans reported yesterday, that General Taylor had fought at Agua Nueva and killed two thousand, but that the Mexicans had taken eight cannon in the battle. That he again fought at Saltillo and killed that number or more, and that he had finally fallen back onto Monterray. —

Mar 4

I heard this morning of one of the enemies pickets nine miles out on the Matamoros road. This intelligence was brought me by two parties of Mexicans I directed Lieut Patterson of the Mississippi Volunteers[59] to ride out and burn the ranch. — Another party approaching from Meir was fired on by my picket and driven to the chaperal. —

I passed an order to the companies of my regiment to turn in their entire baggage and be ready to march at a moments warning and directed my comissary to have the train prepared and twelve days rations loaded into the wagons. —

A Mexican direct from the region of Chiny brings intelligence that he was buying horses at the Ranchos near that place and was surprised by a band of thirty or forty robbers who took his horses and carried off his servants tied. That he also saw a party of about one hundred Rancheros collected at the city and in that neighbourhood, who were en route for General Urrea, who he understood was encamped at Guadeloupe[60] near Monterray with his forces.

My party came in from the Rancho Baldase at six Oclock this evening, bringing five or six prisoners. — A party also came in from Meir, informing me that most of the stores left by Lt. Col McCook are still there.

At eight Oclock, Lieut Burget with ten men started to Meir with orders to bring away the Alcaldes, and the Prefect, and also if possible to bring away our stores or burn them if they are in danger.

The Mexicans at Meir say that Col Morgan is still at Marine. That he was there attacked by Urrea and that he by some means fortified himself there and still holds out. — They also say that General Taylor has fallen back on Monterray.

Another Mexican report states that General Urrea is at Guadeloupe which is almost joining the City of Monterray.

Mar 5

The extraordinary express sent by me on the night of the 1st-2nd might *possibly* have returned before this time. I have therefore looked for him during the night but yet the drum for guard mounting has arrived and we have no tidings yet. Lieut Burget arrived with the Perfect prisoner. No letters however could be obtained. The Alcalda had escaped. The prisoner gave me a pretty plain statement of what he knew in relation to the affairs of the armies. He said that Urrea would be to night or tomorrow night be in Aldamas.[61] That General Taylor has had three or four battles with Santa Anna, and that Santa Annas forces drove General Taylor back to the Rinconada Pass[62] and

A Mexican ranchero (from Thorpe, "Our Army").

then General Taylor drove Santa Anna to the pass of Agua Nueva. That there had been some understanding came to between the Generals. — That the train was taken, and all the guard and drivers put to death. — Knows nothing as to the fate of Col Morgan but thinks he is still in Meir.

An express rider, Ellison, who left here on the 28th Ult has been making every effort to get through but find it impossible to and returns with his letter. He let one copy as directed fall into the hands of the enemy and brings back the other. — He says that all he could get of intelligence satisfied him that General Taylor was at Saltillo that the train is taken and now at Salinas[63] a place on the road leading from Monclova to Monterray.

Captain Marshall returned from his march on the right bank of the San Juan. He went to Aldamas in the night and found no soldiers there. He proceeded to the neighbourhood of the Passa Secatta[64] where he drove in the enemies pickets and hearing the enemies alarm bugle he rode back into the chaperal and soon saw the party in full persuit. My force was strengthened today by the accession of Capt. Hunters Company.[65] — On approaching the outer pickets, the sentinel took the troops for Mexicans, and came in at full speed. Capt Hunter seeing he had alarmed the picket endeavoured to reach him, but the chase only added to the cause of the alarm, the pickets men reported to me that a large Army of Mexicans were close at hand. I told him it might be Americans. — He said no, it was Mexicans a man had passed them and told him so. I caused the long roll to beat and such a jumping, snatching, and running I never saw. —

The Mexican express who took such extraordinary means to conceal his papers was to return at nine Oclock this evening at the furthest.

Mar 6

So much business about the lines preparing defenses serving requisitions and hearing complaints I could do nothing at my register.

FOUR

Victory at Saltillo

"NEWS came at last," wrote Curtis on March 7, 1847. "An express arrived conveying the intelligence of General Taylors [sic] extraordinary success against General Santa Anna." With no more than 4,600 effective soldiers, Zachary Taylor won the most important victory of the Mexican War. Santa Anna, a good strategic planner, was deficient in the practical tactics needed to win a battle. The small American army was stretched thin, too thin to cover the one-mile width of Angostura Pass through which the road from Saltillo to San Luis Potosi passed. Throughout February 23, 1847, the principal day of the battle, Taylor's forces had to shift to reinforce weak spots in the American defensive line that stretched across the pass. Santa Anna's attacks were aimed first at the San Luis Potosi road on the American right, then at the left wing of the American defenses and finally at the American center. Taylor was able to concentrate his meagre forces to counter each Mexican thrust, barely avoiding disaster each time. And victory without the effective use of American field artillery would have been impossible. Fragmented remains of the many

Mexican dead found on the battlefield bore mute testimony to the effectiveness of American cannister and grape shot.

Had Santa Anna used his most powerful resource — the overwhelming superiority in troop strength (according to most observers Santa Anna could count on some 15,000 to 19,000 men) — he could likely have won the day with a simultaneous assault on all fronts. The piecemeal attacks exhausted and depleted Taylor's forces as they rushed from one side of the battlefield to the other, but they managed each time to sustain their defensive positions. Most of the green and undisciplined American volunteer regiments panicked and ran at one time or another during the chaos, but almost always regrouped to fight again.

The defensive strategy employed by American forces was the key to their survival. Taylor, who had been ordered to remain at Monterrey, disobeyed his orders by moving south of Saltillo — a location chosen to deny Santa Anna's Army an opportunity to resupply and rest at Saltillo after a grueling 250-mile march across the high deserts of central Mexico. If forced to defend Monterrey, Taylor's forces would have been easily encircled by the larger — and by then rested — Mexican army. With American supply lines to the Rio Grande cut off by Urrea and Canales, Santa Anna would simply have to surround Monterrey and starve Taylor into submission. As it was, Taylor could defeat Santa Anna by merely denying him passage to Saltillo for food and water.

The American defensive position at Angostura Pass was ideal to neutralize Santa Anna's abundant resources. The large force of Mexican cavalry could not be used to flank American defensive lines and, in fact, could operate in the rugged environment of Buena Vista only with the greatest exertion of horses and men. The many deep gullies and ravines that crisscrossed the battlefield served as natural shelters for American forces against the artillery brought to bear by Santa Anna's men. In the end, however, the issue had to be settled by the soldiers and their generals.

Mexicans fought well; their general was to blame for the defeat. If Santa Anna had renewed the battle on February 24, many felt, including "Old Rough and Ready" himself, that a Mexican victory might have been possible. Such a victory would have had

A page from the Curtis diary — the image bears some likeness to
Zachary Taylor (Curtis Diary, Bancroft Library).

a profound effect on the American war effort and the final shape of the territorial map of the United States.

Mar 7

News came at last. — An express arrived conveying the intelligence of General Taylors extraordinary success against General Santa Anna. A terrible battle has been fought, and General Santa Anna has fallen back on Agua Nueva. — News also arrived of General Urrea. He was last night at a pass 25 miles above this place and moves to day over towards Seralvo [Cerralvo]. — After consulting with some of the officers, I have considered it best to march against him, on my way to Monterray. — The forces of General Urrea are variously estimated but from all I can learn they cannot be over four thousand all cavalry. These may annoy my train very much and I really dread the lumber I am obliged to carry along with me, but a reinforcement to General Taylor will give new vigour to his exertions; and I must try the success of the movement.

My force consists of the following numbers and corps:
Cavalry under command of Col Fontelroy —

Capt Hunter	60
Capt Marshall	30
Capt [?]	60
3rd Regt of Ohio Volunteers Commanded by McCook	629
Battalion of Virginia Volunteers Lt Col Fontelroy	360
	1139
Various say	120
	1259

With this force under arms and in good spirits; we move off at 12 Oclock at night

We arrived at the Rancho Wardaw — 7 miles from the place of our departure about 3 Oclock. Am being very wary. We all laid down without pitching tents and got a few hours sleep. At eight or nine Oclock I again moved forward and arrived at Meir at sundown. The country becomes rolling as we approach Meir, and very rocky and barren.

We see nothing of Meir until we arrive within about one mile of the place. The hills and dales become vast and beautiful. In the far off horizon we see the mountain ridges and the wide valley of the Rio Grande and tributaries. Passing many sharp places we finally arrive at a right turn of the road and on a sloping side of the lomas Meir comes in full view. — The white washed grave yard walls, and white stone houses, added to two large churches, near the center of the town: gave to this picture the appearance of a beautiful city. — A party of my mounted men had a little skirmish with the rancheros this evening and drove a part to a ranch some distance from Camp. Here the enemy was reinforced and our boys had to retreat to camp. The hard march of last night and this day quite exhausted many of the men. — They had to lay down immediately on arriving here overcome with heat and fatigue. The thermometer must have stood at 80 or 90 degrees and the dust was from five to six inches deep. Broken wagons, dead mules, and weary soldiers make a sad picture indeed. I am hoarse with giving orders. My wagon masters and wagon drivers seem to be totally ignorant of parking a train and I toiled till eight or nine Oclock to get my teams in some line of order for a defense. Two men are here in Meir who have just arrived from a train coming this way from Monterray.

They report that Major Giddings[1] with 400 men and two pieces of artillery started some days since with a train, and that he was attacked near Pont aguda day before yesterday by about 800 cavalry. The train was broken up at the point of attack, and some of the wagons were burning when these men escaped by flight.

Mar 9

Some of my heavy wagons were traveling all night, and one or two wagons were broke down and are not yet in at eight Oclock this morning. I have no way of deciding otherwise I must lay by to day as the next water is 17 miles off at a place called Canales Run [Chicarrones].[2] — Nine Oclock. — A party of three or four Mexican cavalry were discovered reconnoitering our line. I have sent out mounted parties to persue them and discover if possible any main body. Every aspect of affairs looks dark and gloomy enough, five more men have been able to reach this place they say that Major Giddings was charged on and as they believe cut to pieces.

I went with Lieut Waynewright to bath in the beautiful stream which flows at the foot of our encampment, the Rio Alcantro.[3] There was a beautiful pebble beach to walk into the water upon, and the bed of the stream is solid limestone rock. The water has a very rapid current and several feet fall within a few rods. This is the first rippling water and stoney shore that I have seen in Mexico and it reminds me of dear scenes with my wife and children on the beautiful banks of "Old Muskingine" [Muskingum].

Mar 10

I made a very early start this morning with my Brigade better arranged than formerly. Two or three more of the unfortunate command of Major Giddings, who made their way to our column, give sad accounts of the butchery inflicted on those who came in contact with the lancers.[4] We also met a Mexican who says the road is a terrible picture of obscene and horrid exhibitions of the dead. Poor Giddings, I fear he has met with a sad fate.

I camped on Canales Run 15 miles from Meir, where I found space enough to make a triangular park of my wagons. —

Mar 11

Spies that I sent to Ponte Aguada returned safe at four Oclock. They report that there is no signs of American or Mexican force in that place, and that the ranch is quite deserted. I started at 6 Oclock, and arrived at Ponte Aguada at about three. The road has been quite level, but exhibited a rolling landscape on the north and west. Our road leads along a high plane parallel to the valley of a beautiful stream the same one we encamped on last night. The shrubbery on the road is principally the white thorn, and vegetation appeared very dry and the earth very sterile. But the valley of the stream presents a green line of thick foliage, and beyond a rolling rising country that is backed by a mighty pile of blue and cloud caped mountains. No landscape can exceed in beauty the front view of the vast scene. Over to the right and resting on the edge of a high hill is the white stone buildings of the town of *Agua Leguas*.[5] It is a beautiful town, on a beautiful stream of the same name. No enemy came in sight during the day. The village or large Rancho of Ponti Aguda is almost entirely deserted[6] — Some articles of American property, evidentaly taken from Major Giddings train have been found in the rancho and chaperal, and being property recaptured I have taken charge of them. We recaptured near Meir several cart loads of provisions which have been taken from Meir.

Mar 12

My anxious forebodings and fears for Major Giddings and his command were gloriously relieved on my approach to Cerralvo. The star spangled banner waved gloriously over a large stone building, we were greeted by officers of the 1st Ohio coming out to meet us. The affair was soon told. Major Giddings had been charged in front by Mexican lancers, and they had persued their way down the train, frightening and killing the wagoners, and showing every act of ferocity they could exhibit: till the cannon opened a shower of grape and cannister on them, which put them to flight. Some sixteen wagoners and soldiers were found dead on the field, and 52 wagons are missing. — The major and men remained on the field during the night, but marched into Cerralvo unmolested the next morning.[7] Here they have remained since the 7th and no doubt had they left this place, they would have been attacked. Major Giddings made a requisition for rations, cartridges, and two Companies of Infantry, all of which I furnished. — The two companies were detailed from the Virginia regiment. — This town of Cerralvo is quite a pretty place situated in full view of the mountains which now begin to show their rough and majestic grandeur. Pile after pile of rough and barren peaks rise in wild and terrible majesty in every direction.

Mar 13

After further consideration, and at the earnest appeal of the officers of the Virginia companies, Major Giddings expressed a preference for a company of mounted men and I gave him in stead of two companies of the Virginia Volunteers, a small company of Texian Rangers under the command of Lieut Jett.

153

Our column was *enroute* at nine Oclock or earlier and no doubt Major Giddings started immediately after on his way to Comargo. Our road leads over a rolling rising country. The hills are barren lime stone ridges, crossed by bright streams of clear running water.

No Mexicans are met on the road. We arrived at our camping ground at an early hour the *old ranch* or *Rancho Viejo*. It is an entire ruin. Major Giddings, as I am informed, had it burned to ashes. We passed to day several dead bodies (the effects of Major Giddings attack) in a putrid and half decayed condition. They had some of them been partly buried, but the wolves have dug them up, and made a mangled carcass of them.

On arriving at my encampment, I was informed that some of my spies had discovered suspicious conduct and circumstances at a ranch about half a mile off: and I sent a party under Lt. Arnold,[8] U.S. Dragoons, to search the premise. The inhabitants all escaped except one old sick man and two or three servants. On searching about the Rancho some guns cartridge boxes and hid in the woods the soldiers found a considerable quantity of corn. Some Mexican soldiers were also discovered and our men persued them for some distance unable to kill or ketch them.

Another one of the wagoners attached to Major Giddings train came into our camp this evening. Poor fellow he has been six or eight days playing hide and seek with the Mexicans and comes in to us half starved and weary with watching and wandering. He says he saw yesterday the Mexican lancers about fifteen miles from this place going towards Monterray and that there were three or four thousand. That the column extended two or three miles and was two or three hours passing the place where he lay concealed. I suppose the poor fellows fears may have magnified the numbers very much, but straws show which way the wind blows. General Urrea is either retreating or concentrating his forces near Monterray to prevent my entrance into that place. —

Mar 14, Sunday

Our outer pickets were twice driven in, either with the approach of force or fear. The first time the pickets came in, I merely directed the men to go back and reconnoiter and if the force approached to return. The second time the pickets fired, came in at full speed, and I really thought the lancers were onto our lines. It was very dark, and the roll of the drum created the greatest *stampede* I have every witnessed. I succeeded however in getting the lines formed around the park of wagons, and my artillery under command of Capt McLaughlin, Allen, Lt. Higgins,[9] was posted ready to receive whatever might come from the dark shadows around us. Nothing came, and I ordered the men to sleep on their arms.

My column is so long when drawn out, I feel sensible of its weakness at several points. I have it arranged as follows. At the head of the column I have a detachment of cavalry under command of Lt. Col Fontelroy. — Next a piece of artillery supported with eight companies of infantry arranged so as to form a square in an instant. Then come in the rear of this, some 35 loaded wagons drawn by mules. Then another six pounder supported by four companies of infantry. — Then another long line of wagons say forty, and here I have "Higgins battery" [named in honor of Lieut. Higgins?] two rampart guns rigged at my own instance and according to my own plan on the head of pork barrels. This battery is supported by two companies of infantry. Then we have some eight or ten wagons and this is followed by a rear guard of cavalry. Scouts and spies are kept out day and night, and I hope under this arrangement to avoid surprise and do all that can be done to secure a large train. My whole train when drawn out cavalry artillery infantry and wagons must always exceed a mile in length and in hilly places it draws out three or four miles long in spite of every exertion. Capt Patterson in advance detected the tracks of mounted men and footmen where they had approached our pickets in great numbers.

We camped this night at what is called the deserted ranch. It is a ruin: like that of last night it has fallen before the fiery element. The fresh ashes and the corn strewed about the place show that we occupy the ground where our foes encamped the last night. This camp is on a bright sparkling stream of clear water, which runs over a thick ledge of limestone rock. . . .

I heard the plaintive sound of a dove and the song of many birds, but the danger of meeting lurking Mexicans induced me to entail my walk [and] return to camp. — My train is well parked, and I lay down quite easy and confident in the system of defenses I have established.

Mar 15

I got under way at half past six Oclock and persued the road with great care and caution lest my train would get extended. Some very bad hills intervene between this place and the next encampment; and here has been a field of skirmishing for almost every train that for the past month that has ventured through. I sent out Col [Louis P.] Cook and others to reconnoiter. Col Cook is a Texian Ranger well acquainted with the country and I use him as a spy. He found a mounted armed Mexican and brought him in. On being closely questioned he states that Generals Urrea and Canales and Col. Ramaro [Romero],[10] are encamped about six miles below Ramos[11] and on the same stream Ramos is on. I therefore determined to encamp at Ramos and if I find it true attack them. Ramos is another ruin. The place must have contained more than a thousand inhabitants. Many of the houses were made of stone and therefore resisted the effects of the element. No Mexicans made their appearance but all is desolate and foresaken.

I ordered out a party to bury the dead. The bodies are strewn from this place two or three miles. These bodies are the wagoners and men under command of Lieut Barbour[12] attacked on the 23rd February. They were attacked on a side hill, and the massacre continued throughout the entire length of the train. The party that I sent out was approached by Mexican cavalry and I had to reinforce it. We saw from the heights a long column going towards Caderita[13] no doubt the retreating army of Urrea. This column is variously estimated at the long distances of from four to five miles at 3 to 4000.

I walked out with Capt T. F. Marshall to see the beautiful cultivated grounds near this place. Very large level fields are surrounded with a ditch of clear running water used for irrigation; and along the side of the ditch; a hedge of musquete, fig, and orange trees decorate the country. The devastation committed by our soldiers is painful and mortifying. I see the smoke of many sad tenements of the women and children who had fled to the hills and mountains. — There were many appearances of hostility around our encampment and I have made every preparation for fighting tomorrow morning.

Mar 16

I moved forward this morning with great caution towards the valley of Ramos where we yesterday had been engaged burying the dead bodies. Not a Mexican was to be seen in the vast field of view that spreads out before us. As we descended into the valley a few heads are seen gathering on the opposite hill at the very place I anticipated an attack. Establishing one gun and 2 companies under Capt Allen on the East hill, I ordered the cavalry to fall back, and the infantry forward for the purpose of making a charge with the infantry designing to follow it up with my artillery and cavalry. As we approached the west hill the force increased and we were short of a hard fight. The infantry in rear under Col. McCook was ordered forward and all was moving to the ascent when a small party approached us, and lo and behold it is General Taylor and his staff!! It was a mutual surprise. The General had heard of Major Giddings difficulties and marched out to relieve him. The Mexican forces seeing the united army under General Taylor with my force had no doubt fled. I met General Taylor about eight Oclock A.M. He was very plainly dressed, but well enough for a hard journey. He wore a plain forage cap, overcoat, black pants, shoes, and spurs. He was riding an indifferent horse with plain saddle and bridle and every way was one of the plainest men I have seen. I knew him the instant I saw him from his resemblance to his brother Col. [Joseph P.] Taylor. The General enquired for news. None of the express carriers have reached him and he knew nothing of all that had been thought, said, or done on the Rio Grande since about the 23rd of February. — On being informed of the direction taken by Urrea, the General immediately ordered matters to follow and he therefore countermarched his escort and directed me with my command to follow. After a few miles march we came to Marine [Marin] a place partly destroyed with fire but being constituted of stone many of the houses still stand. This must have been a town of two or three thousand people. We divided our baggage here, and I took only a blanket for each man and directed my commissary to take provisions for three days. At this place I met my friend, Col. Belknap and I also met Major Bliss,[14] and the other officers of General Taylors staff. — They pointed out a white spot at the foot of the mountains which they told me was Monterray. The clouds hide the tops of the huge mountains that rise in the back ground, and between my station and Monterray is a vale which shows at a distant view many signs of cultivation.

We changed directions to the left and followed a road leading along the side of this wide vale. On our right the country shows signs of considerable cultivation. At a few miles distance we came to Guadeloupe,[15] a very large and rich Hacienda, where there was a fine dashing stream of water, stone houses, and every thing comfortable and quiet. The people appeared very shy but did not desert their avocations. — We crossed two branches of the San Juan, both of them clear and beautiful water with rapid currents. We encamped on the bank of the second. Or rather we bivouacked, for I have no tent and sit writing in the open plain on the bank of a beautiful stream with no bed but a blanket and no cover but the sky.

Mar 17

My bed was rather hard for comfort, but I found rest in a comfortable nights sleep. General Taylor ordered the column to march forward at about 7 Oclock and we pushed forward towards Cadereta in almost a South direction. General Urrea had passed our last nights camp six hours before we arrived at it. Our road leads us across two or three branches of the San Juan all rapid and clear water. The country along the road is generally dry and barren, but in the region of the streams the ground seems to bear a fine coat of grass. Cattle are still quite numerous and generally in good order. After going about 11 miles and crossing a low ridge of mountains called the Masa, we came to the main branch of the San Juan and saw in the middle of a grove on the south side the massive stone church and other large stone buildings of the town or city of Cadereta. — The houses are generally of stone, and many of them large and elegant. The fences too are generally of cut stone and the streets are paved with round stone. In the center of the town is a large plaza paved with round blue and white lime stones and in the center of the plaza there is a fine fountain. —

Cadereta is the largest and most wealthy city I have ever seen in Mexico. It must contain many thousand inhabitants. — It has not been plundered or impaired by soldiers, but remains an ancient Mexican city of some two hundred years antiquity. General Urrea passed through this place night before last on his way toward the mountains which here rise up to the clouds. — I would have been pleased with a continuance of persuit, and believe if we had made forced marches for the next two days we would have caught his mules and baggage at the entrance of the pass. —

Mar 18

General Taylor marched forward leaving us to follow at our leisure. We found the road smooth and much worn leading parallel and near to the mountains. — The soil is much more fertile than I have found it for many days, and on each side of the road larger fields were fenced and apparently well cultivated. Each field is surrounded by a running stream or arrangements made to let in a stream for irrigation. The people are all busy ploughing and planting. Sugar cane seems to be the principle article of culture, but there are also many very large and fine cornfields. Approaching Monterray the first prominent object is the *Bishops castle*[16] which is on a high ridge near the town. An other prominent object rises in view exhibiting a lofty spire and dome and majestic walls. It is the church and its venerable appearance at a distance is exceedingly commanding. The round arch fringes of an old monastery rises up on the right and a little further to the right is the *Black Fort*[17] in where I am to be stationed. The near or distant view of the city would only give a view of shrubbery jacals. Before entering the city we crossed the San Juan a beautiful rapid stream of clear fresh water which skirts the mountain side of the city.

On entering the streets we begin to perceive the magnitude and strength of the place. The streets are very narrow and all paved with hard round stones. On either side stone houses with thick walls appear like old forts to command these narrow streets. The fences are of thick stone walls so high that I could not reach the top of them as I rode through. The plazas are all paved and every thing has the appearance of solid masonry. The houses are silent and lonely. The people are on the hills. — A description of this city would occupy many pages and I will not therefore attempt a description.

I marched my regiment through town and encamped at the black fort. — I received the order of General Taylor to take command of the city and relieve Col Ormsby[18] of the Ky Legion. I met the 1st Ohio which by the order of General Taylor was placed under my command. After so many days hard marching my men were very weary. Our last few days march by Cadereta had been unusually hard. Capt Ramsey[19] of the 1st Ohio invited me to his tent, and gave me a good bed to lay down on. It was the first I have enjoyed for a long time.

Mar 19

I started out this morning on horse back with Capt Ramsey and Lieut Grubb[20] for the purpose of visiting the Commanding General who went directly for his old encampment at "Walnut Grove".[21] — We first took the road to a ranch one league North at the foot of a large mountain for the purpose of visiting the hot springs *Agua Caliente*.[22] The ranch is a very peaceable one and all the road was surrounded with fields quite full of oxen, wooden ploughs, and people planting. At the foot of a round head land mountain, we found the hot spring. A small stone house is erected on its bank, and the spring is walled in on the side of the house, so as to appear like a large stone vat. Some Mexican women were bathing or rather dressing when we came, and they gave way for us except one who lay on a cot. She was ill with rheumatism but able to sit up and talk to us while we stripped and entered the bath!! The pool is about five feet deep and the water just about the heat you would wish a hot bath. I never saw so fine a place for bathing and after a long march I enjoyed it exceedingly.

After our bath Capt Ramsey prescribed some medicine for the senora who had been an interested spectator of an amusement and we bid adieu to the *Agua Calientes*.

Taking the road leading south we reached the camp of General Taylor at Walnut Springs. — There were many troops encamped around in a beautiful grove of large trees resembling oak or walnut, but very different from either of those trees seen in the north. They are some 3 feet in diameter the stumps and green shoots and branching almost from the ground. They are beautiful shade trees, and I could not wonder at the Generals selection of this grove for his head quarters. His tents were placed in a line, and the ground neatly swept around them, giving the place a rural and delightful appearance. The General received us at the door of his tent, where he had two benches for the accomodation of visitors. I have had three or four long and familiar conversations with the General, and begin to understand his character well. He is a plain frank man easily understood. He speaks very freely and feelingly on the subject of his command. He thinks General Scott ought to have seen him, or consulted him before reducing his ranks as he has done. He says that he would readily have cooperated with General Scott, but has had no opportunity. That his letters written to Washington suggesting a march on Vera Cruz have never been replied to, and that his march to Victoria was in persuance of a plan of operations which he had proposed to the Department, and which he was obliged to relinquish under the movements and orders of General Scott. — The General had seen Col Ormsby who desired to remain here, as his term of service will soon expire and the General directed me to be ready to march forward to Saltillo so as to be ready to fight if General Santa Anna returned upon that point. . . .

Mar 20

I visited many parts of the city, and made myself somewhat acquainted with the plat of it. It is situated between two mountain head lands, the Saddle and Mitre Mountains, and the streets running east and west are on the line connecting these two mountains. — The river runs round the south and east side, and there is a large stream of water partly drawn from the river but mostly rising from springs, which runs nearly east and west through the North part of the city. — Over this river there are three or four stone bridges, and the beautiful clear water is carried through the gardens and used for irrigation. It was near these bridges and near the North east corner of the city that our troops were so riddled by the grape of the enemy. Every bridge and street was defended by batteries which raked the streets and approaches in all directions.[23] The trees, fences, houses, and old fragments of

forts show the effects of the conflict. Captain Hamilton[24] accompanied Lt. Col McCook and myself in a long ride around the
city, in which he pointed out the position of each particular
object or person during the battle. — The elevations on the west
side gave to General Worths movements the entire advantage.
The Mexicans seem to have supposed we would try to enter only
at the plane where we approached the city, and hence located on
the east and north the major part of their defenses. The west and
south were therefore poorly prepared, and offered the best point
of attack. Every step of the movement on the west was made with
clear regard to science and skill. On the east everything was
masked. The shrubbery, low ground, and tougher topography
made every spot difficult for the assailants. After passing the most
dangerous batteries and pushing into the main blocks of the city,
it is really surprising that an army should think of yielding. Their
whole city near the center is a system of stone walls that could be
used as so many traverses to resist our approach. The battle of
Monterray was well fought, and after seeing the strength of the
city, and the black fort, no one will doubt the propriety of accepting the surrender on terms somewhat favourable to the be-
sieged.[25] —

I also visited "Aristas Garden". — On the west side of the city
and on the street leading to Saltillo you find a long building of
one high story, presenting like all these houses a plain *fascade*
with large doors like gate ways. The entrance is either for footmen or carriages and you find after entering that the house is
composed of a suit of small rooms in front, and in rear of them
a broad portico extending the whole length of this building. This
portico must be 100 feet long and forty feet wide. The floors of
the rooms and portico are cement, and like all such floors in
Mexico, they are quite smooth and elegant. The stone work of
which the house is composed is similar to all the stone work seen
in this region. It is composed of lime stone. This stone is quarried
in rough blocks about fourteen inches by twenty eight. The
blocks are at first quite soft and become hard by exposure. They
are roughly cut and laid up with mortar, smooth coated and
white washed. Immediately in rear of the portico, there is a yard
beautifully and expensively ornamented with walls, shrubbery,
water pools, and paved walks. This yard covers about the same

U.S. soldiers on a street in Saltillo. Evidence suggests that these men, dressed in new uniforms bought by Curtis, may be from the 3rd Ohio (courtesy of the Amon Carter Museum, Fort Worth, Texas).

area as the building, and all the fountains, walks, and plants are arranged with the utmost symmetry and mathematical precision. The plan is neat and the execution superior to most of the architectural performances in this country. Beyond this yard the garden extends several hundred paces. This is also laid out very carefully, but the shrubbery has been recently planted, and presents no extraordinary beauty. I was delighted with the place and the excellent state of preservation it is in. Thousands visit the garden, but the beauty of every thing prevents its disturbance. A few flowers are handed to you and the domestics are very polite and ready to introduce every body. We can readily associate this pretty house, garden, flowers and fountains with the family of General Arista; and it is natural to conceive of those who are the true owners and once the occupants: that the man is a Gentleman, his wife an elegant lady, and his children bright and beautiful as the flowers that bloom in their absence.

Mar 21 Sunday

Three companies A, B, and C marched forward towards Saltillo in persuance of orders and under command of Major Love; for the purpose of escorting a large train of wagons. After breakfast I visited the church. This building, as I have before remarked, is one of the grand objects that presents itself to your view when you approach the city. The interior is also grand. Lofty arches and massive columns sustain the roof and the sides, and front view after you enter, are decorated with paintings, images, and altars.

The mummery of the service was proceeding under the direction of a dark little priest who read a few words of latin and made a great many crosses. The mechanical performances usually adopted by the priest and laity must require much time and attention to acquire. The ringing bells and learning the signals they convey must require a long course of drilling. The floor of the church is composed of large rough wooden panels easily raised and constructed no doubt as covers to vaults for the dead.

I cannot describe the outside or inside of this church. It is a moorish architecture very well executed and had a clock on one of the spires which strikes the quarters of each hour.

I visited and dined with General Taylor at camp. He was in

good health and humor, and as usual talked freely of the war and the prospects of peace. He has received a letter from the interior which states that Arista has marched to the City of Mexico and erected a new government, putting Herrera at the head of it. The General thinks that this may be true, and if so, that peace may be grow out of it. After dinner Col Belknap, Maj Mansfield,[26] Major Craig[27] of the Genl staff, Col McCook, and myself rode over to the hot spring ranch Agua Caliente. — During most of our way our road lead through a forrest of large trees similar to those about Walnut Springs — The country has now the appearance of Ohio than any other part of Mexico. These trees are the largest seen any where except on the tops of some high mountains where the pine groves are similar to those of other mountain countries. — We found crowds of Mexicans about the hot springs and therefore did not choose to bathe. —

The officers of whom I have just spoken have been with the General most of the time since he arrived at Corpus Christi. He has Major W. W. S. Bliss as his Asst. Adj. General, and he could not find one in the army so capable of filling the post. — He is a small man in stature, with rather small agreeable face and bald head. — He must be indefatigable in his labors and untiring in his energy.

I marched at six Oclock. The road passes Aristas garden, the Bishops Castle, and following up the San Juan we soon come into a pass where the valley is about a mile wide and the mountains on each side at least a mile high. About six miles from the city are the celebrated mills of Arista. The water is conducted to the mill in a stone culvert, supported near the mill on arches. The mill is stone and attached to it is a large stone vat covering perhaps 100 feet square used for roasting the wheat and leaching off the water it is used for drying it [wheat?]. The mill is propelled by about 12 feet perhaps 15 feet fall. The wheel is percussion or commonly called reaction with a vertical shaft attached to the mill stone. I did not stop to enquire particulars. The whole mill property was coated and whitewashed giving every thing a neat and substantial appearance. It is a little below the mill that the water is taken out to irrigate the city of Monterray. There is a little wing dam angling up and partly across the river, which throws the water into a small race which meanders along the side of the mountain. Passing the mills the valley continues nearly the same width. The mountains are huge rough masses thrown up in vertical strata and presenting rough projecting points on the sides and summits. There is a mass of headlands through which the San Juan penetrates from the left side. This pass is said to be very crooked narrow and its sides perpendicular. I was tempted to stop and examine it, but the day is very warm and the wind throws clouds of dust into our eyes, till we are all glad to stop at our watering place near the town of San Caderina [Santa Catarina],[28] about twelve miles from Monterray. — There is a mine hole through a shaft of the mountain near this place that will always attract the eye of curiosity. Looking at it from the road it would seem to be only ten or fifteen feet from the top and about three feet diameter. But when you compare these distances with a pine tree that at the same height appears like a little shrub, it is easily perceived that this hole must be larger than a house and several hundred feet below the top of the mountain.

Mar 23

Major Dix[29] came into camp late last night, with a considerable amount of money which he is taking up to Saltillo to pay the troops with. I made an early start, and marched over a rough road to the Rinconada Ranch.[30] The country is the most barren in the earth. Mountains on each side and rocks between the mountains. The road was on an ascending grade of from thirty to sixty feet to a mile till we came within four or five miles of this ranch. Then the inclination is changed, and we descend at sixty or 100 feet to the mile. This is a large valley, surrounded by high mountains. — The grounds are poor but have been well cultivated and irrigated. Long stone fences are seen running up the side of the mountains where the soil is perfectly barren. The street leading to the buildings is beautifully shaded by two rows of poplar trees the branches of which interlock over the road. Wheat and corn and magay are cultivated but the ranch is now deserted and the fields are going to waste. — These poplar trees are a great relief to the eye, after looking all day on nude bare mountains, stony roads, and a rocky plain studded with dusty shrub brush about three feet high.

Mar 24

Our march for the first four miles of this day was on a rising plane protected on each side by high mountains. At the distance of say four miles, we come to the summit. It is the celebrated pass "los muertes" some times called the pass of the Rinconada, confounding the pass with the name of the ranch. The pass is protected on each flank by high impassible mountains, and a high ridge crosses between these mountains. This ridge is ascended going westward skirting the North side of the mountain where the road leads up at an angle of five to seven degrees. On this east side the ridge is quite precipitous, and a small line of breastworks on the brink of the cross ridge would render the pass impregnable except at the North end of the ridge, where two guns could so fortified as to render the whole east side absolutely impassible. With two pieces of artillery and three hundred men this pass could be protected against the world moving from the east against it. On the west side the plane is of easy descent. It could be raked with artillery perhaps better than the east side, as the angle of inclination is nearer that to which a cannon can be depressed, but it offers an easier approach for a very large force, and to protect this side against great numbers, much more work and more men would be required.

The water is nearer the west side, and works erected on the bank of the stream could hold the water and defend this west ascent or rather (going westward) the descent. — I have thus minutely spoken of this pass because it it the only way of passing all arms of the service across the Sierra Madre. There are several passes between this place and Tampico but they are represented as exceedingly dangerous for a simple defile of men and mules. A few men and a few pieces of Artillery; are all that would be required to resist a passage through the *Sierra Madre*. As for going over it that is out of the question. The passes east of this one were made by the Spaniards by blasting rocks, and cutting the sides where streams wend their way through. — The mountain ridge itself is composed of vertical strata of volcanic rock and most of the points are quite inaccessable. It is a succession of sharp points and like every thing in Mexico it seems armed with thorny projections.

The country along the valley is very barren. Wherever there is a level spot and even on sidling places you see the work of the agriculturist, but the little ranches are all deserted. Every thing shows the value of water and its universal scarcity. All these little side hill places are watered by carrying ditches along paralled to the sides of the main mountain and thus catch the water and thence conveying it in other little drains through the gardens or fields. — Fences are made by hedging with the cactus plant or by erecting walls of stone. We are camped at a vacant ranch about 18 miles from Saltillo, Ojo Caliente [hot water spring].[31] There is a fine stream of water in front of the old house, and on the opposite side of the stream there is a large field containing perhaps one hundred acres all walled in and cultivated by irrigating the ground. At the upper end of the field we found a stone spring house and in one room a fine spring of clear water which I expected to find very nice and cool: but found it quite warm. — I never witnessed a more splendid sunset. In a distant gorge of the rough mountains, the golden orb seemed to nestle for the night. The clouds and mountain peaks all tinged in the brightest colours, seemed to exhibit a mass of volcanic fire. I never expect to see the like again. . . .

Mar 25

I marched at seven Oclock over a desolate and barren road. — On our right for six or seven miles we have a stone wall running from mountain to mountain enclosing a very large piece of barren ground cultivated in spots where earth and water can be accumulated sufficient to admit of culture. —

We passed a considerable town *Santa Maria*[32] which lies north of the road, and perhaps a mile from it. — The road was better to day and we are encamped in sight of Saltillo and opposite to a large factory establishment. The mountains have appeared smaller to day, and the pass has been wider. Our route has been nearly South West ever since we left Monterray. I visited with Lt. Col McCook [concerning] the cotton factory near this place. It is a joint stock establishment owned by Mr. Hale of Matamoros and others. On arriving at this place we were met by American men, women, and children, who seemed quite glad to see us, as we were delighted to see them. They are the managers of the factory and very intelligent persons from New York and New Jersey.[33]

The factory is a large long two story building, made of adobe brick rough cast and quite well finished. The establishment runs about 15 hundred spindles and makes about forty pieces of brown muslin in a week. The work men are Mexicans under the direction of American overseers and I am informed they are very easily learned [taught] and quite faithful.

After visiting the factory which seems to be in a very neat and orderly condition, we went to the house of Mr. Bentley who seems to be the principal manager of the establishment. We were introduced to Mr. Bentley and seated at a fireplace with a wood fire, brass andirons, quite like home. To make matters entirely delightful, a clean table clothe was spread china plates, coffee cups, knives, forks, coffee, bread, and *butter* were before us. I declare the transition can hardly be imagined. I have been using an old tin cup, iron spoon, and a little box for my dining establishment, and in all Mexico I have never seen such coffee or anything like good *butter* before. I began to think butter could not be made here, but at the table of Mr. Bentley I found this essential article in all its profusion. It is strange but true, that the Mexicans have no idea of real butter or cheese. In a country where cattle are so numerous and so easily raised, I can hardly imagine how it is the people neglect the most valuable use of cows. We stayed some hours at the fire side of this family. It seemed like a dream contrasted with the cold realities of a soldiers life. I see the little community is in the power of Mexicans and in case our army is defeated the fate of all foreigners is sealed. Mr. Bentley gave me much intelligence of the condition of things here among the Mexicans. He thinks there is no doubt of a revolution in Mexico, but thinks the Mexican army is recruiting for the purpose of again attacking us.

FIVE

Northern Mexico after Buena Vista

W ITH the coming of darkness at Angostura Pass on February 23rd, 1847, and the last parting volleys between Mexicans and Americans, the war in northern Mexico came largely to an end. Zachary Taylor's army was destined to stand on the defensive in a guerrilla campaign for the remainder of the war, while General Winfield Scott and his men advanced from Vera Cruz along the National Highway to the City of Mexico.

Taylor's army was filled with one-year volunteers whose term of service was to end by May or June, 1847. Polk's administration had sent out a second call for volunteers to the various states, but the ranks were slow to fill. The American public, ever impatient, had begun to weary of the conflict. A quick victory over the Republic of Mexico would not be possible, and the United States military might be required to occupy Mexico for many years. With the a volunteer's enlistment now specified "for the duration of the war," few of the idealistic young men who had swarmed recruiting camps a year earlier were now eager to sign up. Their places in the volunteer regiments were now filled with a harder set of men, often criminals and felons eager to escape justice in the United States. The new regiments that were to garrison northern Mexican towns for the remainder of the war were, for the most part, undisciplined and poorly led — often eager to rob and plunder. Bored by the tedium of garrison duty, many volunteers committed acts of murder and rape that went unpunished because of an inadequate code of American military justice.

With the end of the official war in northern Mexico came an undeclared guerrilla war. The actions of this conflict were much smaller, but what they lacked in size they made up for in cruelty and brutality. Accounts of these clashes often did not appear in official records, newspapers, or histories because of the savage and often illegal methods employed by both sides.

By April, 1847, "Citizen Mariano Salas" issued a proclamation from Mexico City to incite Mexican citizens:

> I have obtained permission to raise a guerrilla corps, with which to attack & destroy the invaders in every manner imaginable. The conduct of the enemy, contrary both to humanity & natural rights, authorises us to pursue him without pity. *War without pity unto death!* will be the motto of the guerrilla warfare of *Vengeance.* [1]

Guerrilla fighting in northern Mexico had been a reality for almost a year by this date, with some minor successes by Mexican troops. Much of the action, however, was treated by Americans as banditry. The most notable guerrilla success occurred on February 24, 1847,[2] when José Urrea's cavalry division waylaid and burned a large supply train of wagons near the village of Marin. Captured American teamsters were barbarically put to death, shocking and enraging the occupying American troops. Mistakenly, U.S. troops blamed the forces of Canales and Romero for the savagery. Retribution was swift in coming.

On March 22, 1847, Zachary Taylor issued a directive to the inhabitants of Tamaulipas, Nuevo Leon, and Coahuila:

> [Taylor] has used every effort to cause the war to bear lightly upon the people of these States, and he has hoped by this means to retain their confidence, and to assure their neutrality in the strife . . . his kindness has not been appre-

ciated, but has been met by acts of hostility and plunder. The citizens of the country, instead of pursuing their avocations quietly at home, have in armed bands waylaid the road, and under the direction and support of government troops, have destroyed trains and murdered drivers, under circumstances of atrocity which disgrace humanity. . . . The undersigned requires from the people of the country an indemnification for the loss sustained by the destruction of the trains and the pillage of the contents. To that end an estimate will be made by the proper officers of the entire loss, and this loss must be made good either in money or in the products of the country, by the community at large of the States of Tamaulipas and of Nueva Leon, each district or juzgado paying its just proportion.[3]

The two states were finally assessed $96,000 for the loss of the wagon train, but payment was made contingent on the future conduct of the people.[4] Revenge for the murder of American teamsters was unofficial but swift and sure. On March 28, 1847, a party of men, believed by Taylor to have been composed of "Texas Rangers, teamsters, and other persons not soldiers" summarily executed the men at a small rancho near Marin.[5] The assassins could not be identified by American authorities and went unpunished. A fanciful account of this crime is related by Samuel Chamberlain, who probably was not in attendance, but had heard enough from those who were there to piece together a story of some accuracy.[6] This incident caused Antonio Canales to propose a general uprising of all citizens in northern Mexico:

With the greatest indignation I have learned that the Americans have committed horrible murders on the Guadalupe Ranch, hanging twenty-five peaceful men in their homes and by the side of their families, and shooting them almost immediately. Reprisal is the only recourse left to us to repel this warfare, which is not war, but atrocity in its greatest fury. . . . You will immediately proclaim martial law, with the stipulation that eight days after the publication of said law all individuals who are capable of bearing arms and do not do so will be considered traitors and will be shot immediately.

In accordance, then, with what has been stated, you are authorized to give no quarter to any Americans whom you may find, or who may present themselves to you, even though they be unarmed.[7]

General Taylor grimly realized that an enraged Mexican populace had the means to expel all American forces from their borders; therefore he attempted to keep the peace and punish lawless Americans. But he was well aware that his efforts as a military governor were inadequate and wrote on June 16, 1847, to the office of the adjutant general:

> I deeply regret to report that many of the twelve months' volunteers in their route hence of the lower Rio Grande, have committed extensive depredations and outrages upon the peaceful inhabitants. There is scarcely a form of crime that has not been reported to me as committed by them; but they have passed beyond my reach, and even were they here, it would be next to impossible to detect the individuals who thus disgrace their colors and their country. Were it possible to rouse the Mexican people to resistance, no more effectual plan could be devised than the very one pursued by some of our volunteer regiments now about to be discharged.
>
> The volunteers for the war, so far, give an earnest of better conduct, with the exception of the companies of Texas horse. Of the infantry I have had little or no complaint; but the mounted men from Texas have scarcely made one expedition without unwarrantably killing a Mexican. . . . The constant recurrence of such atrocities, which I have been reluctant to report to the department, is my motive for requesting that no more troops may be sent to this column from the State of Texas. . . .[8]

Northern Mexico would remain in this state of attack and reprisal for the remainder of the war. The result was apparent to one observer. Major Luther Giddings described the road from Monterrey to Camargo on June, 1847,[9] as "dotted with the skel-

174

etons of men and animals. Roofless and ruined ranchos, and many a dark and smouldering heap of ashes, told the disasters. . . ."

Mar 26

After a short march of two hours we came to the skirts of Saltillo. The view presents you a town on a side hill. The houses [are] generally of adobe brick, and the color of the earth. Four or five spires rise among the low dull looking masses. One large church presents itself as the great object of magnificence. It has a large dome with two high towers like that in Monterray but apparently much lower. The streets of Saltillo are generally narrow and paved, and their appearance more Mexican than we found at Monterray. In passing through town we rose at a rapid inclination till we arrived at the summit of an extensive level plane on the edge of which the town appears to terminate. I only stopped to return the salute of some Illinois companies that met and escorted us into the city. After resting a few minutes on the top of the hill, I marched forward in a south direction towards *Buena Vista* where General Woll [Wool] is encamped.

The long line of tents soon made their appearance and I reached the position about 12 M. The encampment is on the edge of the battle ground and the lines of tents entered across the pass. The mountains on either side are not precipitous as we have seen them at other places, but sufficiently precipitous to sustain the flanks of a line of battle. — I was ordered to take the right of a new line in rear of one now occupied and on higher ground. I have therefore a beautiful location on a dry plain overlooking the battle field and also overlooking the entire men present. —

Two regiments of Illinois two of Indiana one of Kentucky several Ky Companies of Cavalry and Washington and Shermans batteries of Artillery are in full view before me[10]. —

Mar 27

I called on General Woll who gave me a long and very interesting account of the battle. I will not attempt a description.

Those who were here and participated in the terrible struggle are the only proper persons to describe it. The general has written a detailed and graphic account which I hope will be published.[11] His own actions and daring aid in the whole matter gave him the right to a fair share of the glory of the victory. He does not however feel disposed to detract from the preeminent position which this last battle gives to the "Hero of the Mexican war". His opinions of General Taylor are the most exalted and he speaks of him as the great General in the United States Army.

General Wool is a very easy active gentlemanly officer. He is exceedingly rigid in enforcing discipline and I believe he is the most devoted officer in our service. —

Mar 29

I am a member of a court of enquiry composed of Brig. General Marshall, Col Morgan, and myself ordered by General Wool for the purpose of enquiring into the conduct of Brig. General Lane[12] of Indiana in the battle of Buena Vista. The 2nd Indiana retreated and fled in confusion, and it has been said they were ordered to retreat. The question arises as to who gave the order to retreat, General Lane or Col Bowles.[13] — This afternoon I rode out with General Wool and staff and Col Morgan to reconnoiter our position and give the General another opportunity to show the battle ground. We returned by way of our line of encampment on the hill. This line is in rear of the Generals position on a beautiful rise of ground on where we have a delightful plane for drilling. Col Morgans Regiment and the 3rd Ohio were out and both appeared very well. General Wool said he gave it to us. My 3rd Ohio is decidedly best in the field, and Col Morgans is close upon my heels. — While in Matamoros I had been told the Illinois Regiments were my strongest competitions: but now that we come together there can be no doubt among all judges the 3rd Ohio stands decidedly first the 2nd Ohio next and Illinois next. I see it would be an easy matter to make the Illinois regiments entirely equal to any. Their conduct in battle was so distinguished as to place them high enough on the temple of fame. — There is an order for a general review tomorrow which is designed to bring out all arms of the service.

Mar 30th

As the proceedings of the court martial or rather the court of enquiry seems to bring up the whole matter of the retreat of the 2nd Indiana Regiment and especially brings up the conduct of Col Bowles the commander: it seems to me the investigation of General Lanes conduct is a mere incident to more important matter, and I have therefore proposed to be relieved from the hearing of the case. — A court of enquiry is always an ex parte matter, I dislike to be the means of propagating error. After I made the motion the court adjourned.

The great matter of the day was the Review of all the troops by Brig. Genl. John E. Wool. — The line was formed in front of our line of tents and a long long line it was. On the right were two batteries of Artillery under command of Capt Washington.[14] — A squadron of cavalry under Captain Eustice,[15] next the Second Regiment of Ky commanded by Major Fry,[16] next my 3rd Ohio under Lt. Col McCook, then the 2nd Ohio commanded by Col Morgan, next two regiments of Illinois commanded by Col Churchill[17] and Col Wethard,[18] next and last two regiments of Indiana under Col Bowles and Col Lane. The whole under my command as Senior Colonel.

It was the largest force I ever saw, and decidedly the most splendid. All arms appeared well represented. The Ohio regiments were evidentaly superior in many respects. Especially the 3rd Ohio. — The whole line would not have fallen under my command had General Marshall or General Lane been present; but they were both excused and absent. The line was organized and formed by Col Churchill Acting Inspector General of the U.S.A. He is my senior in rank, but being a staff officer he is not expected to take command and therefore declined unless I *requested* it. This I could not do without placing myself in a false position, and would not, though as I told the gallant and brave old Colonel, I would have prefered to give him the command without a request which would leave ground for the inference that I did not feel competent of my ability.

I was interrupted writing by General Wool calling with Capt [William W.] Chapman, a very gentlemanly and agreeable quartermaster. The General seems delighted with the review and was pleased to compliment me on my success. —

Indeed the troops all appeared well and worthy of any service.
the General says he would like to go forward if he had say two
regiments of regulars to add to the four regiments now here on
the hill. It is probable we may yet be required to visit San Luis
before our time expires.

April 1

All fools day amuses soldiers. One is sent to the Colonel another to the General for orders, and poor fools, all are in anxious
fear lest they are fools.

General Wool sent me word to be ready to go with him to a
review of troops in Saltillo. — I was not very well and had but
little pleasure in the review.

Two companies of Illinois under Lieut Col Warren[19] and one
company of Cavalry and one of Artillery were drawn up on the
plain this side of the City. The General and staff made quite a
display, but what is the use of it? Three thousand miles from all
creation displaying lace plumes and epulettes does appear almost
ridiculous. Yet we never were more anxious to excell each other
and my whole regiment seems unusually ambitious.

April 2

Our court of enquiry into the conduct of Brig General Lane
still requires a few hours session each day. We are determined to
bring it to a close soon and adjourned to day for the purpose of
examining the ground on which the Second Indiana operated.

General Marshall, General Lane, Col Bowles, and others with
myself went out and looked over the ground. I consider it a plain
matter that the position taken by the regiment was one that
should not have been taken, and could not be held. A powerful
battery raked it with grape and there was an overwhelming force
of Infantry in front. The matter of regret is that more of the
regiment could not be rallied.

An express came from Col Doniphan at Chihuahua.[20] — He
met the Mexicans about 15 miles from that place on the 27th
Feby and took their baggage and 10 pieces of Artillery. The
volunteer force under Col Doniphan was about 900 strong, and
that of the Mexicans about three thousand. Mexican loss 300
killed 500 wounded. Our loss 2 killed 9 wounded!!

April 3rd

Lt O'Brien,[21] U.S.A. having heard that testimony had been introduced before the court of enquiry and "recorded" which related to his conduct on the day of battle wrote a note to the recorder of the court requesting the court to grant him the right to be heard by introducing opposing testimony. — I insisted on his right and the court adjourned to give him an opportunity to be heard. All the objections that I anticipated arise from our proceedings. The conduct of every officer is in some way inter-woven with that of his commander and when General Lane asked for a court of enquiry he brought up the conduct of the 2nd Regiment and all the officers and men under his command.

I was afflicted with head ache and fever and during the after noon confined to my bed, or rather to my blanket, in my tent. I took rhubarb and in the evening my fever and head ache sub-sided. The nights are quite cold but the days are exceedingly hot.

I am better to day but not well enough to find incidents to write about. The idea of getting sick and laying on the ground under a tent covering is enough to give any one the horrors.

April 5

Sick! Sick! A slight chill very early in the morning and then a burning fever. — By keeping a wet handkerchief on my head and bearing patiently "the ills that flesh is heir to" I passed the paroxysm so that by supper time I found myself ready for my allowance. I am determined to go to town Saltillo in the morning and procure a room which will exclude the burning rays of this *intemperate* sun.

News arrived through a Mexican that General Scott marched into the plaza of Vera Cruz on the 8th March. The same man states that Santa Anna has been declared dictator and part of the army goes for and part against him.

April 6

Moved into the city and got a room at the American kept by woman who seems to be a part of the army, Mrs Bourjette.[22] She is commonly called the "Great Western" for her size. She is nearly six feet high and well proportioned. She distinguished herself at Fort Brown during the bombardment in attending the sick and wounded and is said to be a useful soldier. She has several servants Negro and Mexican and she knocks them around like children. While I am writing she is watering her horse. A fine white horse that Lincoln was killed on.[23] —

I have a comfortable room and bed and have taken ten grains of quinine. So if the ague comes tomorrow I am ready for him. There was an evening shower, enough to lay the dust — attended with thunder and lightning.

Apl 11 Sunday

I attended high mass at the Cathedral with Captain Allen. The altar at the east end and in front of the Great Gilt frontispiece was covered with a rich lace cloth beautifully and richly embroidered. The Priest had on a tunic of the same kind of work which hung from his neck almost to his feet. During the Performance his back was almost always towards the audience and the dazzling gilt frontispiece and burning tapers so blended the colours of the embroidered linen and curtain of the Altar that you could hardly distinguish anything but the Priests black head with a bald spot on it. The long hall was full of men and women all kneeling during the most of the ceremony. There must have been from ten to fifteen hundred in the Cathedral. The Priest had for his attendants two little Mexican boys dressed in red and white. They stood back generally but stepped forward to remove the large Bible from one corner of the Altar to the other apparently an important and essential part of the service. The priest entered from a side door and standing with his face to the audience made the sign of the cross with his hands which was repeated in hasty and singular activity by the entire audience. He immediately turned his back to the audience and fell on one knee, rose instantly made signs, stepped a little to the right and *fumbled* over a vase returned to the center kissed something before him on the altar made signs stepped to one corner of the Altar where the Bible was open and read in a low solemn voice a few words that no one could hear. Shut the book turned his face to the audience and made the sign of the cross faced about again stooped and touched his knees rose stooped and kissed something stepped to the other corner of the altar where the same Bible had been conveyed and read a few lines in the same solemn incomprehen-

sible tone — stepped back to the center stooped and kissed —
faced the audience made the sign of the cross. — The boy shuts
the Bible and walks out with it the Priest stoops and puts on a
black miter cap and retires; and so closes High Mass in the Great
Cathedral at Saltillo.

During the performance the audience generally kneeling keep
their eyes fixed on the priest and occasionally one of the little
boys rings a bell which puts the entire audience into a simultaneous performance of making crosses in swift spasmodic succession. Everything is conducted with the utmost propriety and the
men and women show the most perfect devotion. —

The great congregation scattered in all directions each person
persuing his amusement or avocation and no further notice appears to be given to religious service during the day. —

Apl 13th

We closed the proceeding of our court of enquiry after taking
the testimony of our witness to balance the testimony of Col
Bowles which seemed to reflect on Lieut O'Brien.

I called with Captain Allen on General Wool who entered
largely into the matters of his own life especially his travels in
Europe and his reception by the King of the French and others of
the Nobility. The Generals history is very interesting. His father
and uncles were Whigs in the time of the Revolutionary War and
participated in that eventful struggle. For a considerable period
the General lived with an uncle, but was his own master at the
early age of twelve years and has since that time been the arbiter
of his own fortune. For some time he was clerk in a store and
afterwards went into the book business in the employment of a
Mr. [left blank] the editor of the Troy [New York] Budget till he
lost all his little earnings in a fire. He then under the direction
of this man acquired a considerable degree of education and no
doubt in the *book store* acquired a sense of the value of knowledge
which lead to his future advancement — Having been thus prepared for study and reduced by fire to a new beginning; General
Wool entered the Law office of [blank] Livingston and afterwards
persued his studies under [blank].

During the period of his law studies young Wool entered into
the political disciplines of the day and became acquainted with

Dewitt H. Clinton[24] the Governor of New York. The Governor proposed to him the idea of entering the army; and War soon after being declared young Wool at the age of 22 years entered the service as a Captain.

Apl 17

An order was sent to me directing me to allow none to pass to town as the small pox is in Saltillo. We had some days since been informed that it exists in the City of Monterray and among the troops coming up particularly the Mississippi volunteers. — Such an epidemic is much to be dreaded in a camp of soldiers and I am glad to perceive the General is using his exertions to prevent an extension of its ravages. The dangers that surround us must create the greatest anxiety among our friends at home and the idea of Small Pox in the Army will no doubt add very much to that anxiety. — More rain fell last night and I think we may safely say the rainy season is on us. As yet the dashing showers have been swallowed up by the dry earth, and you can see no running water or appearances of its effects except the appearance of small blades of grass and other herbage which begins to show life reviving in the vegetable kingdom

Apl 19th

A prisoner arrived from San Luis reports that most of the troops heretofore stationed there have been ordered to meet General Scott. The proclamation of General Santa Anna also arrived dated at Mexico and called on the people to make [a] last struggle against our advancing columns. I never read so stirring a report.

I called on General Lane and General Marshall for the purpose of considering the propriety of moving forward.

General Wool had expressed a fear, that the volunteers would revolt if they find their time expired at some remote position. I told the General I thought the volunteers would submit to any emergency that the service placed them in. That they are all reasonable men and would require no unreasonable discharge. That if the generals consider it necessary to move forward they should do so and the volunteers would so far as I knew and believed sustain them with all their efforts. The Indiana officers assured me their troops would and the Illinois also expressed a willingness to Capt Chapman. The Kentucky regiment prefer to go back towards the Gulf. I take it for granted the Ohio boys will obey any order to advance without a murmur and after getting the best evidence of the spirit of the volunteers I reported to the Commander General Wool who said the whole matter would be for General Taylors decision: but the great difficulty anticipated is the want of *transportation*.

Apl 20th

Field officer of the day and therefore busy. I regret to find the guard generally indifferent in the performance of duty. Volunteers appear to require a great deal of instruction and constant attention to get them in the way of doing guard duty. It seems the most difficult matter to teach them.

Apl 21st

Very warm indeed. I have nothing to write because I see and hear nothing. The Saltillo "Picket Guard"[25] dated April 14th speaks so favourable of my regiment I will here attach the paragraph so as to preserve it. I also received a few days since a letter from my friend the Senr Alcalda of Matamoros. The Generals interpreter has translated it for me and I will therefore attach it to this "blank book".

THE BUCKEYES. — We shall not be charged with making invidious distinctions between the different regiments now here. In saying that Col. Curtis' (3rd) Ohio regiment is the finest looking body of men we ever saw. All uniformed alike, in dark blue, and their uniforms kept remarkably neat and clean, on a dress parade or review, they certainly outshine anything we have ever seen dressed in soldiers clothes. We should doubtless be able to say the same of Col. Morgan's (2nd) Ohio regiment, were it not that a good part of this regiment, in coming up from Comargo, were obliged to destroy their baggage, owing to their coming several times in contact with the whole force of Urea. Both these regiments are under superior discipline, and drill like automatons, equaling if not beating anything on the ground — always excepting the two Illinois regiments (we belong to the 1st Illinois *ourselves*) which, either in marching, drilling, or regular hard fighting of course, *can't be beat*.

Apl 22

A large mail arrived bringing papers and letters in great abundance. The Congress has exhibited unhappy divisions on the subject of this war and many speeches have been made there which will be republished in Mexico.

Apl 25 Sunday

I rode over to the Encampment of a company of Arkansas troops commanded by Capt Preston.[26] This Capt is a very gentlemanly man and has a very good corps. I went over with my old school fellow and class mate Lieut Sitgreaves[27] of the Topographical Engineers. The encampment is near the city on the bank of a small irrigating ditch. The country admits of no interest. The rains here have not yet advanced vegetation so as to beautify the barren surface. We therefore see only the broad plane covered with short dry grass, and on either side the volcanic dark iron looking mountains thrown up in irregular masses.

Apl 27

The speech of T. Corwin,[28] Senator of Ohio, on the subject of the war with Mexico, has been received and it creates considerable excitement. I seated myself on the corner of my bed in the corner of my tent and read it through. It seems to me unequal to the fame of Corwin in every point of view. I dislike the premises, the argument, and the style. — It is almost universally condemned here. While reading the speech I was interrupted by being called to dinner and I seated myself on the ground by the side of an ammunition box where I feasted on a little salt meat fried, greens and bread. While discussing [digesting?] this dinner, I discussed Corwin's speech and I confess on the subject of supplies it struck me he would hardly be for withholding them if he had to share our humble fare. I expect that the boys have burned Corwin in effigy. The matter was got up in the 2nd Ohio but my

Regt. many of them went to see and it was nearly over before I saw it.

Apl 28

Went to town and spent the day shopping and visiting. I had a long conversation with Capt Davis[29] of the quartermasters department. He has resided twelve years in Mexico and is well acquainted with the manners and customs of the people. He thinks there will be no peace till a more vigorous course be taken in the prosecution of this war.

Apl 29

I remained in town during the night and paid 2.50 for my entertainment at the boarding house of the Great Western.[30] Every thing is very dear in this country. Eggs 50 cents a doz., chickens 50 cents, and all kinds of provisions very scarce and very dear. The dry weather still prevails. The few showers have not yet been able to start vegetation to any considerable extent. We hear of rain below on the valley of the Rio Grande and the clouds continue to hover around here and occasionally give us a dash of rain.

I took tea with Genl Wool and conversed freely on the subject of the deplorable prospect of this line. It is time now that we were on our way toward home, and there seems to be no force to take our places. This point cannot be sustained and the General thinks the army will be compelled to fall back onto the Rio Grande. — Our regiment is 622 strong at this days muster. —

May 1

Attended a meeting of Free masons. We met far up in the valley of the mountain. The officers seated themselves on rocks and the walls of our lodges rose up in terrific grandeur to the clouds that overshadowed us above. —

The sound of the gavel has not been heard among these mountains for many years past. Masonry has been interdicted in Mexico and the workman have for many years been obliged to conceal their implements and hide themselves from the persuit of their foes. —

Two cases of small pox in the 2nd Ohio.

May 2

I am again detailed as Field officer of the day and no doubt I shall find enough to keep me busy. Some rain this morning rather drizzling. Lieut Tidball[31] arrived from his jaunt to Vera Cruz.

May 3

Rumor is afloat and giving news of a great battle between General Scott and Santa Anna on or about the 12th Ulto.[32] It is not probable however that any thing has been done on that line at so early a period.

May 4

Walked over and around the battlefield with Capt McDongal of 1st Ia,[33] and Capt Allen. Found many articles, the implements of the strife still strewn over the field.

General Wool sent for me in relation to a letter which he was writing to General Taylor on the subject of our going forward. The General said that Col Morgan had said his Regiment was willing and anxious to go.

I told the General I had reported to him on the 19th or 20th ulto. that my regiment would readily obey orders to go forward and I still believe they would do so without murmering if the Generals thought a movement necessary but I suggested that such move if contemplated should be made within our time and without any delay; because after the period of our service we all consider that we have discharged our duty and can only be prevailed on to move forward by the certain prospect of immediate brilliant service, or extraordinary circumstances requiring our delay in the field. I also told the General that I saw no possible way of moving. General Taylor has neither men or means to make a useful or decisive movement. — It is therefore needless to talk of a forward movement during the period of our time which for some of my companies expires on the 27th day of this month. When that day expires then companies are entitled to an honourable discharge, and they should be in the state of Ohio. —

I perceive however that our term must expire while we are in Mexico, and our men will have to wait patiently and obey orders till they get to New Orleans. I see in this as in every other matter there is a want of foresight. The men to fill our places will not be here. — The orders and movement will not be in time for us to reach the states before the termination of our term: and our men will be crowded together at Brasos and New Orleans without any adequate provision of medical or other stores; and very like without any means for transporting us.

May 5

Went to town with Lt. Col McCook and spent the day. I met Major Crossman of the Quartermasters department, Col Wilson[34] of the new North Carolina Regiment[35] and Lt. Col Wright[36] of the Massachusetts Regt. Maj Crossman thinks there is no probability of General Taylor having force enough to go on towards San Luis. The Major is well acquainted with the condition of the line and has rendered the most active and energetic services in securing its present resources.

I can really see the difficulty of anticipating the requisite means of transportation in this country but there can be no excuse for neglecting the period for our relief. Troops should have been mustered and marched long before our time expired so that we could be at home even a month before our term expires. Thus giving us a little time to look about and prepare for entering upon business which most of us left without the best arrangement. The laws passed by Congress have made provisions to grant lands to "non commissioned officers, musicians, and privates" which will compensate for their destroyed affairs: but officers, who leave their business in the same "hot haste" have the same compensation granted to Regulars of the same grade who retain their places when peace renders their office almost a scarcity.

May 7

A mail arrived with letters from the states giving a terrible account of the feeling excited in the states on receiving intelligence of General Taylors position.

May 8

News arrived from Mexicans from General Scotts column giving intelligence of the entire rout of the Mexican forces under General Santa Anna at Cerrogorda [Cerro Gordo]. — It also reported that the soldiers have deserted the garrisons at Perota,[37] Puebla, and the City of Mexico. I rode to town with Lieut Sitgreaves, and Col Warren commanding the city, has the same news of our success.

May 9

I stayed in town and obtained the benefit of the shade during this hot day. The whole theme of conversation is the rout of the Mexican forces. The battle of Buena Vista seems to have entirely prostrated the *morale* of the Mexican army. I regret exceedingly that we are not able to follow in the chase. General Scotts movements are merely the advantage of General Taylors victory. If we could move all together or in separate columns to the City of Mexico, the campaign would be deeply interesting and our war could close gloriously. All we want is a little more *force* on this line. No doubt General Scott has every thing necessary to carry his line forward.

I visited today a beautiful garden in the east part of Saltillo. The buildings are plain, but the garden has been the work of considerable taste and expense. There is a shallow circular fountain of water. In the center a *jet* deau which throws the water against a little time [?] machine which is carried round like a wind-mill. There are seats made of cement around the fountain and the seats are shaded with the pear, apple, and peach trees interwoven beautifully with verigated honey suckle, multiflora roses and various other shrubbery. Poppies, pinks, and various other garden flowers were in profusion all through the garden.

May 12

The report of General Canalizo[38] second in command of the Mexicans at Cerro Gordo is published giving a doleful statement in regard to the disasters of the Mexicans. It seems to me extraordinary that a Mexican General should report so plainly in relation to his weakness and especially that he should say he had no way of preventing the advance of our troops. — It looks a little like "drawing us on".

May 13

Major Fry has orders to march his regiment home to Ky. I and Lieut Sitgreaves went to town to assist in the disinterment and

preparation for transportation of the bodies of Col McKee and
Lieut Col Clay[39] both of whom fell in the Battle of Buena
Vista. — Clay was a classmate and companion of ours at the
Academy and we rendered this sad service to last remains which
revive many early recollections. — In the palmy days of our
youth we had wandered among the hills and vales of the Hudson
and passed many happy days together. We had met again after a
separation of sixteen years — and here among the ragged mountains of the Cordeillaras we part forever! In my last intercourse
with Clay he talked of his bereavement in the loss of his wife and
of his fond attachment to his children. Alas! they are now or-
phans and are deprived of a father who was one of Gods noblest
specimens. Peace Oh Peace to thy ashes Clay. We have lived to
see the ways of mortals in peace and war. You fell as you lived
Honourably, faithfully, bravely. You never turned your back on a
friend or a foe and your memory and fame will be cherished as
long as the Battle of Buena Vista shall be memory of our National Glory.

May 14

I went out to the factory with Capt James M. Love for the
purpose of procuring vacsin virus.[40] I have before mentioned that
place and gave a pretty clear idea of it. I saw to-day the whole
matter in operation. It is a wonderful machine. Mexicans, men
and women, appear to work like parts of the machine from the
picking of the cotton to the measuring and folding the muslin.
Major Fry in command of 2nd Ky marched homeward. I met near
Saltillo and bade him farewell he is good officer and in battle
proven himself brave and gallant. —

May 15

Orders came for my Regiment to march homewards on Tuesday the 18th Inst. I directed every thing to be ready for marching
at sunrise of that day. I feel much regret at the prospect of our
returning without being [in] battle but such is our fate. I have
done all I ought to do to get my regiment forward for the purpose
of participating in every contest; but I have been assigned to a
part of the field less exposed. My men have always exhibited the
utmost anxiety to press forward and deserve as much credit for

their express desire to do so as though they had met their wishes. — Another mail brings news from the states down to Apl. 11 from home.

May 16

Lt. Col Mitchell[41] of Col Doniphans command arrived from Chihuahua. The main body of the troops is marching on their way but they are expected in two or 3 days.

May 17

Two Mexican officers accompanied by two lancers came into camp in full uniform with a package directed to General Taylor.[42] They say they come direct from San Luis but evade answering any questions which relate to the army, or the nature of their communication. They were quite rudely handled by the outer picket but received politely as soon as their business was perceived.

I was in General Wools tent after they arrived and thanked him for the kind notice he had taken of our Ohio troops. The General said he had only rendered simple justice to our deserts and regretted exceedingly that we could not stay. I told the General I disliked very much indeed to leave him but supposed he would soon be reinforced. The General then told me he wished I would stay in his staff, that if I would do so he would appoint me Inspector General in the place of Col Churchill who has recently been ordered to New Orleans to muster out the troops. I told the General I had not expected such an offer, but that I would accept it and remain if he thought my services needed. The General then wrote a letter to General Taylor recommending me in high terms and soliciting my services to be retained. I then concluded that I would go with the express direct to General Taylor and if he will comply with the request made by General Wool I can return to this place for duty. —

I started with Lieut Franklin[43] and Capt O'Brien; and we arrived at the Rinconada ranch about 8 Oclock in the evening. We passed Col Morgans Regiment which started to day for their home.

May 18

We arrived at Monterray about 12 Oclock after a very warm ride. This is the day my regiment starts homeward from Buena Vista.

May 19

I called out and visited General Taylor at his camp at the Walnut Springs. The General called me aside and told me he had received a letter from General Wool on the subject of appointing me and that he was willing and anxious to comply with it: but that after my time would expire it might be a question as to his right to retain me and I could see for myself, the only difficulty that seemed to present itself. — After consulting with Major Bliss who told me that General Johnson [Albert Sidney Johnston] of Texas had held over for the purpose of being at the battle of Monterray I concluded to obey orders directing my return to Buena Vista if they saw proper to give them designing to remain at my post at the head of the army at least till the expiration of my years service. The order was written accordingly directing Lt. Col McCook to take command of the regiment and me to report for duty in General Wools staff.

May 20

My regiment arrived early in the day at "The mills" five miles out. One man was killed and another wounded near Santa Catarina. They had separated from the regiment and were attacked by two armed Mexicans who succeeded in killing one of them [Private A. D. Lewis, Company H].[44] We become so used to walking and riding about alone that we forget danger and these men had foolishly put their guns in the wagon.

May 21

My Regiment marched through town and encamped at Walnut Springs. — After the attention shown us by General Wool I thought it might be possible that General Taylor would ride out to our camp or in some way manifest a parting regard. But the old General sits "at the door of his tent" in his old dark overcoat, conversing very kindly and amicably with those who call on him. He says he designs to march forward as soon as enough force arrives but cannot go with less than 6000 and would like to have 10000 men. — He seems to consider himself doomed to sit and wait as General Scott indicated in his letter of November last; and he bears his fate with more fortitude than I could expect to find in one thus situated.

May 22

I have informed my officers last night of my design to remain, and most of them called to see me and expressed their regret but at the same time their assurance in the propriety of my remaining. I accompanied the regiment on their way for a mile or two and then gave them a parting address. I alluded to the long faithful and dangerous service we have performed especially our sustaining a position where the loathsome diseases of the south had carried off hundreds around us and when the pale images of death were constantly passing in defile before us. That while others shunned the positon or deserted the field in boat loads, we had remained at the harrow of our lives to perform our hard and daily duty under the sad sound of muffled drums. I alluded to the efforts we have made to secure a more brilliant post in the field of battle and the disappointed hopes that we had suffered by the plighted promises of our Commanding Generals — I declared to each and all their just right to all the honours due to the most distinguished in this service, since they have pressed forward with every possible occasion without a moments regard to consequences performing every duty required of them and earnestly desiring and seeking more. I feel all I said because I knew it was all true. The Ohio troops go out of the field with less of the blare of glory but with the eternal glow. They never turned their back on the foe and whenever they have approached the enemy he fled or fell. In drill and discipline they attained preemminence and they have sustained among their associates a distinguished and honourable fame.

I was much affected and could not restrain tears when I parted with my officers. They too seemed many of them similarly affected and the large tears that darted in the eyes of some of the men when I alluded to their privations suffering and sorrows shows that all of my command was equally excited.

May 23d

I procured a wagon from the quarter master designing to go on towards Saltillo last night but I was too late to reach a party of recruits that had started in the morning, and therefore "put up" at Mr. Faddens boarding house here in Monterray to wait till another force is going up the road and thereby render my journey safe. — It is very warm and I have spent the day writing to my wife and children who will no doubt hear with anguish at my having remained. It pains me exceedingly to think of their anxiety and almost unmans me. — It is hard, very hard to stay so long from those so very dear to us. There is constantly an aching void in my bosom that almost stifles me. If the army was only moving I should find enough to excite and interest me; but for the span of two or three weeks during which time I hope the General will be prepared; I shall suffer intense torture. — I also wrote to my wifes brother, Rev G. Buckingham, giving him an idea of the motion that impelled me forward rather than back. — I wrote to my brother, H. B. Curtis that he may understand my motives. I have been falsely and villainously assailed by a corrupt and political press for various things I have done[45] and while there are foes in front I prefer to fight them rather than to go so far to fight *assassins* in my rear.

Their vile arrows I fear may pierce the bosom of my wife and children when I am too remote to avert their deadly aim. But I hope I get to live long enough to disarm the cowardly vultures who seek to feast themselves on my reputation.

May 26

I understand the 2nd Mississippi Volunteers[46] start up the country to day and I am camped at the Mill five miles out. I have two Mexican servants well armed and I am in company with two merchants, who are going with two wagon loads of goods to Saltillo. I have also a wagon and drive along, so that we muster six Americans and two Mexicans all tolerably well armed. The 2nd Mississippi Regiment has passed us and encamped two miles above us at Santa Catarina.

May 27

The smallpox rages in the Mississippi regiment and I therefore determined to start very early so as to get the lead. We passed the regiment before day and traveled hard till we arrived at the watering place south of the pass Los Muertos. We learned by one who had overtaken us, that the Mississippi Regiment did not march forward to day and we are therefore obliged to encamp twenty five or 30 miles distant from all American forces in a country noted for bands of robbers and Mexican Guerrila parties. We put our wagons together near an old Rancho to which we design to resort for the purpose of fighting against any odds that may dare to intrude on us.

May 28

Started very early, and arrived about 1 P.M. at Saltillo. General Wool appeared very much pleased with my return, and desired me to take the post of military commander and Governor of Saltillo. Said it should not interfere with my position when the column takes up its line of march for San Luis. The General said he wanted some rules made out to Govern the city, and therefore particularly desired my aid in the matter but wished me to consider till morning without deciding.

May 29

I called at camp and dined with General Wool. His offer of the appointment to command Saltillo could not well be declined and I accepted it believing I can be of more service in that station during the delay of the movement on San Luis Potosi. An order appointing me "Governor and Military Commandant of Saltillo" was therefore published. — This is not the first time I have been appointed Governor. — I have now been appointed Commander of Matamoros, Comargo, Monterray, and Saltillo; all the important points on this line of operation.

May 30

Some trouble and excitement arose last night among the Arkansas troops[47] — one of their men was murdered near the Alameda and I had to direct patrols to scatter the groups of Americans and the multitudes of Mexicans. —

I published my order No. 1 assuming the duties of Governor and Military commandant of Saltillo. — Two Mexicans were found killed.

May 31

Those Mexicans were killed by Americans last night and today. — One a notorious villain. There are so many rogues about
the city I am told it is hard to shoot a miss. General Wool has
ordered the Arkansas troops commanded by Capt Pike[48] to take
up their line of march and I hope they will now cease to seek
indiscriminant or doubtful vengance.

June 1st

Two companies of the Va.[49] and 2 of the North Carolina
Regiments arrived and passed through town. Col Warren started
with the last of the Illinois troops and I am therefore left in full
possession of the large block of buildings and all the servants and
furniture the property of Sanchez[50] the richest proprietor in all of
Mexico.

June 2

I sent for the prisoners and had the entire establishment po-
liced and fitted up to my own liking. My private chamber is that
formerly occupied by the proprietor who is a Gentleman Bachelor and who seems to well understand the luxuries that wealth
can drape around us. His ward robe dressing case bed stead and
other chamber furniture are quite splendid. — My office is the
room adjoining, and all my rooms are on the first story enclosing
a well paved square where a few pots of flowers and other shrubbery evince the handy work of a skillful master. Two old women,
a man and his wife, a lady looking young woman very pretty and
perfect in her deportment a young girl of about 10 and a boy John
(Juan) about 12 are the servants who attach to the premises, and
whom I employ for myself as laborers. They seem very honest
simple and obedient and I have reason to rejoice in the appearance of wealth and magnificence. — I feel how ever that it is all
a vain show and that the tenure held by American force is so
temporary I can make no permanent arrangements for the Government of the place or the accomodation of the executive office.

I have employed an interpreter Mr. Frister and a collector Mr.
Riddle[51] who are generally near me and make a part of my staff.
I have had a great number of cases brought before me today and

I have made short work of all of them as all such matters in this country are disposed of.

June 4

Sen. Don [Jacobo Sanchez] Sanches the owner of this country house and proprietor of the lands almost every where that our army has marched: called to report himself and take up his lodgings here. He is quite a young man apparently not over 28 years of age small in stature, dark complexion with a round receding head. He was dressed with neat french boots, check pants, a yellow buckskin jacket somewhat indian in style, and a white hat. As he had been sent for by General Wool, he seemed uneasy and very humble. I saw that he was a stranger in his own house and tried to make my self as agreeable to him as possible. — The ravages of war have no doubt visited many of his haciendas and he sees many places here on his homestead where the rude hand has devastated his propery.

My time is fully employed in hearing complaints, disposing of grievances, and consulting and considering as to the best mode of governing this place.

June 5

The news circulating among the Mexicans is, that General Santa Anna is in the city of Mexico presiding over the affairs of state and negociating with two American commissioners who are said to be there with 3000000 of dollars.[52] The Mexicans now think there will be peace, and that Santa Anna is there for the purpose of handling the three millions of dollars.

Our Government had best watch Santa Anna his leading trait no doubt is treachery, and he will surely make some display of his duplicity before he gets through with a treaty. General Scott is said to have marched through Puebla without opposition and that his army is now at Agua Frio or Rio Frio forty miles from the captiol.

June 9

I have been too busy the few days past to occupy myself with my blank book. I have every day complaints of various character brought before me, and have to hear and determine them. I have also been drawing up rules designed to regulate the affairs of government and in the tangled condition of state and city affairs and laws, I find it very difficult to define rules suited to the circumstances. I have written a letter, transmitting a few principals which I desire to have promulgated through the General. I see a troop of Mexican officers, connected with the tribunals of justice all of whom must draw their salaries from the taxes levied on the people and account to no one unless it is to the foes of the Americans.

June 10

More rain. We have rain every [day] in showers. Generally they come about the same hours two or 3 Oclock P.M.

I got further rumors of an accumulating Mexican army in front of us. No doubt Valencia[53] is at San Luis Potosi trying to reorganize the scattered fragments of the Mexican forces and if they cannot come and fight us here, they can hold us in check.

In conversation with Captain Davis of the quartermasters department, I am often instructed in the nature of Mexican institutions. He has lived long among them and understands these affairs. The clergy has the power and wealth 5 per cent on Capillania or Finca is allowed the church, and many a poor sinner who has accumulated a fortune leaves his estate on his death bed incumbered with a Finca of from 1 to ten thousand dollars. This is like a mortgage which rests on the estate, and the lands are never released except it be by passing the incumbrance over onto another estate equally valuable. By this means most of the lands pay an annuity to the Church and thus the Church has acquired the ascendency in wealth. When will the people of Mexico shake off their fetters? How vain the effort under their present organization!

Marriage cost at least 32½ dollars. — Out of this slavery grows. A man wishes to marry and sells himself off to a master for that sum and thus begins a service that lasts from one generation to another.

June 15

My office for a few days past has been a regular and constant court. All sorts of crime are tried before me. In one case of

murder I found so many implicated I had to yield the persuit. —
It was likely to occupy a summer campaign.

I had one case between a Padre and a little Irish doctor [Dr.
Emmit]. The Padre and the Dr. had bet against each other at
the cock pit and the Padre having held the stakes and "heeled"
the chicken decided to matters in his own favor and carried
off the Doctors 10 dollars. The Doctor had more ruin than religion in his heart and denounced the padre without strict regard
to the ten commandments.

The Padre therefore came to complain of insolence and
threats and the Doctor answered by charges of fraud at the cock
pit. As the controversy was between those who had the care of
the body and the soul of men, I concluded to commission two
officers to try it and therefore ordered Captains Davis of the
quartermasters and Lieut Waynewright of the Ordnance department to hear and decide. — The Padre is an old, tall slender and
feeble man, and the Doctor is a little, old, pockmarked slanting
noses green eyes Irishman. — The Rev Padre shows by several
witnesses that the Doctor used harsh words at the Cock pit and
afterwards at his house made an assault on his front door with
sundry knocks kicks and oaths to the great terror of the Padre and
the disturbance of the peace of the city. The little Doctor per
contra shows that he and the Padre bet at the cock pit 10 dollars
and that both bet on the the same cock and by this error both
won. That a friend seeing the mistake had advised them to settle
the matter by each taking his own money: but the Padre had too
much regard for the fund of the church and held onto the stakes
which were in his hands. The Doctor fired up at the loss of his
money and admits that he made some hostile demonstrations to
bring the priest to bay. As the case is not yet decided I leave the
sequel for another days writing.

News came yesterday through Mexicans, that General Scott is
dead. As such reports often get circulation we hope it is not true
in this instance. Such a fall would indeed be a sad disaster to us
and the Mexicans would regard it in the light of a victory. —

The decision of the court was that the Priest pay over the
money to the Doctor and the Doctor should pay the money over
as a fine for a breach of the peace and that it be applied to the
benefit of the poor and that the parties go hence and cease to

gamble especially on Sunday — They returned grumbling — at all — Not a one e'er felt the halter draw with a good opinion of the law.

June 22

The few days past have been interesting and very exciting. We had news that the Mexican army was moving rapidly against us and consequently every arm of the service had to be overhauled and prepared for action. We have now learned that the force has fallen back after coming within 60 or 80 miles of us.

June 23

As my years service has now fully expired and the Mexicans are again retreating, this seems to be the proper period for me to leave. There is now sufficient force to render an attack here exceedingly improbable and not sufficient to go forward. Troops are getting discharges and leaving off about as fast as recruits are coming out. This line has nothing but garrison duty to perform and I despise that.

I have therefore written to General Wool asking to be relieved determined now to go home to my family and friends.

Major Washington is ordered to come in and relieve me. I am busy making out discharges for some Ohio volunteers sick and teamsters. My being here is fortunate for them, for I apprehend they would never have got their papers adjusted if I had not been ready to prepare them. General Wool has written me a very flattering letter on the occasion of my leaving him and issued an order giving me an honourable discharge. I have therefore acquitted myself as well as the fortune of war would permit. — I have filled every station assigned me to the entire satisfaction of my commanding General and this is all my offices can do. —

June 26

Having made all my arrangements to leave, I dined yesterday with General Wool and bade him farewell. Col Hamtramack,[54]

Va. Col Payne[55] N. C. and Major Early[56] of Va. dine at the same table. — I bid them all farewell together with the staff.

June 28

I sold my horse Jack to Major Stokes[57] of the N. C. volunteers. I dislike to leave you old companion, but I fear you would fare worse than your master on the water and therefore a last farewell. You have borne me over vale and mountain and always bravely borne the toil and danger. I leave you in good health and spirits and recommend you to the kind care of your new master.

Mounted on a mule, in company with Capt of Train — Lafayette Porter and Mr. Easten of the quartermasters department and with smiles to my old friend Capt Montgomery;[58] I came on my way homewards as far as Santa Catarina 12 miles from Monterray.

June 29

I arrived at Monterray at 9 Oclock. It is a Holly day San Pedra and all the Mexicans are making a fine showing in their best Sunday attire. Put up at the house of Mr. Peters formerly of Capt T. F. Marshalls Cavalry. A man who distinguished himself as a brave and gallant Sergeant.

I rode out to General Taylors camp where I found him as usual surrounded by his staff and comfortably stationed at Walnut Grove. The General thinks there is little or no prospect of this line having sufficient force upon it to permit him to advance this fall. Certainly not before the first of September. He is very much disappointed in the failure of troops, but bears his adverse fortune with the utmost coolness.

He says he must go to the states in November and will apply in time for relief.

An artist has taken an excellent portrait of the General and Major Bliss.[59] The same artist has taken a view of the Genl Staff and in the front ground his [Gen. Taylor's] horse and orderly. The picture is a suitable size and elegantly adapted for an engraving. The faces of the entire group are readily recognised and the whole picture is to the life.

It is very sultry here in Monterray. The climate is entirely different from that at Saltillo.

General Taylor (third from left) and his staff at Walnut Springs after the
Battle of Buena Vista (National Portrait Gallery, Smithsonian
Institution, Washington, D.C.).

June 30

Make my arrangements here for the journey to Comargo. — A train leaves tomorrow for that place and I will move my baggage out as far as General Taylors camp.

I bade farewell to General Taylor and staff. The General said if I had not been in battle it was not my fault but attributable to the interferance of General Scott with his designs.

He said he wished I had command of the new Regiment ordered from Ohio. As that regiment is now on its way out, I have no reason to hope to be its commander and so informed the General.

July 2

I joined a party of Texian Rangers who are going down as an escort to protect the train. I was readily accepted by the sergeant in command and I found the whole party a sort of jolly good fellows all fair specimens of "Texian Rangers" all acquainted with border warfare and have a thousand tales to tell about fights with Indians and Mexicans.

In company with three others I took a route north of the main road which leads through the noted valley of Ramas in order to search for the lurking places of Guerrilla parties. Our route lead us behind a mountain ridge along the valley of a creek which crosses the main road at Ramas. By gliding in indian file we slipped through the chaperal unnoticed and came onto a number of huts in the bushes where we surprised the people in some instances before they had time to fight or run. I took a musket and Mexican cartridge box and gave it to a Ranger who was poorly armed, but as our party was very small and we were some two or three miles from our comrades we did not think it safe to stop to search the huts or take prisoners.

The Mexicans were frightened terribly and gave us many *adieus* when we proposed to *Bamose*.

July 3

We heard of a party of Canales men being located south of Pappagias [Pappagallos][60] near the spurs of the mountain and 14 of us *Rangers* commanded by Capt Wilkison [Wilkinson][61] of the 16th Inf mounted our horses and took the trail in that direction.

Our road was through the chaperal twisting and turning in many directions till we had gone some seven or eight miles from the main road.

When we came to a parcel of huts — mere roofs made of cane or hides and very soon put to flight a party which was armed and evidently some of the Ranchero force of Canales. They threw away their arms without firing and most of them escaped. Two prisoners on being threatened with instant death and promised favors if they would give up their arms showed us where their comrades had thrown theirs and told the best tale they could to excuse themselves. We recaptured wine, brandy, soldiers clothing and many other articles that had been taken by these men on the occasion of the slaughter of the wagoners. We heard of another party about 6 miles off but having loaded our men with comissary captured at this place we again determined to turn our faces toward the main road. We did not reach the wagon train till it arrived at Cerralvo. I was very weary and glad to accept a good matress at the quarters of Major Arthur[62] who is stationed at this place in charge of the Comissary department.

July 4

This glorious day we could not stop to celebrate. It was Sunday also and it seemed to me sacrilege to march but we thought duty required us to do so and constrained us to proceed without accepting the invitation offered us to participate in the enjoyments preparing for the occasion by the officers stationed at Cerralvo. After a long tedious and warm days march we encamped at Canales Run or Chicharonnes. I spread my blanket under a white thorn bush and rested after the toilsome 4th of July in the Republic of Mexico.

July 5

We passed Meir and camped at the Rancho Wardo twelve miles from Camargo on the bank of the Rio Grande. I was glad to find myself again on this noble river. I have spent so much time on its sickly shore that I have a kind of grave yard attachment for it. I look forward with a sad delight at the little hillocks which mark on its banks the sleeping companions of last summers campaign.[63] Peace oh peace to thy sacred ashes. You have

long since ceased to assemble to the call of the drum. Our comrades are now many of them returning to the bosom of their
families to tell the sad news of your untimely fall. Oh peace to
the bosom of thy fathers and mothers thy sisters thy brothers
and Oh God provide for their widows and fatherless children.

July 6

I arrived at Camargo about 12 M where I found many of the
officers who were stationed here three months ago when we were
all surrounded with foes on all sides and anxiously stood behind
the dark curtains which hid from us the dreadful travails of the
slaughtered wagoners and battle of Buena Vista. Major Chapman, Capt Britton, Capt Hunt, Lt. Brerton[64] and several officers
whose names I regret to have forgotten are still toiling on and
discharging the responsible and necessary duties of this disagreeable post. The place is now in command of my friend Col
Belknap who has had much trouble in regulating the affairs of
the place but who persists in a rigid persecution of all persons
guilty of vending a drop of the water of life. — There is a new
encampment being established near Meir which is to be under
the command of Brig. Genl. Hopping.[65] Col Belknap is going up
on a steam boat and desired me to join the party: but I excused
myself desiring rather to get to the mouth of the river where I can
determine whether I will go home or to Vera Cruz. My friends
here think it very sickly down there and oppose the idea of my
exposing myself so much.

July 8

Having visited all my old friends at Camargo and given my
Comanche Mule to my friend Capt Britton I took passage on the
steam boat "Del Norte" commanded by Captain K. Bowen[66] of
Zanesville, Ohio. I was very much surprised to find this boat and
in command of an old acquaintance. The captain has preserved
his life and narrowly escaped a complete wreck in bringing a light
draft river boat over that dangerous and stormy water that lies
between the Rio del Norte and the Mississippi. The captain is yet
a young man, but he has already made and lost two or three
fortunes. He possesses the most extraordinary business talent and

retains the most unyielding energy. — He is now in a favourable gale with his ill fortunes and I hope he may continue to prosper.

July 10

We were beating about the river all day yesterday and part of the night reaching this place, Reynosa. — The water is quite low and therefore the boating very difficult. It is very windy, and the boat is driven against the bends with much violence. The captain has to stop to repair his rudder and wheel and we therefore remain all day at the landing. We passed a depot of stone yesterday guarded by only 12 men at a place called St. [left blank]. At this place there is an immense quantity of stores protected by about 50 bayonets. News has just arrived from the interior giving us intelligence that General Urrea is en route from Victoria against this place.[67] Certainly the large amount of stores here unprotected is calculated to tempt an attack.

I have just drawn a plan for fortifying the post and Mr. Parker, the Commisary agent is going to arrange *pork and beans* to suit Mexican stomachs. An express has been sent to Camargo giving news of the intelligence and no doubt before Urrea can reach here the forces at or near Meir will be so arranged as to repel Urreas attack. There must be considerable of cavalry at Matamoros and that will be very useful in defending this country against *lanceros*.

I am so sick of the marches and counter marches of Urrea and Canales that I never hear of their names without regarding them as scare crows destined to keep this border in perpetual alarm.

I have a fair chance of seeing more trouble, and probably more loss of property than lives. This war is daily becoming more sanguinary and more irregular. News from General Scotts army is exceedingly gloomy. Every train is attacked by Guerilla parties and considerable loss of life and property is the result of each recontre.

July 11 Sunday

We got underway again at about 7 Oclock A.M. The country along the river is the same everywhere. On one side we have a perpendicular bank and on the other a sandy beach. The bank is now about 12 feet above the surface of the water. At very high stages the whole country must be slightly innundated. Thick chaperal grows on the bank so thick a man can hardly crawl through it. Ranchos are passed occasionally and we get plenty of corn and plenty of watermelons. — Notwithstanding the continued dry weather, corn looks very well and I see it is of all ages of growth some quite ripe and some of it just rising with life.

July 12

Arrived at Matamoros landing at my old place of encampment. It is a deserted spot. No tent or tenant except the little grave yard that still remains though the living have long since deserted the place.

I leave my box and other baggage at the first Mexican house. It being the residence of my old friend the senora that used to send me marketing. She was very glad to see me and I knew my cumber would be safe at her house for the time I should stay at Matamoros.

July 15

I have spent the last three days with my friends making my home at Capt Kidders. I was very sorry to find that I had passed Hicks Curtis on the river. He was going up and I passed the boat he was on some 50 miles above. I have stayed here longer than at first I thought of doing, hoping Hicks would get news of my having passed and come down, and also hoping the steam boat from New Orleans would bring a mail by which I could expect letters from home. Whether I will go to Vera Cruz or to Ohio I will not determine till I get to the mouth of the river, but think I will go to Ohio.

The Alcaldas Senr. Don Augustin Menchaca and a Senr. Longora [Longoria] called on me and spoke of giving some public acknowledgement of my services and kindness to the inhabitants when I commanded here: but as war still frowns upon us and any such testimony might be miscontrued against us all I declined the least intimation. They said they hoped the time would come when our friendship could be safely manifested and I heartily concurred.

News from New Orleans gives but little index to the affairs on the other line.

July 17

Taking leave of my old and new friends in Matamoros and shipping every thing on a steam boat I bade fare well to all the relations I hold this attachment to, my old camp ground, the graves of my comrades — and behold me again under way either for Vera Cruz or the United States as circumstances may seem to incline when I reach the Brasos.

We arrived at the mouth at dusk and accompanied by Doctor [left blank] of the army. We called on my old friend and class mate Capt Ogden.[68] There have been many great changes made in the appearances about the mouth. A great number of large ware houses sutlers stores and other buildings have been erected.

The captain has erected himself comfortable quarters and has brought his family to reside with him.

As luck would have it I met here the captain of the "James L. Day"[69] the fastest steamer on the Gulf. There are three boats ready to start to New Orleans but none going to Vera Cruz. By this combination of circumstances I can readily see the consent of my destiny. It is to go home wards and I at once determined to follow the current. In fact I could not go to Vera Cruz sooner than to go to New Orleans and then take the steamer to Vera Cruz which does not always come by Brasos.

But after getting to New Orleans, I will go home; and I will then be able to recruit my health at a season when I feel that here it is constantly being impared. Perhaps I may then have orders from Washington to recruit my Regiment and should this be the case I think I can serve my country best in raising reinforcements in Ohio.

July 18

I started from the mouth in an open wagon with Dr. [left blank]. The rays of the sun reflected from the sun and water (the road leads close along the edge of the Gulf) soon became sickly and oppression and the horror of Brasos Sant Iago was full before me.

I made the acquaintance of Major Eastland[70] the new quartermaster at this place. In him I think the president has made an excellent selection. He has already much improved this abominable place and persuing his zeal and industry I hope he and Capt

Eaton of the Comissary department who is also stationed here; will soon make troops a little more comfortable than they were on arriving last year.

I also became acquainted with Col Davis of the 2nd Mississippi[71] who is going home tired of the war. My old friend Capt Davis and his clerk Mr. Clark, Mr. Easton brother-in-law to Capt Montgomery of Monterray are all going on the same boat so that I hope to find friends and an *audience* who will see my sickly performances on the "dark blue sea".

We started at two Oclock and had not got a mile from Brasos before I was heaving over the railing and grinning a ghastly smile at any images which fluttered in the waves below. —

It is horrible to know one has to undergo several days this dreadful sickness!

July 19

To add to my misery the symptoms of the ague are again upon me and finally I have a tremendous chill and fever. The passengers all laugh at me when I stick my head out of my stateroom. My hair in terrible confusion over my bald head, my beard five days old. My poor skeleton half dressed person I deserve the cognomen of the "Knight of the rueful countenance".

July 20

Thanks to a kind providence I am again in the waters of the Great Mississippi. I have shaved, dressed, and quite recovered from sea sickness but the ague still lingers as a dull memento of a campaign in Mexico.

Aug 3

I arrived safe at home where I found my family and friends all well and rejoiced to see me. All express astonishment at my slender appearance. I was myself surprised to see their astonishment. Well I am 40 lbs lighter than when I started; but I feel quite well as I have done for many months past.

I wrote from New Orleans to the President of the United States requesting orders to reorganize my regiment raise a new one or an appointment in the staff. — In the event of the Pres't giving me either of these stations I expect again to join my friends in Mexico, and in that event I shall renew my journal.

Having returned to my home in Wooster, Ohio and enjoying all the blessings of civil life, in the circle of my family and friends I have great reason to rejoice in my safe return and to return sincere and hearty thanks to the creator and Governor of all things for his kind protection and care during a long perilous and tedious campaign. —

Saml R. Curtis

Notes

Introduction

1. Dumas Malone, *Dictionary of American Biography* (New York: Charles Scribners' Sons, 1933), pp. 619–20 (hereafter cited as Malone, *DAB*). The biographical sketch of Samuel R. Curtis is drawn from this source.

2. A copy of the Polk letter is found in a collection of letters and newspaper clippings located near the end of the Curtis diary.

3. Milo M. Quaife, *The Diary of James K. Polk* (Chicago: A. C. McClurg & Co., 1910), vol. 2, pp. 436–39.

4. Justin H. Smith, *The War With Mexico* (New York: The Macmillan Company, 1919), vol. 1, p. 562.

5. Curtis diary entry for May 23rd, 1847.

6. Herman J. Viola, "Zachary Taylor and the Indiana Volunteers," *Southwestern Historical Quarterly*, vol. 72, no. 3, pp. 335–46.

7. Amelia W. Williams and Eugene C. Barker, *The Writings of Sam Houston* (Austin: University of Texas Press, 1941), vol. 5, pp. 169, 172. In a speech on June 12, 1850, before the United States Senate on the Texas-New Mexico Boundary, Houston expressed a feeling that "The people of that State [Texas] have been unwarrantably assailed, traduced, and defamed by the present Executive of the nation when a general in the field."

8. The quotes are taken from undated newspaper clippings appearing at the end of the Curtis diary. The *Louisville Journal* article is not included, but written rebuttals of this article are of sufficient detail to determine the major contents of the article.

9. Curtis to "Dear Captain," September 11, 1848, in miscellaneous letters and notes at the end of the third volume of his "Diary."

Chapter 1: From the State of Ohio to the State of Tamaulipas

1. Luther Giddings, *Sketches of the Campaign in Northern Mexico by an Officer of the First Regiment of Ohio Volunteers* (New York: George Putnam & Co., 1853), p. 19. Camp Washington, near Cincinnati, Ohio, was designated as a place of rendezvous for the various companies

wishing to volunteer for service in Mexico. Samuel Ryan Curtis, then adjutant general of the State of Ohio had selected this site. Camp Washington was three miles west of Cincinnati, near old Fort Washington and the canal. The grounds were a mile in circumference, encompassing a hilly portion on which soldiers' tents were pitched, and a nearby level field for drills. Frank Hardy, a member of the 3rd Ohio fondly remembered camp life, "There was lots of fun there, fiddling, dancing, singing, negros playing the banjo &c. &c." Crowds of people from all parts of Ohio were in daily attendance, "attracted by various motives." See, Steven Bruce Michael, "Ohio and the Mexican War: Public Response to the 1846–1848 Crisis," dissertation (Ohio State University), 1985, p. 19.

2. Fredrick Way, Jr., *Way's Packet Directory, 1848–1983* (Athens: Ohio University, 1983), p. 460. The *Tuskaloosa* was a sidewheel wooden hull packet of 320 tons. She was built in 1844 in Cincinnati, Ohio, and was lost in a boiler explosion at Mobile, Alabama, January 29, 1847, in an accident that claimed twelve lives.

3. Francis B. Heitman, *Historical Register and Dictionary of the United States Army, From its Organization, September 29, 1789, to March 2, 1903* (Washington: Government Printing Office, 1903), vol. 2, pp. 60, 124. George W. McCook was originally the captain of the Steubenville City Greys, elected to the rank of lieutentant colonel. During the Civil War, he served as colonel of the 157th Ohio Infantry.

4. Ibid., vol. 2, p. 59. John S. Love, originally the captain of the Morgan Volunteers, was elected to the rank of major.

5. William M. Lytle and Forrest R. Holcamper, *Merchant Steam Vessels of the United States, 1790–1868* (Staten Island, New York: The Steamship Historical Society of America, Inc., 1975), p. 155. The *New Era* was a sidewheel wooden hull packet of 263 tons, built in Cincinnati, Ohio, in 1843, and retired from service by 1848.

6. *Official Roster of the Soldiers of the State of Ohio in the War of the Rebellion, 1861–1866, and the War with Mexico, 1846–1848* (Norwalk, Ohio: The Laning Company, 1895), vol. 12, p. 438. The dead soldier was Private George Kitchen, thirty-one years of age, a member of Company B.

7. [John A. Scott], *Encarnacion Prisoners. Comprising an Account of the March of the Kentucky Cavalry From Louisville to the Rio Grande . . .* (Louisville: Prentice & Weissanger, 1848); Henry Benham, "Recollections of Mexico and Buena Vista," *Old and New*, vol. 3, no. 6, and vol. 4, no. 1, pp. 49, 51. The First Kentucky Cavalry, departed from Louisville, on July 4, 1846, and traveled by steamboat to a point opposite Memphis, Tennessee, on the Mississippi River. From there they rode

overland on a harrowing journey to Camargo, Mexico. In response to the anticipated attack by Santa Anna on Saltillo, the Kentuckians were moved to a camp outside that city by January 10, 1847. The Kentucky Cavalry participated in the Battle of Buena Vista on February 22–23, 1847, and performed well on the actions of February 22. On the second day of the battle, the Mexicans continued their attack on the American left wing and broke through those defenses to pose an immediate threat to the American supply depot and wagon park at Hacienda Buena Vista. Mexican cavalry in columns of fours advanced on the Hacienda, but, in the eyes of a competent observer, ". . . [Col. Humphrey] Marshall, though repeatedly urged by others, could not be prevailed upon to order an advance or charge." Colonel Archibald Yell, junior in rank to Marshall, organized an abortive and feeble advance on the Mexicans by Arkansas cavalry but with no success. "The Mexican lancers . . . overwhelmed him [Yell] at the charging pace, when Yell with several of his officers and men went down, and the lines of Marshall in his rear turned at once, without waiting the shock, and rushed pell-mell between and around the buildings of the ranch, followed by Mexicans." The Kentucky Cavalry, or more properly termed by now as just Marshall's men, continued to congregate near the Hacienda for the remainder of the day after the Mexicans had been driven off. General Taylor went to the Hacienda during the day for an inspection of the defenses. At this site, "He also went to the cavalry under Marshall, then near the ranch, and commanded, urged, and implored them to come up close to the plain, to be ready to assist us, begging him in the homely farmer's phrase, though with inverted meaning, to 'stand up to his fodder, rack or no rack.' But all his efforts were in vain; for I recollect hours after, during the last conflict, the General told me to look with my glass, and tell him what men those were in our rear, beyond the ranch. I could only answer, 'I see they are our cavalry, as they are not in uniform;' when his earnest, feeling exclamation was, 'I wish in God's name they would only come up and show themselves. I would not ask them to fight.'"

8. Scott, *Encarnacion Prisoners*, p. 3. The Kentucky Cavalry was assembled at Camp Marshall, probably named either for Colonel Humphrey Marshall or Brigadier General Thomas Marshall. The camp was at Oakland, a suburb of Louisville, Kentucky, near the locks on the Ohio River.

9. Heitman, *Register*, vol. 1, p. 690; Malone, *DAB*, pp. 310–11. Humphrey Marshall graduated from West Point, September 1, 1828, and served in the First Dragoons until April 30, 1833, when he resigned from the service. He served as colonel of the First Kentucky cavalry

from June 9, 1846, to July 7, 1847. According to one biographer, ". . . he took a prominent part in the battle of Buena Vista, in which he executed some brilliant cavalry charges." He served in Congress from 1849 to 1852, when he resigned to accept the position of minister to China. He returned to Congress to serve from 1854 to 1859; with the outbreak of war received a commission as brigadier general in the Confederate Army. In 1863 he resigned this commission and was elected to the Second Confederate Congress. He returned to Kentucky to practice law after the war and died there in 1872.

10. Heitman, *Register*, vol. 2, p. 52; Scott, *Encarnacion Prisoners*, pp. 34–36. Major John P. Gaines was an officer in the First Kentucky Cavalry. Gaines led a notable command of Kentucky and Arkansas mounted troops on a reconnaissance of the region south of Agua Nueva. The party was captured by Mexican cavalry under Colonel Miguel Andrade, on January 23, 1847, at the hacienda of Encarnacion without a shot being fired. Although not mentioned by Scott, it was suspected that Major Gaines had failed to post any pickets or sentries, and was encircled without warning by the Mexicans during a foggy night. Also captured were Cassius Marcellus Clay the noted Kentuckian and Solon Borland, well-known in Arkansas. These prisoners were released at the end of the war.

11. George H. Yater, *Two Hundred Years at the Falls of the Ohio: A History of Louisville and Jefferson County* (Louisville: Pinaire Lithographing Corp., 1979), pp. 38–41. Louisville, Kentucky, and its sister city, New Albany, Indiana, are located on opposite sides of the Ohio River at the falls. Both cities developed because water borne freight and passengers had to be carried by land conveyance around the falls. As early as 1804 the Kentucky legislature approved a charter for the Ohio Canal Company to build a canal on the Kentucky side, but the project lacked the necessary funds. The success of the Erie Canal, then partially completed in 1824 stirred new interest in a canal. A private stock company, The Louisville and Portland Canal Company, was chartered by the Kentucky legislature in 1825 to construct the locks. The company was heavily subscribed in by business interests in Philadelphia. The narrow, three-flight lock of the Louisville and Portland Canal opened in 1830, built at a cost of $743,000 — more than twice the anticipated cost of construction. The canal continued in use until 1870.

12. Oran Perry, *Indiana in the Mexican War* (Indianapolis: Wm. B. Burford, Printer, 1908), pp. 58, 73. The 2,553 men of the First, Second, and Third Indiana Volunteer Infantry Regiments were camped in tents on the northern side of the Ohio River near a wooded island at the foot of the falls of the Ohio between the towns of Jeffersonville and New

Albany. They named the site "Camp Whitcomb" in honor of Governor James Whitcomb. Camp Whitcomb was broken up on July 5, 1846, when the volunteers — destined for Brazos Island off the south Texas coast — were loaded onto steamboats.

13. Smithland, Kentucky (at the mouth of the Cumberland River), is a village with a current population of about 2,500.

14. The village seen from this general location on the Ohio River was most likely Metropolis, Illinois.

15. Dunbar Rowland, *Mississippi* (Atlanta: Southern Historical Publishing Association, 1907), vol. 1. p. 399. The Chickasaw Bluffs begin north of Memphis, Tennessee; the original site of Memphis was on one of these bluffs.

16. Heitman, *Register*, vol. 2, pp. 57, 117. Captain John Kell, Co. I, 3rd Ohio, served during the Civil War as colonel of the 2nd Ohio Regiment.

17. Ibid., vol. 2, pp. 51, 101. Captain Thomas H. Ford, Co. C, 3rd Ohio, was colonel of the 32nd Ohio Infantry during the Civil War.

18. Ibid., vol. 2, p. 64; Perry, *Indiana*, p. 94. Captain John Patterson, originally raised the Belmont County Company which became Company D of the 3rd Ohio. Patterson became ill in New Orleans and remained behind to recuperate. Recovering his health, he took passage with a party of Indiana volunteers, whose small vessel wrecked on the coast of Texas. Patterson was seated in one of the few lifeboats when a voice from one of the Indiana officers still on the sinking ship paged him: "Captain, if you get on shore safe will you inform my family of my death and how it came about?" Patterson, a single man, heroically surrendered his seat on the lifeboat to the married Indiana officer. Fortunately, both were picked up from the sea by a revenue cutter.

19. Malone, *DAB*, vol. 20, pp. 513–14. General John Ellis Wool was born in Newburgh, New York, on February 29, 1784. At the age of four, with the death of his father, he was taken to be raised by his grandfather. His formal education was limited and at the age of twelve he became a store clerk. When the War of 1812 was declared, he raised a company of volunteers in Troy, New York. On April 14, 1812, Wool was commissioned a captain in the Thirteenth Infantry. He was severely wounded at the battle of Queenstown and was promoted to major in the Twenty-ninth Infantry on April 13, 1813. For bravery at Plattsburg, Wool was promoted to brevet lieutenant colonel, and on April 29, 1816, was again promoted to the rank of colonel and inspector general of the army. On April 29, 1826, he was promoted to brevet brigadier general for ten years service in one grade. At the outset of war with Mexico in 1846, he was ordered to Cincinnati where he prepared

and mustered in 12,000 volunteers in six weeks. On August 14, 1846, Wool arrived in San Antonio, Texas, to lead his command on an invasion of the Mexican state of Chihuahua. His force of 1,400 men marched more than 900 miles through enemy country, arriving at Saltillo on December 22, 1846. Wool served gallantly at the battle of Buena Vista and was voted a sword by Congress "for his distinguished services in the War with Mexico and especially for the skill, enterprise, and courage exhibited at Buena Vista." He was promoted to brevet major general for his services to the country. He retired on August 1, 1863, at the rank of regular major general. Wool died on November 10, 1869, in Troy, New York.

20. Turner J. Fakes, Jr., "Memphis and the Mexican War," *West Tennessee Historical Society Papers*, vol. 2, 1948, pp. 119–44. The Tennessee volunteers found at Memphis by Curtis were soon to be members of either the Second Tennessee Volunteer Regiment or the Tennessee Cavalry Regiment. The Tennessee volunteers were frustrated by the apparent inaction of their governor, A. V. Brown, to muster in the troops camped near Memphis. They sat idly in camp and watched volunteer regiments from Missouri, Kentucky, Ohio, Indiana, Illinois, and even Nashville float past them down the Mississippi to New Orleans to embark for Mexico. The Missourians even had the gall to order their band to strike up "Oh, Take Your Time Miss Lucy" as they passed the inactive Memphis camp. The first mixed contingent of three companies of infantry and a company of cavalry left Memphis by June 10, 1846, for New Orleans; the remaining companies of both regiments tarried behind for some unexplained reason. By late November, 1846, the Tennesseans were at Matamoros and formed part of the column under command of General Robert Patterson that was marching from that city overland to capture Victoria. From Victoria the regiment became a part of General Winfield Scott's army and participated in the capture of Vera Cruz. On April 17, 1847, the Second Tennessee suffered heavy casualties during the battle of Cerro Gordo when General Gideon Pillow ordered them in advance of his brigade to attack a strong Mexican position. Pillow was later censured for ordering this attack by Colonel [William T.] Haskell and the majority of the officers of the regiment, who published a statement demanding Pillow's immediate court martial.

21. *Forest Trees of Texas*, Bulletin 20 (Texas Forest Service, College Station, Texas, 1980), p. 76. The sweet gum or red gum (Liquidambar, styraciflua L.) is a valuable and sometimes troublesome forest tree that also grows in East Texas.

22. Haskell M. Monroe, Jr., and James T. McIntosh, *The Papers of*

Jefferson Davis (Baton Rouge: Louisiana State University Press, 1981), vol. 1, p. 307. Fort Gibson (in present-day Oklahoma) was located about fifty miles northwest of Fort Smith, Arkansas Territory. The post was established in 1824 to protect travelers and to maintain a military presence among the Indians. Fort Gibson was closed in 1890.

23. James W. Leslie, *Land of Cypress and Pine: More Southeast Arkansas History* (Little Rock: Rose Publishing Co, 1976), pp. 35–46. The site of Napoleon, Arkansas, at the confluence of the Mississippi and Arkansas Rivers, was selected by Frederick Notrebe around 1833. The town abounded in warehouses because the freight from large Mississippi steamers was transferred at Napoleon onto shallow-draft steam boats. These smaller vessels were able to ply the Arkansas River, which at low stages could be no more than two or three feet deep. At its heyday the town had a population of around 7,000, "a U.S. bank, a U. S. Marine Hospital, several two story brick stores. . . ." But at the confluence of these two rivers flooding and bank erosion was a constant problem that finally spelled doom to the town.

24. Dunbar Rowland, *Mississippi* (Spartanburg, South Carolina: The Reprint Company, Publishers, 1976), vol. 2, p. 296. The city of Natchez, Mississippi, has a long history that extends back to 1716. A traveler to Natchez in 1835 gives us this fleeting glimpse, "our port is in sight — a pile of gray and white cliffs with here and there a church steeple, a roof elevated above its summit, and a light house hanging on the verge. At the foot of the bluffs are long, straggling lines of wooden buildings, principally stores and storehouses; the levee is fringed with flatboats and steamers . . . but this is not Natchez. The city proper is built upon the summit level, the tops of whose buildings and trees can be seen . . . rising higher than the cliff. The road up, cut on a gentle incline along the side of the cliff for a quarter of a mile. The city proper consists of six streets at right angles with the river, intersected by seven others parallel with the stream."

25. Mississippi Archives and History Department, private communication. Jesse Edwards of Wilkinson County, Mississippi (adjacent to the Mississippi River), had a will admitted to probate during the December, 1839, term of the court. He listed his wife as Elizabeth and sons Charles A. and Hughes M. Edwards and one daughter, Emily, in the will. Edwards was a landowner, both in Wilkinson and Amitie County, Mississippi, and in the Republic of Texas. Jesse Edwards was quite likely a kinsman of the famous Texas land empresario, Hayden Edwards. Elizabeth Edwards, widow of Jesse Edwards, is listed in the Amitie County records for 1840 as a head of a family consisting of three females and one male. Elizabeth Edwards was born in South Carolina in 1799.

In Amitie County she held no slaves, but the 1840 Wilkinson County records list her as owning fifteen male slaves and ten female slaves. She was still living in Wilkinson County in 1850.

26. Heitman, *Register*, vol. 1, p. 557. Lieutenant Colonel Thomas F. Hunt, quartermaster at New Orleans, joined the service in 1813 and was promoted to colonel on May 30, 1848, "for meritorious conduct particularly in performance of his duties in prosecution of the war with Mexico."

27. Brazos Santiago, literally "the arms of Saint James" is a narrow pass between Brazos and Padre Islands, which leads from the Gulf of Mexico into Laguna Madre. This pass is directly opposite Port Isabel and about eight miles from the mouth of the Rio Grande.

28. Harnett T. Kane, *Queen New Orleans: City by the River* (New York: Bonanza Books, 1949), pp. 136–40. Construction on the magnificent St. Charles Hotel began in 1836. Under the supervision of the Irish architect Gallier, a structure — upon which the city could be justly proud — rose on a site two squares away from Canal Street. The facade had a projecting portico of fourteen Corinthian columns topped by a tall marble pediment. A circular colonade of heavy marble supported a white dome topped by an open turret. For the more practical traveler there was a magnificent oval barroom seventy feet across and twenty feet high that was reached by a double flight of stairs. A traveler reported that the St. Charles was "not only the largest and handsomest hotel in the United States, but the largest and handsomest hotel in the world." The building burned in 1851; the present St. Charles Hotel is built on the site.

29. Curtis must have been mistaken. The St. Patricks Cathedral he refers to must have been the familiar twin spires of St. Louis Cathedral.

30. Heitman, *Register*, vol. 1, p. 207. Captain James Belger, assistant quartermaster at New Orleans, joined the service in 1832 as an enlisted man and received a brevet to major for the meritorious "performance of his duty" on May 30, 1848.

31. Brian Robertson, *Wild Horse Desert* (Edinburg, Texas: New Santander Press, 1985), p. 58; *American Flag,* July 19, 1846, April 18, May 26, 1847. Brigadier General Romulo Diaz de la Vega, and his aide, Lieutenant Mejia were prisoners of the United States, having been captured at the battle of Resaca de la Palma on May 9, 1846. General de la Vega had given his word as a gentleman that he would not take up arms until exchanged and was taken to New Orleans. His proposed trip to Kentucky and Ohio was allowed and he met Senator Henry Clay while in Kentucky. The general's brigade band, during the opening hostilities at Palo Alto, on May 8, 1846, had struck up "Los Zapadores de

Jalisco," a lively regimental tune, when an American shell exploded in their midst and silenced the music.

32. Dr. Jenkins, 3rd Ohio surgeon, is not listed on the official roster of the 3rd Ohio. Benjamin Stone is listed in that capacity.

33. According to *Webster's Dictionary of the English Language* (1989 Edition), Mother Carey's chicken is any one of several petrels, especially the storm petrel.

34. *Vicksburg Whig*, August 18, 1846. Rufus K. Arthur, a soldier from the 1st Mississippi Volunteer Infantry writes in a letter home that the bar across Brazos Santiago was only six to seven feet deep and that the pass and the beach was littered with shipwrecks and cargoes that had been washed ashore. The harbor at Point Isabel contained "50 to 60 vessels of every class from ship down to sloop."

35. Lytle, *Merchant Steam Vessels*, p. 17; *American Flag*, February 3, 1847. The *Cincinnati* was a 276-ton sidewheel steamboat chartered by the United States for use as a lighter. She was reported as wrecked on the bar at Tampico in early 1847.

36. *Official Roster*, p. 448. Curtis is mistaken in the name. There is no man by the name of Cameron on the official roster. However, in Company H, the Zanesville Company, Private D. S. McCammat is reported as having died on July 21, 1846.

37. *American Flag*, August 12, 1846, recorded that "Captain Young of the steamer *Panama* was wrecked on the passage from New Orleans to this place. . . ." Young reported that his ship broke her "steam pipe" and that the boat leaked so badly three pumps were kept continually in action. By the next day she could not be kept afloat with five pumps, so the captain ordered the ship to be abandoned. All hands were saved and the vessel was "fully insured."

38. *Vicksburg Whig*, September 24, 1846. A Mississippian commented that, "We lie on the sands and the strong winds keep it whirling about and over us . . . it fills our hair, mouth, nose, whiskers, moustaches . . . and mixes with our victuals, so that I am afraid we should wear out our teeth, had we to stay here."

39. Heitman, *Register*, vol. 2, p. 43; *American Flag*, February 6, 1847. Captain James Allen organized the Mack Rangers which became Company K, 3rd Ohio. This company — to be deployed as skirmishers —was issued rifles instead of muskets. Allen had a good record of service and had made a very positive impression on the town folk of Matamoros by the time he left that city. "All who have ever known the Captain speak favorable of his qualifications . . . and we are inclined to the opinion that the public interest would be promoted by sticking him

up a peg higher than he now stands." Captain Allen had come to Texas once before in 1836 as a volunteer to fight for Texas independence.

40. Michael, "Ohio and the Mexican War," pp. 9, 36–37. On May
20, 1846, Ohio Governor Mordecai Bartley issued a proclamation calling for the enrollment of three regiments of Ohio troops. The men were
to enlist for one year's service. The ranks were rapidly filled and men
had to be turned away. In 1847, a second call for troops was issued, and
the Fourth and Fifth Ohio Regiments, five companies of the Fifteenth
Infantry, and five independent companies were recruited for service in
Mexico. The ranks of these new regiments filled more slowly though
because the term of enlistment for soldiers was "for the duration of the
war" and the public perception was now that the conflict was not to be
won swiftly and would proceed on for years.

41. *American Flag*, July 7, 16, 19, 1846. The Louisiana volunteers
consisted of four regiments under the command of Colonel P. S. Smith.
They were the Andrew Jackson, Montezuma, Washington, and Louisiana regiments, commanded respectively by Colonels F. S. Marks,
Horatio Davis, Walton, and Dakin.

42. Heitman, *Register*, vol. 1, p. 442; James W. Silver, *Edmund
Pendleton Gaines, Frontier General* (Baton Rouge: Louisiana State University Press, 1949), pp. 258–67. General Edmund Pendleton Gaines
joined the service in 1799, rising to the rank of brevet major general on
August 15, 1814, for "his gallantry and good conduct in defeating the
enemy at Fort Erie U C," and received the thanks of congress with the
presentation of a gold medal for "repelling with great slaughter the attack
of the British veteran army superior in numbers. . . ." Gaines was in
charge of the Western Military District of the United States with
headquarters in New Orleans prior to the Mexican War. In August,
1845, rumors of the encirclement of Taylor's forces at Corpus Christi by
a strong Mexican force prompted Gaines to take unauthorized actions.
He contacted the governors of Louisiana and Alabama to requisition
militia that he felt were needed for Taylor's defense. There was no legal
authority for his actions. When informed by the adjutant general of the
army to cease and desist, Gaines ignored the order and continued
requisitioning militia from the states in the Western District. Before his
recruiting efforts could be halted, more than 6,000 troops from the state
of Louisiana alone were mustered into federal service for an enlistment
period of six months. By the Militia Act of 1795, men were obliged to
serve for only three months. This unexpected flood of volunteers created
massive supply problems for Taylor, requiring tents and hardtack then
in scarce supply in south Texas. With the massive cost to the taxpayer

created by their enlistment, they barely reached the shores of south Texas before their enlistment expired and they had to be shipped back to New Orleans. Gaines was summoned before a court martial on August 14, 1846, to answer charges that he misused his authority. He was found guilty, but the tribunal recommended that "in view of his long services and his undoubted patriotism and purity of motives, no disciplinary action be taken." President Polk upheld the recommendations of the court.

43. Heitman, *Register*, vol. 1, p. 725. Colonel George Washington Morgan was a cadet at West Point from 1841 to 1843. He served as colonel of the 2nd Ohio Volunteers until this unit was mustered out of service in May, 1847. He was appointed colonel of the 15th United States Infantry and was promoted to brevet brigadier general for his gallantry at the battles of Contreras and Churubusco. Morgan was discharged in 1848 but reentered the service as brigadier general of volunteers in 1861. He resigned this rank in 1863.

44. Ibid., vol. 1, p. 308. Lieutenant Colonel Henry Clay, Jr., son of the famous Kentucky politician, graduated from West Point second in his class but resigned from the service by 1831. He was elected lieutenant colonel of the Second Kentucky Volunteers in June, 1846, and was killed leading his fellow Kentuckians at the battle of Buena Vista, February 23, 1847.

45. Ibid., vol. 2, p. 52. Major Cary H. Fry, Second Kentucky Infantry.

46. Ibid., vol. 1, p. 902. Colonel Persifor Frazer Smith was appointed brigadier general of Louisiana volunteers in May, 1836. He became colonel of the Mounted Rifles in May, 1846, brevet brigadier general in September, 1846, for "gallant and meritorious conduct in the several conflicts at Monterey, Mexico," and brigadier general for his actions at Contreras and Churubusco in August 1847.

47. Executive Document No. 65. Point Isabel was a small village on the Laguna Madre about five miles northwest of Brazos Santiago Pass. This village, originally named Fronton, was a Mexican customs station serving as a port of entry for the city of Matamoros and a large portion of northeastern Mexico. An extensive supply depot was established there during the Mexican War and an earthen fort, Fort Polk, was thrown up around the depot. The only wall of the fort remaining today forms the embankment upon which a lighthouse is situated in the resort town of Port Isabel.

48. Heitman, *Register*, vol. 1, p. 446. Major John Lane Gardner entered the service in May, 1813. He was promoted to lieutenant colonel in April, 1847, for "gallant and meritorous conduct" at the

battle of Cerro Gordo and to colonel in August, 1847, for his services at the battle of Contreras.

49. Ibid., vol. 1, p. 939. Capt Henry Swartwout graduated from West Point in 1827 and served in the artillery. He died on July 1, 1852.

50. Ibid., vol. 2, p. 73. Captain Chauncey Woodruff organized the Huron Cass Guards, which later became Company G, 3rd Ohio.

51. *Official Roster*, p. 446. Private Charles Burr a member of Company G, died July 28, 1846, on Brazos Santiago at the age of eighteen.

52. Ibid., p. 438. Private John Darne of Company B, twenty-four years of age, died on July 29, 1846,

53. Heitman, *Register*, vol. 2, p. 61. Captain Jesse Meredith organized the Coshocton Volunteers, which later became Company B of 3rd Ohio.

54. Executive Document No. 65. Boca Chica, literally meaning "little mouth," was one of two major outlets of the Rio Grande. This opening formed the south end of Brazos Island and was only about three feet deep during the time of the war; it could be forded by wading. At the latter stages of the war, a bridge was built across Boca Chica. The outlet has since silted over.

55. Heitman, *Register*, vol. 1, p. 757. Captain Edmund Augustus Ogden graduated from West Point in 1827. He served as quartermaster until May, 1848, when he became brevet major for meritorous conduct. He died August 3, 1855.

56. The houses at the mouth of the Rio Grande on the south side of the river were the start of the Mexican city of Bagdad, which would be so important during the American Civil War as a terminal for the Confederate cotton trade. All that currently remains at this site is a lighthouse erected by the Mexican government.

57. Heitman, *Register*, vol. 1, p. 361. Lieutenant Samuel Kennedy Dawson graduated from West Point in 1835 and was promoted to brevet captain in 1847 for his actions at the battle of Cerro Gordo. He was promoted to the rank of colonel for gallantry at the battle of Chickamauga in September, 1863.

58. The 1850 Census of Cameron County, Texas, lists James Selkirk, a native of Scotland, as the pilot at the mouth of the Rio Grande. Perhaps Selkirk was this man.

59. Executive Document No. 65. Burrita is a small Mexican village on the south side of the Rio Grande about ten miles from the mouth of the river. An 1847 map indicates only about eight huts in the village and a small American army camp.

60. Roger Torrey Peterson, *A Field Guide to the Birds of Texas* (Boston: Houghton Mifflin Company, 1963), p. 79. The whooping crane

(Grus americana) is a large white crane with black primary wing feathers that winters on the coast of Texas. This bird is now perhaps the rarest North American species.

61. *Forest Trees of Texas*, p. 87. The western honey mesquite (P. juliflora var. torreyana L. Benson) is a shrub or small tree that grows abundantly in the southern and Trans-Pecos regions of Texas.

62. This site, known as Camp Belknap, was located about five miles from the mouth of the Rio Grande on the left side on a rise about three-quarters of a mile from the river. The site is now on open land that is densely wooded with ebony trees.

63. Milo Kearney and Anthony Knopp, *Boom and Bust: The Historical Cycles of Matamoros and Brownsville* (Austin: Eakin Press, 1991), pp. 15–25. The city of Matamoros was founded in 1774 by ten powerful ranching families living in Camargo. By 1796 the growing village was known as Nuestra Senora del Refugio de los Esteros (Our Lady of the Refuge of the Lakes). In 1826, the city received its current name in honor of Padre Mariano Matamoros, who was killed in the struggle for independence from Spain. Matamoros grew and became the official port of entry for all trade goods entering northern Mexico. The actual port was the village of Fronton near Brazos Santiago. Goods were carted overland from Fronton to Matamoros. By 1844 Matamoros had been laid out in the Spanish style of squares filled with many governmental buildings, markets and a large and attractive church. The city had a population of 11,823 on the eve of the Mexican War.

64. John Frost, *Pictorial History of Mexico and the Mexican War* (Philadelphia: Thomas, Copperwait and Co., 1848), pp. 266–68. Camargo is a small Mexican town situated on the east bank of the Rio San Juan about four miles above the junction of that river and the Rio Grande. Camargo is about 140 miles from Matamoros as the crow flies but is at least twice that far for a steamboat traveling on the Rio Grande. The town consisted of about 2,000 inhabitants in early 1846 but many fled after a disastrous overflow of the Rio San Juan in June, 1846, that destroyed a large portion of the town. An American volunteer soldier wrote, "The town was once very beautiful; and from the ruined walls, we saw the houses must have been quite pretty. It contains three plazas, in the middle one of which are situated the finest buildings, and where still stands a neat little church." Camargo became a vast supply depot during the Mexican War. Supplies transported by steamboats from the mouth of the Rio Grande were off-loaded there for transport by vast trains of wagons and mules to Monterrey and Saltillo. At times the tents of thousands of American soldiers lined both sides of the Rio San Juan for miles about Camargo.

Chapter 2: American Military Rule of Matamoros — 1846

1. 30th Congress, 1st Session, House Executive Document No. 60. Mexican War Correspondence. Headquarters, Army of Occupation, Matamoros, Orders No. 94, p. 497.

2. Letters of Samuel Curtis, "Dear Brother," November 14, 1846, The Huntington Library, San Marino, California.

3. Winfield Scott, *Memoirs of Lieut.-General Scott, LL.D.* (Freeport, New York: Books for Libraries Press [1864]), vol. 2, pp. 392–96.

4. *American Flag*, August, 3, 1846. A typical day at Matamoros was reported by the editors of the paper, "Passengers who came up from Burita yesterday, on the steamer Enterprise, report seeing several dead bodies floating in the river." "A murder was committed . . . [by] a member of the company, [McIntosh's Company of Louisiana Volunteers] named William Overton, it is said, without provocation, stabbed another member of the company, named King who died immediately. . . ." On the same day, the paper also reports three assaults, two by Mexicans on volunteers and one by a volunteer on a Mexican. Finally, there is an advertisement announcing that a bowling alley had been opened opposite the American Hotel, and the proprietor, Dan Murphy, states that ". . . if while there, any one should by accident, feel inclined, to participate in a glass of the wholesome beverage, they offer a BAR well stocked with the best Liquors the country can produce."

5. The "large fleshy woman" who ran the "American," also ran this advertisement for her establishment: "AMERICAN HOTEL Mrs. Phillis Hamblin, having opened a house under the above name, in the large and commodious building in Teran street, near the northeast corner of the Grand Square (opposite Gen. Arista's Head Quarters) is prepared to accomodate Boarders either by the Day, Week, or Meal. The house is roomy, and Sleeping Rooms will be fitted up as well as circumstances will permit. No expense will be spared in bringing upon the table every delicacy to be procured in market, and in having it served up in a superior style. Matamoros, July 10, 1846." *American Flag*, July 21, 1846.

6. Ibid., August 6, 1846. The paper reports the murder of Jack Haynes, a well respected citizen, by a Texas Ranger named McCanan, belonging to Tom Greene's [sic] company from Lafayette, Texas. Haynes' life was dispatched by a knife slash across his jugular vein. McCanan immediately left town.

7. D. E. Livingston-Little (ed.), *The Mexican War Diary of Thomas D. Tennery* (Norman: University of Oklahoma Press, 1970) p. 27. Fort Paredes was built by the Mexicans to defend the Anacuita Crossing of the Rio Grande. A volunteer described the fort on September 26, 1846,

as ". . . built in a circular form containing about an acre; the wall is dirt or clay thrown up eight or nine feet high, mounted with cannon, and a deep ditch around the outside; it is occupied by soldiers at the present."

8. Heitman, *Register*, vol. 2, pp. 60, 125. Captain William McLaughlin organized the Mansfield Boys, which later became Company A, a rifle company in 3rd Ohio. During the Civil War he led McLaughlin's squadron of Ohio Cavalry.

9. Smith, *The War with Mexico*, vol. 1, pp. 467–68. Fort Brown, originally named Fort Texas, was a large earthen fort built across the Rio Grande from Matamoros prior to the opening engagements of the war. The fort had "six bastion fronts, which made a perimeter of 800 yards, a strongly designed wall of earth 9½ feet high from the natural ground, a parapet 15 feet thick, a ditch about 8 feet deep and from 15 to 22 feet wide, a gate and a drawbridge . . . the magazine was made of pork barrels filled with sand, seven tiers thick and four tiers high, with a timber roof covered with 10 or 12 feet of sand."

10. Heitman, *Register*, vol. 1, p. 307. Colonel Newman S. Clarke joined the service in 1812, and was promoted to colonel on June 29, 1846, six days later than the date on Samuel Curtis's appointment, making Curtis his senior in grade. Clarke received a promotion to brevet captain in 1814 for his services at the battle of Niagra, and brigadier general for gallantry at the siege of Vera Cruz.

11. *American Flag*, November 4, 1846. Captain Norman is not mentioned in Heitman, but he is described in the newspaper article as "Captain Norman of Company H, 1st Regiment of Artillery, stationed at Fort Brown."

12. Heitman, *Register*, vol. 1, p. 644. Captain Allen Lowd entered the service in 1814, and promoted to major in 1846 for gallant conduct in the defense of Fort Brown. He died November 25, 1854.

13. Heitman, *Register*, vol. 2, pp. 62, 130. Captain Robert M. Moore organized the Montgomery Guards of Cincinnati, which became Co. E, 3rd Ohio. During the Civil War, he served as lieutenant colonel of 10th Ohio Infantry.

14. *Official Roster*, p. 439. John O. Derstine was first sergeant of Company C, and discharged from the service on September 5, 1846, at Matamoros on a surgeon's certificate of disability.

15. Thomas W. Reilly, "American Reporters and the Mexican War, 1846–1848," Dissertation (University of Minnesota), pp. 145–149. The *American Flag* appeared twice weekly on Wednesdays and Saturdays. The first issue appeared on July 4, 1846, and the paper continued operations in Matamoros until October 9, 1848. On this date

the paper moved across the river to Brownsville and continued to publish on the American side of the river. The first editors were J. N. Fleeson and John N. Peoples, New Orleans printers; Peoples was later replaced by J. R. Palmer. The paper was initially published from temporary quarters and printed on a captured Mexican government press. By January 17, 1847, however, the editors boasted that their offices had been moved to "Abasolo street, first house below Bravo Street — into Captain Smith's building (known as the "Steamboat House") next door west of Bigelow's Livery Stable."

16. *Official Roster*, p. 450. Private William Christmas, musician for Company K, died August 12, 1846, at Matamoros. He was twenty-one years of age.

17. Jose R. Alvarez, ed., *Enciclopedia de Mexico* (Cuidad de Mexico, 1978), vol. 9, p. 295; Maurice G. Fulton, *Diary and Letters of Josiah Gregg* (Norman: University of Oklahoma Press, 1944), vol. 1, pp. 358–59. Monterrey lies more than 150 miles west of Matamoros astride the principal pass through the Sierra Madre that connects northeastern and central Mexico. The city was named for the Spanish Viceroy of Mexico, the Conde de Monterey, who established it about 1600 as the first colony in the province of Nuevo Leon. At the time of the Mexican War the name was spelled "Monterey" but has since been changed. Gregg reported that the city — originally named Valle de Extramadura was founded in 1596 by Don Diego Montemayor — had a population of 10,905, by 1821. The population included all the neighboring villages and ranchos.

18. Heitman, *Register*, vol. 1, p. 1013. Captain Lucien Bonaparte Webster graduated from West Point in 1819. He was promoted to brevet major for his actions at the battle of Monterrey on September 23, 1846, and brevet lieutenant colonel for gallantry at the battle of Buena Vista on February 23, 1847.

19. Ibid., vol. 1, p. 378. Lieutenant James Lowry Donaldson graduated from West Point in 1832. He was promoted to brevet captain for service at the battle of Monterrey and to major for meritorous conduct at the battle of Buena Vista. He was promoted to colonel and brigadier general for his services as quartermaster in the actions around Atlanta, Georgia, in September, 1864.

20. Smith, *War With Mexico*, vol. 1, p. 159. Smith indicates two ferry crossings on the river at Matamoros, the upper crossing (Anacuita) near Fort Paredes and the lower crossing (Paso Real) near Fort Brown.

21. Benjamin Franklin Scribner, *Camp Life of a Volunteer: a Campaign in Mexico or a Glimpse of Life in Camp by "One Who Has Seen the*

Elephant" (Philadelphia: Grigg, Elliot and Co., 1847), p. 31, "Entry for September 7, 1846." Scribner, a young soldier from the 2nd Indiana Regiment described these entertainers: ". . . our attention was attracted by music, and a crowd, following a company of rope dancers. We were informed that they came in every Sunday afternoon, and performed at three o'clock. The party consisted of three men and one woman on horseback. They were gaudily dressed, very much after the manner of our circus riders, but, if possible, more grotesque and showy. The music consisted of a clarinet, a drum, and a kind of opeclide painted green and red. The pompous cavalcade, supported by the motley crew of men, women and children, making every gesticulation of delight, presented truly a rich and ludicrous scene."

22. The term "ranchero" was originally applied to the many cow-hands and drovers who populated northern Mexico. During the war with Mexico came to refer to the group of lightly armed irregular cavalry who waged the guerrilla warfare in northern Mexico from 1846 to 1848. Their most novel weapon was the *lazo*, a rawhide or braided horsehair lariat with a loop on the end used to snare unwary Americans. Most Americans had never seen a loop tossed from horseback to snare prey, either bovine or human, and marvelled at the dexterity of Mexican horsemen. These roping skills were adopted by American cowboys, who learned many of their ranching skills from their Mexican counterparts.

23. Heitman, *Register*, vol. 1, p. 655. Captain William C. McCaus-lin, was appointed assistant comissary of subsistence for the 3rd Ohio Regiment in June, 1846, and honorably discharged in 1848.

24. Ibid., vol. 2, p. 63. Captain Asbury F. Noles organized the Union Infantry Company of Zanesville which became Company H, 3rd Ohio.

25. K. Jack Bauer, *The Mexican War 1846–1848* (New York: Mac-millan Publishing Co., Inc., 1974) p. 85; Sister Blanche Marie McEniry, *American Catholics in the War with Mexico* (Washington: Catholic University, 1932) p.66; *American Flag*, July 27, 1846, May 15, 1847, May 22, 1847. In a meeting on May 19, 1846, President James K. Polk discussed with Bishop John Hughes of New York how the government might counter the prejudices of the Catholic priests in Mexico. Polk felt that the idea was widely circulated in Mexico that "our object was to overthrow their religion and rob their churches, and that if they believed this they would make a desperate resistance to our army in the present war." See, Allan Nevins, *Polk — The Diary of a President* (London: Longmans, Green and Co., 1952) p. 96. Polk suggested to the bishop that Spanish-speaking priests from the United States be sent to

accompany the army in Mexico. Bishop Hughes agreed and Reverends John McElroy and Antony Rey were dispatched to Mexico. Father Rey followed the army to Monterrey, and conducted several services in the great cathedral. He was murdered by bandits near the town of Marin on January 15, 1847. Padre Rey was traveling with a servant near Marin when they were attacked by bandits who killed the servant. The clerical habit worn by the good father caused the bandits to halt further violence, but Rey was finally killed on the command of the bandit leader who wished to leave no witnesses to the earlier crime. The populace of Marin, in tears of indignation and regret, received the body and interred it near the village. The *American Flag* reported as early as July 27, 1846, that, "Rev. Mr McElroy officiated in divine service yesterday in the Cathedral on the Plaza . . . the service was well attended by both citizens and soldiers." But by May 15, 1847, McElroy had returned to the United States because of failed health.

26. Heitman, *Register*, vol. 1, p. 947. Lieutenant Colonel Joseph P. Taylor entered the service in 1813 and became brevet colonel in May, 1848, for "prosecuting the war with Mexico." Promoted to brigader general in 1863, he died on June 29, 1864. He was a brother of General Zachary Taylor.

27. *American Flag*, August 26, September 2, 1846. The steamboat *Enterprise* burst her boilers a little above Reynosa on the Rio Grande while transporting Wood's Company of Texas Volunteers and two companies of Tennessee Volunteers to Camargo. The accident probably occurred on or near August 23, 1846. Two were killed and twenty-six were scalded, burned, or bruised. The steamboat captain, D. S. Kelsy, is listed among the casualties, but otherwise was considered blameless for the accident.

28. Heitman, *Register*, vol. 1, p. 388. Thomas Duncan, First Lieutenant, Mounted Rifles, entered service in May, 1846. Promoted to brevet colonel on April 8, 1862, for actions near Albuquerque, New Mexico, he retired a brigadier general.

29. *Diccionario Porrúa de Historia, Biografía, y Geografía de México* (Mexico City: Editorial Porrúa, 1965) vol. 1, p. 101; Wilfrid Calcott, *Santa Anna, the Story of an Enigma Who Was Once Mexico* (Norman: University of Oklahoma Press, 1936). Antonio Lopez de Santa Anna Perez de Lebron was born in Jalapa, Vera Cruz, on February 24, 1794. After a limited education he was apprenticed to a merchant but elected the life of a soldier and was accepted as a cadet in the Fijo de Vera Cruz Regiment. Santa Anna joined forces with Agustin de Iturbide, late in the struggle for independence from Spain, helping him to drive the Spanish from Mexico. Shortly thereafter, Santa Anna led a revolt that

toppled the government of Iturbide. In 1829 the Spanish attempted to retake Mexico and Santa Anna led the Mexican army that expelled the invaders. For his services he was elected president in 1832, but he seized control of the government, assuming dictatorial powers that violated the constitution. Several Mexican states revolted and Santa Anna headed an army to crush the uprisings in Zacatecas and Coahuila de Tejas. Santa Anna's army marched into Texas but was defeated by an army of Texas settlers led by Sam Houston at the battle of San Jacinto on April 21, 1836. Santa Anna was captured by the Texas army and while a prisoner signed a treaty acknowledging the independence of Texas. The treaty was later rejected by the Mexican Congress. Returning to Mexico, Santa Anna took up arms for his country in 1838 to repulse the French from the city of Vera Cruz, where he lost a leg to a French cannonball. He was elected president of Mexico again and served from 1841 to 1844, but a revolt against his government forced him to flee the country. In 1846 after war was declared by the United States against Mexico, Santa Anna returned from exile to resume control of Mexico. With great energy he organized an army at San Luis Potosi and marched north to oppose General Zachary Taylor. The two armies engaged in the battle of Buena Vista on February 22–23, 1847. Victory was in the grasp of Santa Anna, but the outnumbered and gallant American forces repeatedly blunted the Mexican attacks and at the close of the day on February 23rd still held the field. Santa Anna abandoned the battlefield on February 24th and retreated to San Luis Potosi. He continued to command the Mexican army until the fall of Mexico City when he again fled the country. He returned to Mexico in 1853 and became president for the third time but was again overthrown and exiled. After the death of Benito Juarez, Santa Anna was allowed to return to Mexico, where he died in Mexico City in 1874.

30. *Diccionario*, vol. 2, pp. 1577–78. Mariano Paredes y Arrillaga (1797–1849) was the interim president of the Republic of Mexico from January 4, 1846, to July 28, 1846.

31. Consular Dispatches from Matamoros "To the Honorable James Buchanan," July 18, 1846. J. P. Schatzell was appointed Consul of the United States for the Port of Matamoros, on December 23, 1844, and acknowledged on his letter of acceptance that his country of birth was Germany. The consular despatches from the years 1844 to 1846 are mostly missing, no doubt due to steps taken by the Mexican Government to expel all foreigners from Matamoros. J. P. Schatzell wrote that ". . . on the 12th of April last, all the resident citizens of the United States, as well as myself, were forcibly expelled from this city and directed to proceed to Victoria, by order of Genl. Ampudia. . . . The

order allowed only 24 hours for our departure, and was so vigorously executed, with open threats of violence, that our citizens were compelled to abandon their property and effects and leave the city on foot. Having received information on the route to the interior of the reappointment of Genl Arista to the command of the Mexican Army, I and those who accompanied me opened a correspondence with him on the subject of our expulsion . . . which resulted in a modification of the order, giving us permission to embark at Tampico. Two or three Americans were permitted to remain at stock farms (Ranchos) in the vicinity of this place, and several others at San Fernando and Santander. It is almost useless to add that we incurred great personal risk and fatigue on this journey to Tampico, the roads thither being generally infested by robbers and at the time we passed through the country the inhabitants were extremely exasperated at our countrymen on account of the approach of the American Army. . . ."

32. Kearney, *Boom and Bust — The Historical Cycles of Matamoros and Brownsville*, pp. 33, 37. Mrs. Kidder was the wife of Sanforth Kidder who came to Matamoros from Connecticut in 1825 and established a boardinghouse. Captain Kidder was accused of smuggling by the Mexican government in 1833 and forced to tear down several warehouses and a wharf that he owned on Punta de Isabel. (Also see chapter 3, note 27.)

33. Heitman, *Register*, vol. 1, p. 297. Lieutenant Leslie Chase graduated from West Point in 1834. He was promoted to brevet captain for his actions at Palo Alto and Resaca de la Palma. He died on April 15, 1849.

34. Rio San Juan headwaters rise in the mountains south of Saltillo and flow northward about 150 miles before emptying into the Rio Grande near Camargo.

35. Bauer, *The Mexican War*, p. 89. The Second Division, led by General William Jenkins Worth, was the vanguard of the American army that marched overland from Camargo to attack Monterrey. Worth was ordered to march to Cerralvo, a village halfway between Camargo and Monterrey, and there set up a supply depot and await the arrival of the remainder of the army. Worth left Camargo on August 19, 1846, and arrived in Cerralvo by August 25.

36. Smith, *The War With Mexico*, vol. 1, pp. 229–30. Cerralvo is about fifty miles southwest of Camargo along the main line of advance of the American army to Monterrey. During the war the town claimed about 1,800 citizens. Buildings were mainly of stone; many private residences contained formal gardens watered by the numerous springs of crystal clear cold water that emerge from the ground south of the town

and are circulated throughout by a system of canals. B. F. Scribner offered this view of Cerralvo, "We pitched our tents near the old Spanish town of Ceralvo, which bears the impress of an antiquated fortress, and reminds one of the dilapidated castles we read of in romances. The houses are built of gray stone, with loopholes for windows. Through the centre of town runs a beautiful clear stream, spanned by bridges and arches. There is also a cathedral with chimes and a towering steeple. It is said to be 166 years old." See, Scribner, *Camp Life of a Volunteer*, p. 49.

37. 30th Congress, 1st Session, House Executive Document 60, Mexican War Correspondence, No. 1, p. 774. The Polk administration allowed Santa Anna to enter Mexico from exile in Cuba. A confidential document to Commodore David Connor, who commanded the fleet blockading the east coast of Mexico, from Secretary of the Navy George Bancroft ordered an undisputed passage: "Navy Department, May 13, 1846 . . . Commodore: If Santa Anna endeavors to enter the Mexican ports, you will allow him to pass freely. . . ." On August 16, 1846, Santa Anna returned to Vera Cruz.

38. Heitman, *Register*, vol. 1, p. 183; *American Flag*, September 5, 1846. Colonel Edward Dickinson Baker was born in England and elected colonel of the 4th Illinois Volunteer Regiment in July, 1846. He was honorably discharged in May, 1847. Appointed major general of volunteers on September 21, 1861, Baker was killed the same day at the battle of Balls Bluff, Virginia.

In early September, 1846, Colonel Baker was seriously wounded in a scene of riot and murder that occurred at Camp Belknap on the Rio Grande across from the village of Burrita. While trying to break up a melee between two companies of Georgia volunteers on board the steamboat *Corvette*, Baker was reportedly shot through the neck. One Georgia volunteer was killed and fifteen wounded before peace was imposed on the Jaspar Greens, an impetuous company of Irishmen from Georgia.

39. Heitman, *Register*, vol. 2, p. 63. Patrick H. Mulvaney was assistant surgeon for the 3rd Ohio.

40. Private Henry Ray of Company G died on September 13, 1846.

41. Pat Kelly, *The River of Lost Dreams — Navigation on the Rio Grande* (Lincoln: University of Nebraska Press, 1986), p. 108. The *Corvette* was a sidewheeler of 149 tons built in Brownsville, Pennsylvania, in 1846 and purchased by the Army Quartermaster Corps expressly for moving troops and supplies on the Rio Grande. After the war, the *Corvette* was retained by the army to carry supplies to Fort Brown and Fort Ringgold.

American Flag, October 7, 1846, gives the following account: "ATTEMPT TO LASSO A BOY. — The steamer *Corvette*, on her trip down from Camargo, stopped for the night at a rancho on the river, and a small boy attached to the boat went ashore and strayed some distance from the bank. He was espied by a Mexican who thought to entrap him with a lasso and drag him off. The Mexican was no doubt expert in the use of this weapon, but somehow he was not quick enough in his movements. He succeeded in encircling the boy with his noose, but before he could throw him from his feet, the youngster fired two pistol balls into him which hurried Mr. Mexican off, no doubt quite sick at the stomach. The boy was not over thirteen years of age. The Mexicans must think the Yankees are 'born veteran' pistol shooters."

42. Lytle, *Merchant Steam Vessels*, p. 157; *American Flag*, September 16–19, 1846. The *New York* was a wooden hulled sternwheeler of 365 tons, built in New York, New York, in 1837. The ship, under the command of Captain Phillips, foundered and was lost on September 5, 1846, about seventy miles from Galveston, on a run from that city to New Orleans. Seventeen lives were lost in the accident; her survivors were rescued by the steamship *Galveston*.

43. Heitman, *Register*, vol. 2, pp. 51, 101. Captain Thomas H. Ford organized the Bartley Guards, which became Company C of the 3rd Ohio. He was colonel of the 32nd Ohio Infantry during the Civil War.

44. Ibid., vol. 1, p. 928. Benjamin Stone served as surgeon of the 3rd Ohio.

45. Ibid., vol. 1, p. 172. Major John T. Arthur was quartermaster for the 3rd Ohio. He was discharged in October, 1848.

46. Walter P. Webb, *Handbook of Texas* (Austin: Texas State Historical Association, 1952), vol. 1, p. 406; *American Flag*, September 16, 19, 23, October 17, 21, 31, November 7, 1846, April 3, 1847. Louis P. Cooke was born in Tennessee in 1811. He entered the United States Military Academy but left before graduation to go to Texas and fight in the revolution. Cooke arrived too late to participate in the battle of San Jacinto but stayed to serve in the army. He rose to the rank of lieutenant colonel in the Army of the Republic of Texas before seeking political office. He was elected and served in the Third Congress. In the administration of Mirabeau B. Lamar, Cooke acted as secretrary of the navy from May 2, 1839 to December 13, 1841. He served in the Sixth Congress where he introduced the Texas Homestead Exemption Law and worked on the committee to select a site for the capitol. He and his wife, Mary A. Cooke, were both victims of a cholera epidemic, dying at Brownsville in 1849.

To retaliate for the attack on Harrison W. Davis and others as reported by Curtis on September 22, Colonel N. S. Clark furnished the necessary arms to the citizens of Matamoros to form a "rescue party" under the command of Louis P. Cooke and Lloyd Tilghman. Mexicans claimed that Davis and his party of discharged soldiers were on a mule-stealing expedition and that the fight resulted when the Mexicans tried to stop the Davis party. The rescue mission of Cooke's party became one of vengeance, with Cooke and his men burning the Rancho de los Animos, the Ranchos of the Masa, and the Rancho "Surestio." Rancho de los Animos was owned by the reported murderer and bandit Juan Antonio Byene; the Ranchos of the Masa were owned by Chica Trevino. One of the men captured at Rancho of the Masa, "Marteas Garza," was identified as a bandit and murdered by the Cooke party. The Cooke "rescue party" was never punished for these actions and the inquiry made by Curtis was deemed sufficient and the matter dropped. However, on September 23 in broad daylight, a lone Mexican rider entered Market Square, rode up to Señor Jesus Garcia, the man who acted as a guide to the Cooke party and shot Garcia dead. Onlookers were too stunned by the sudden action to respond and "The assassin, a large fine looking Mexican, wheeled his horse as soon as he had discharged his pistol and galloped to the further corner of the Square, where he halted and turned round to see if he had made sure his aim; being satisfied, he cooly replaced his pistol in his belt, put spurs to his horse and was soon out of sight."

Colonel Cooke operated a store on the corner of Calle Teran and the Public Square in Matamoros with a partner named Humphreys. He remained interested in military matters and attempted to organize a company of Texas Ranger volunteers to serve in Jack Hays regiment but the effort appears to have failed. Compton Smith offers a brief description of Colonel Cooke, "[Cooke] had figured largely as an Indian fighter; and carried an evidence of his acquaintance with the Camanches, in an ugly scar, made by an arrow-head, which crashing through the cheek bone, had entered his right eye, tearing it completely from the socket." Compton Smith, *Chile Con Carne or, The Camp and the Field* (New York: Miller & Curtis, 1857), p. 341. For Cooke's revenge on the Indian that loosed this disfiguring arrow, see Robert H. Ferrell, *Monterrey is Ours!* (Lexington: The University Press of Kentucky, 1990), p. 13.

47. Harrison W. Davis is not listed on the muster rolls of any company of the 1st Texas Foot Riflemen. His story sounds a bit suspicious. The regiment was disbanded on August 4, 1846, not on September 4.

48. Heitman, *Register*, vol. 1, p. 671. Colonel William Robertson McKee graduated from West Point in 1825 but resigned his commission

by 1836. He was elected colonel of the 2nd Kentucky Cavalry in June, 1846, and was killed leading his men at the battle of Buena Vista on February 23, 1847.

49. Malone, *DAB*, vol. 3, pp. 371–72. William Orlando Butler (1791–1880) won the praise of Andrew Jackson for his actions at the battle of New Orleans. Butler was appointed a major general of volunteers by President James K. Polk and was second in command to General Zachary Taylor at the battle of Monterrey. He received a leg wound during the action in the Monterrey streets on September 21, 1846. After recuperating, Butler joined General Scott's army and participated in the capture of Mexico City. In 1848 he was the Democratic candidate for vice-president of the United States but his ticket, led by Lewis Cass, was defeated by Zachary Taylor and the Whig Party.

50. Charles Spurlin, *Texas Veterans in the Mexican War* (Nacogdoches: Erickson Publishing, 1984), p. 7; William P. Johnston, *The Life of Albert Sidney Johnston* (New York: D. Appleton and Co., 1878), p. 136. John B. Williams was enrolled as a private in Company D of 1st Texas Foot Riflemen. The regiment was mustered into federal service on July 7, 1846, and mustered out on August 4, 1846. The men were moved to Camargo to prepare for the attack on Monterrey but their three-month term of enlistment had run out by August 7. Their colonel, Albert Sidney Johnston, mounted a stump and delivered an empassioned speech to the volunteers, begging them to reenlist for at least a year more. But good-natured Johnston, who offered this example to his friends as evidence of what a poor public speaker he was, could only sway the vote of one man. The entire regiment was disbanded.

51. *American Flag*, September 26, 1846; House Executive Document No. 13, 31st Congress, 2d Session, "General Patterson's Route of March." San Fernando is a little town about ninety miles southwest of Matamoros. This rumor found its way into the paper: "Something in the Wind — A Mexican express rider rode into town about dusk last evening, post haste from San Fernando, having killed two horses on the road. The horse on which he rode into town dropped dead as soon as he dismounted. We could not learn the nature of his errand. We have heard it rumored that there are a large body of Mexican troops in San Fernando. Probably his mission has reference to them. . . ." An officer in the engineers who passed through the town in February, 1847, left this glimpse, "San Fernando is quite a handsome, well built town, about 1,000 inhabitants, houses stone; it is on a high limestone bluff — say 150 feet — on the left bank of a stream. . . ."

52. Heitman, *Register*, vol. 2, p. 47. Captain James F. Chapman

organized the Seneca Volunteers which became Company F of the 3rd Ohio.

53. Heitman, *Register*, vol. 2, pp. 49, 94. Lieutenant Isaac Delong. He served as major in 13th Indiana Cavalry during the Civil War.

54. Ibid., vol. 2, pp. 44, 79. Lieutenant Samuel Beatty served as colonel in the 19th Ohio Infantry during the Civil War.

55. Joseph Chance, *The Mexican War Journal of Captain Franklin Smith* (Jackson: University Press of Mississippi, 1991), p. 35. This express arrived in Camargo at 2 o'clock A.M. on the steamer *Aid*. Franklin Smith, stationed at Camargo reported that the messenger was "Lieutenant Armistead only fourteen days from Washington to this place — he left this morning for Monterey about day break . . . when he [Armistead] got to some point on the Rio Grande finding no public boat he gave the "Aid" a thousand dollars to bring him to Camargo." James K. Polk was unhappy with the terms of surrender for Monterrey, especially the armistice that had been mutually declared by the two sides. This express contained orders for Taylor to break off the armistice at once and "resume offensive operations."

56. Kelly, *River of Lost Dreams*, pp. 34, 38, 108; *American Flag*, October 14, 1846; Way, *Packet Directory*, p. 103; Chance, *Mexican War Journal*, pp. 11–12. The *Colonel Cross* was a sidewheeler steamboat of 160 tons built in Shousetown, Pennsylvania, and purchased by the army for use on the Rio Grande. The vessel was brought to the Rio Grande by Captain John Birmingham, but he was discharged on August 28, 1846, for transporting private goods on a government boat. Captain Pratt was promptly hired at Matamoros, Mexico, as the new captain. The *Flag* reported that the *Colonel Cross* was one of the fastest boats in service for the run from the mouth of the river to Camargo. On one memorable run she "Left Mouth of Rio Grande on the 6th Oct. at 47 minutes past 5 A.M., and arrived at Camargo 12 minutes past 7 P.M. Oct. 8th." Subtracting for stoppages, the transit time was 50 hours and 29 minutes. Her most famous captain, Richard King, bought the boat from the army at auction after the Mexican War on April 2, 1849, with financial help from a certain Richard Penny. This boat literally launched King on a career in south Texas that culminated in the founding of the mighty King Ranch. The *Colonel Cross* was reportedly snagged and lost while being operated by private owners at San Francisco, California, on January 29, 1850.

57. Heitman, *Register*, vol. 2, p. 70. William Trevitt served as surgeon for the 2nd Ohio.

58. Ibid., vol. 2, p. 56. Lieutenant Colonel William Irvin served in 2nd Ohio, and later as colonel of the 5th Ohio.

59. Ibid., vol. 2, p. 60. Captain Robert G. McLean was a captain in the 2nd Ohio.

60. Ibid., vol. 1, p. 557. Major David (Black Dave) Hunter graduated from West Point in 1818 and was a paymaster. Hunter was promoted to brevet brigadier general in 1865 for services rendered at the battle of Piedmont and for his notorious scorched earth campaign in the valley of Virginia. He was promoted to major general after the Civil War.

61. Kelley, *River of Lost Dreams*, p. 111; *American Flag*, October 7, 1846, August 14, 25, 1847. The *Major Brown* was a 125 ton sternwheeler built in Elizabeth, Pennsylvania, in 1846. She was purchased by the Quartermaster Corps to transport men and supplies up the Rio Grande from the mouth to Camargo. General John Wool's expedition into Mexico to capture Chihuahua had created supply problems; the only reliable base for resupply was overland from San Antonio, Texas. To shorten this long, dangerous route, the army attempted to open communication with Laredo and Presidio del Rio Grande by water, sending the *Major Brown* on an exploratory trip far up the Rio Grande. This remarkable adventure was recorded by Bryant P. Tilden, Jr., in the monograph *Notes on the Upper Rio Grande* . . . (Philadelphia, 1847). The *Flag* reported on September 30, that the *Major Brown* was sighted near Mier and arrived at Laredo on October 24, 1846. River levels began to drop almost immediately, however, leaving the steamboat stranded at Laredo for almost a year. There is a river island at Laredo named "Major Brown" where the boat remained moored for many months. The river finally rose again and the *Major Brown* was able to escape. The *Flag* of August 14, 1847, reported that, "The steamer Major Brown, which it will be recollected ascended the Rio Grande on an exploring expedition, about a year ago . . . has at length effected a descent and reached here on Wednesday last." The editors credited her extrication to the masterful efforts of the experienced steamboatman, Captain McGowan.

62. George W. Hughes, *Memoir Descriptive of a March of a Division of the United States Army . . . from San Antonio de Bexar, in Texas, to Saltillo, in Mexico*, 31st Congress, 1st Session, Senate Executive Document 32, p. 17. Presidio del Rio Grande was created as a military post and penal colony by order of the king of Spain in 1772. The ruins of an old solid stone Jesuit monastery within a mile of the village testified to the town's colonial heritage. By 1846 the Mexican village — constructed largely of adobe brick — had a population of about 1,200.

63. Robert Lonard, et al, *Woody Plants of the Lower Rio Grande Valley, Texas* (Austin: Texas Memorial Museum, 1991), p. 84. The Texas Ebony (Pithecellobium ebano [Berlandier] C. H. Muller) is a

native tree usually less than ten meters in height with dark green bipinnately compound leaves bearing a thick-walled, woody, legume seed. The blooms are sweetly fragrant.

64. Paul Horgan, *Great River: The Rio Grande in North American History* (New York: Holt, Rinehart, and Winston, 1968), vol. 1, pp. 83–89. The beautiful native palm, Sabal texana inspired the Spanish explorer Alonzo de Pineda in 1519 to name this river "Rio de las Palmas" because of the abundant groves that fringed the banks of the Rio Grande and reached far inland. Of this original stand there remains currently less than twenty acres.

65. Mary Motz Wills, *Roadside Flowers of Texas* (Austin: University of Texas Press, 1961), pp. 33, 174–75. The wild morning glory (Ipomoea trichocarpa) is a beautiful blooming vine common to the lower Rio Grande.

66. Lonard, *The Woody Plants of the Lower Rio Grande Valley*, pp. 140–41. The Capsicum annuum var. minus, or chile piquin, grows in abundant supply throughout the lower Rio Grande Valley of Texas and is used to add zest to insipid foods.

67. Ibid., p. 113. Curtis is probably describing the beautiful scarlet flowered native hibiscus (hibiscus cardiophyllus Gray) found throughout the lower Rio Grande Valley and into northern Mexico.

68. Wills, *Roadside Flowers of Texas*, pp. 15, 125–26. The sensitive briar (Schrankia uncinata) is seen in profusion along the Rio Grande in the Matamoros-Brownsville area.

69. *Diccionario Porrúa*, p. 1842. Saltillo, the capitol of the state of Coahuila, was founded by Captain Alberto del Canto in 1575. The city, known as Leona Vicario at one time, is an important center for agriculture and ranching. The name is derived from the Spanish word "salto" for the little waterfall that fell from a spring around which the city was originally situated. Saltillo lies in the mountains about fifty-five miles west of Monterrey through a mountain pass walled by rugged high mountains.

70. Ibid., vol. 1, p. 101. Pedro de Ampudia was born in 1805 in Havana, Cuba. He came to Mexico City in 1821 and fought against the Spanish, participating in the assault on San Juan de Ulloa Castle at Vera Cruz. After Santa Anna deposed Bustamente as president in 1840, Ampudia became a general in the Army of Mexico. He participated with General Woll in an invasion of Texas in 1842, and led the troops that captured Colonel William S. Fisher and his Texans at Mier, Mexico, on December 26, 1842. During the war with the United States Ampudia commanded the defenses of Monterrey. After the fall of that city to the Americans he proceeded to San Luis Potosi, where he was

appointed quartermaster general of the forces raised by Santa Anna for the defense of Mexico. Ampudia fought in the battle of Buena Vista. After the war, he was active in politics and was elected governor of the state of Nuevo Leon in 1854. He died in 1868.

71. The 1840 Census of Ohio lists a Nehemiah Abbott as a resident of Zanesville, Ohio.

72. *Official Roster*, p. 443. Private George Richard of Company E was discharged at Matamoros on a surgeon's certificate of disability.

73. Heitman, *Register*, vol. 1, p. 509. Lieutenant Joseph Abel Haskin graduated from West Point in 1835. He was promoted to brevet captain for bravery at the battle of Cerro Gordo and to captain for his services in the capture of Chapultepec Castle. He retired on December 15, 1870, at the rank of brigadier general.

74. Ibid., vol. 1, p. 1042. Either Seth Williams or Thomas Williams.

75. Ibid., vol. 1, p. 578. Lieutenant Richard William Johnston graduated from West Point in 1838. He served in the 3rd Regiment of Artillery and resigned his commission on December 4, 1847.

76. Ibid., vol. 1, p. 206. Colonel William G. Belknap entered the service in 1813 and was promoted to colonel for his gallantry at Palo Alto and Resaca de la Palma. He was promoted to brigader general for his services at the battle of Buena Vista.

77. Ibid., vol. 2, p. 53. Lieutenant Oliver C. Gray.

78. *Official Roster*, p. 435. Private Abraham Metz, age twenty, was appointed hospital steward on August 31, 1846, and discharged from the service at Buena Vista, Mexico, on April 13, 1847, on a surgeon's certificate of disability.

79. Heitman, *Register*, vol. 2, p. 48. Second Lieutenant Samuel B. Crowley was a member of the Coshocton Volunteers (Company B) of the 3rd Ohio Regiment.

80. Ibid., vol. 2, p. 46. Lieutenant Peter Burket.

81. Raymond L. Ditmars, *The Reptiles of North America* (Garden City: Doubleday & Company, 1953), p. 69. The Texas horned lizard (Phrynosoma cornutum Harlan) is still abundant in eastern Cameron County, Texas.

82. The Resaca de la Palma battlefield lies on an ancient channel of the Rio Grande and now within the northern part of Brownsville. In 1967, while excavating for the development of a housing subdivision, a mass grave of Mexican soldiers was unearthed. A team of archeologists from the University of Texas at Austin, led by Dr. Thomas Hester, examined the site. The skeletons, or partial skeletons, of thirty-two Mexican soldiers were exhumed. The main artifacts discovered were

shirt and trouser buttons, canteens, buckles, and musket balls, "found in what were evidently lethal locales." A final report on the excavations and subsequent analyses was never prepared. See, "An Exploration of a Common Legacy: A Conference on Border Architecture," Proceedings, Texas Historical Commission, 1978, p. 71. Lieutenant Rankin Dilworth reported on a visit to the battle site on June 3, 1846, that two graves existed in which 150 Mexicans were buried. See, Diary of Rankin Dilworth, unpublished, privately owned. A second burial site has never been unearthed.

83. Peterson, *Birds of Texas* pp. 5, 11. The bird sighted is an anhinga (Anhinga anhinga) commonly referred to as "water turkey" or "snakebird" for the supple nature of its neck. This bird is still commonly seen on the Rio Grande.

84. Heitman, *Register*, vol. 2, p. 52; *American Flag*, October 21, 1846. "DIED, at his hotel in Matamoros, on Monday last, Lieut. OWEN FRANCIS — a native of Sandusky City, Erie county, Ohio. The deceased was an officer in one of the regiments [3rd] of Ohio Volunteers."

85. Heitman, *Register*, vol. 1, p. 940; *American Flag*, October 4, 24, 1846. Captain Alexander Joseph Swift graduated from West Point in 1826. He was in the Corps of Engineers. He died on April 24, 1847.

General Taylor's long awaited pontoon bridge had finally arrived but too late to be of any use where he was — in the Chihuahuan Desert. Captain Swift commanded the company of Sappers and Miners having the responsibility for the pontoon bridge. The *Flag* reported, "We mentioned in our last paper that a steamer was lying off the Brazos Bar with a signal of distress hoisted. The vessel alluded to was the steamer *Neptune*, with the long expected Ponton Train on board. She was in a leaky condition, and the last we heard from her they were arguing the propriety of either running her ashore or attempting to cross the bar, drawing eight feet water, with a heavy sea on." By October 24 it was reported that the *Neptune* could not cross the bar. She went to Galveston, then on to New Orleans with the pontoon bridge still on board. The bridge was subsequently brought up the river to Camargo, only to languish there in disuse.

86. *Official Roster*, p. 443. Private Jacob Flickinger, age twenty-four, of Company E, died on October 21, 1846, at Matamoros.

87. The Palo Alto battlefield is located on private land in a vast prairie about ten miles northeast of Brownsville, Texas. As of this writing, the site is to be purchased by the National Park Service for construction of a battlefield park.

88. Heitman, *Register*, vol. 1, p. 297. Lieutenant Leslie Chase grad-

uated from West Point in 1834 and was assigned to the 2nd Regiment of Artillery. He was promoted to brevet captain for gallant and meritorious conduct in the battles of Palo Alto and Resaca de la Palma. Chase died on April 15, 1849.

89. Ibid., vol. 1, p. 223; T. B. Thorpe, *Our Army on the Rio Grande* (Philadelphia: Carey and Hart, 1846), pp. 75, 90. Lieutenant Jacob Edmund Blake graduated from West Point in 1829. He served as a topographical engineer. On May 8, 1846, before the battle of Palo Alto, Blake made a daring reconnaisance, deliberately riding on horseback in front of the entire Mexican line of battle. From a distance of 150 yards, he made a galloping inventory of the Mexican army and reported the tally to General Taylor. His bravery was the object of admiration by thousands of American and Mexican soldiers. On May 9, prior to hostilities at Resaca de la Palma, Blake dropped his pistol, discharging its contents. The pistol ball struck Blake, killing him.

90. Peterson, *Birds of Texas*, p. 25. The roseate spoonbill (Ajaja ajaja) is a pink wading bird. It is still seen occasionally along the south Texas coast.

91. Heitman, *Register*, vol. 1, p. 797. William Laurens Poole resigned his commission on November 7, 1842.

92. Ibid., vol. 1, p. 367. Major St. Clair Denny graduated from West Point in 1818. He was a paymaster. He died on August 18, 1858.

93. Sellers G. Archer and Clarence E. Bunch, *The American Grass Book* (Norman: University of Oklahoma Press, 1953), p. 207. The native buffalo grass (Buchloe dactyloides) is a perennial deep-rooted short grass that can withstand heavy grazing and prolonged drought.

94. Heitman, *Register*, vol. 2, p. 60. Lieutenant James McMillen.

95. Malone, *DAB*, vol. 14, p. 304. Major General Robert Patterson was born on January 12, 1792, in County Tyrone, Ireland. His father was banished from Ireland and resettled in Delaware County, Pennsylvania. Patterson fought in the War of 1812 and rose to the rank of colonel in the Pennsylvania Militia. After the war, he established himself in business and, in time, became a wealthy commission merchant. With the onset of the Mexican War, Patterson was appointed a brigadier general of volunteers by President James K. Polk. He was appointed commander of the military garrisons on the Rio Grande by General Taylor in August, 1846. In November, 1846, Patterson commanded a force that marched overland from Matamoros to Tampico to join Scott's army for the invasion of central Mexico. Patterson commanded a division at Cerro Gordo and led the advance into Jalapa. After the war, Patterson acquired extensive holdings in sugar and cotton plantations, owning some thirty cotton mills in Pennsylvania. He

served briefly as major general of Union volunteers in 1861 and participated in the Battle of Bull Run. He resigned his commission from the army and returned to Pennsylvania, where he died on August 7, 1881.

96. Heitman, *Register*, vol. 1, p. 586. Lieutenant Philip Kearney joined the service in 1837. He was promoted to brevet major for gallantry at the battles of Contreras and Churubusco. Kearney was killed in battle at Chantilly, Virginia, on September 1, 1862, while serving as a major general of volunteers.

97. *American Flag*, November 14, 1846. "On Wednesday the Tennessee Cavalry, numbering near 900 men and horses, under the command of Colonel Thomas, marched through the streets of our city." The regiment left Memphis on August 27 and marched overland, arriving on the banks of the Rio Grande on November 7, 1846, after a 1,400 mile trip. "They are a fine looking set of young men, and bear a flag, the gift of the young ladies of Tennessee, whose motto is . . . 'None but the brave deserve the fair.'"

98. *Official Roster*, p. 445. Solomon J. Van Treese, age thirty-five, was appointed first sergeant June 26, 1846, and reduced to the ranks on April 6, 1847.

99. Captain Kauman cannot be located in Heitman or other sources.

100. Perry, *Indiana in the Mexican War*, pp. 70, 72, 292–97. General Joseph Lane's brigade consisted of the 1st, 2nd, and 3rd Regiments of Indiana Volunteer Infantry. The brigade was mustered into federal service for one-year's duty, beginning on June 19, 1846. The 1st, under the command of Colonel James P. Drake, saw no active fighting, but spent the majority of its time on garrison duty at the mouth of the Rio Grande. The 2nd, under Colonel William Bowles, fought at Buena Vista, where its reputation was clouded by charges that it "ran from the enemy." The 3rd, under the command of Colonel James H. Lane, fought with valor at Buena Vista and was cited for bravery.

101. Kelley, *River of Lost Dreams*, p. 109. The *Exchange*, a sidewheeler steamboat of seventy-five tons was built in New Albany, Indiana, in 1845 and brought to the Rio Grande by the Quartermaster Corps.

102. Chance, *Mexican War Journal*, p. 240. Major Robert W. McLane was indeed the bearer of dispatches from President James K. Polk and Secretary of War William Marcy. Polk supplied McLane with both written and oral instructions for General Taylor regarding future objectives of the war. McLane left Washington on October 22, 1846, and reached General Taylor in Monterrey by November 12.

103. *American Flag*, November 4, 1846. This "gambling house" placed regular advertisements in the paper: "EXCHANGE HOTEL Bertrand Combe would inform the traveling community and the public generally, that they have fitted up a large and commodious house on Commerical street, a few doors from the Plaza, formerly occupied as a Custom house, and will furnish gentlemen with board and lodging, by the week, day, or single meal. The rooms are large and airy; and the table will be supplied with all the variety the market affords. There is a bar connected with the establishment, where will be kept the choicest wines and cordials, and the usual variety of liquors that are allowed sold in this city."

104. Heitman, *Register*, vol. 2, p. 46. Lieutenant Josiah C. Cable.

105. The Mexicans cast many of their solid shot, grape, and musket balls from copper, one of their abundant natural resources. These balls were thought by many American soldiers to be poisonous and wounds inflicted by them meant certain death. The balls were crudely cast, often having flat spots and rough surfaces that caused them to "growl" and "whistle" while traveling in their trajectories.

106. Lieutenant Miles of the 1st Regiment cannot be located in Heitman or other sources.

107. Malone, *DAB*, 473–74. Waddy Thompson served as a congressman from the State of South Carolina and was appointed minister to Mexico by President John Tyler in 1842. His mission in Mexico was highly successful, and he left that country in 1844, an ardent friend who had won the respect and admiration of the Mexicans. In 1846, his book *Recollections* appeared in print, a "calm, judicious volume still cited by historians."

108. Wilson Popenoe, *Manual of Tropical and Subtropical Fruits* (New York: The Macmillan Company, 1927), pp. 225–40. The papaya (Carica Papaya, L.) is an import to the Rio Grande Valley, but a welcome visitor that is easily cultivated. It is a giant herbaceous plant that is normally dioecious, with both male and female plants bearing sweetly fragrant flowers. The fruit is an orange-yellow melon with a sweet to musky taste.

109. Adolphus Wislizenus, *Memoir of a Tour of Northern Mexico* (Glorieta, New Mexico: The Rio Grande Press, 1969), p. 72. A similar apparatus for drawing water with leather buckets was found by Wislizenus at the hacienda of Don Manuel de Ibarra near Parras, Mexico.

110. Bauer, *The Mexican War*, p. 120. The Home Squadron, under the command of Commodore David Conner captured Tampico on November 14, 1846, after a short period of shelling.

111. San Luis Potosi is the capitol city of the Mexican state of the

same name. The city — almost equidistant between Mexico City and Monterrey (about 250 miles) and connected on both cities by fairly good roads — was of strategic importance in the Mexican War. Santa Anna located the Mexican Army at this site from September, 1846, until March, 1847, to counter American advances into central Mexico from either the north or the south.

112. *Catálogo Nacional: Monumentos Historícos Inmuebles Tamaulipas* (Secretario de Educación Pública, 1987), vol. 1, p. 423. The Ampudia House, at 89-A Abasolo Street, is still standing in Matamoros. General Ampudia lived in this house in 1844 when he commanded the garrison defending the city. In 1845, the building was the site of the German consulate.

113. Kearney, *Boom and Bust*, p. 13; *American Flag*, July 4, 1846. The city of Reynosa, on the banks of the Rio Grande about sixty miles west of Matamoros, was founded in 1749. The original site, now known as Reynosa Viejo, was on low ground and prone to flooding, so the city was moved to its present location on a limestone bluff. By 1846, the population of Reynosa was estimated at 2,000 and Reynosa Viejo about 500.

114. Livingston-Little, *Diary of Thomas D. Tennery*, p. 40. The 4th Illinois Volunteer Regiment reached Matamoros from Camargo, making the journey by steamboats. This regiment was to form a part of the forces under General Robert Patterson which would march from Matamoros to capture Victoria. Patterson's brigade, consisting of the 3rd and 4th Illinois Infantry Regiments and the Tennessee Mounted Regiment, left Matamoros on an overland march for Victoria, Mexico, on December 24, 1846.

115. *American Flag*, November 28, 1846. "We were present at the ball given at the Tremont House, on Thursday last, and were pleased to see a goodly number of fair Senoritas in attendance. There were, of course, a much larger number of the 'lords of creation,' but all appeared to enjoy the festive scene. An elegant supper was prepared under the superintendence of the fair hostess, and ample justice was done to it by the party. — Among the guests were Colonel Curtis, Maj. Gorman, Captain McDougall, and several others. . . ." The management of the Tremont House placed the following advertisement in the *Flag* of November 25: "TREMONT HOUSE Messrs. Gillock & Miller, thankful for the very liberal patronage heretofore bestowed, would inform the citizens of Matamoros and the traveling community in general, that they have opened their house on a more extensive scale; having leased and furnished a number of rooms immediately opposite, they flatter them-

selves that their accomodations are not surpassed by any Hotel in the city. . . ."

116. *American Flag*, November 28, 1846. Private Malone, stationed at Fort Paredes, was attacked by two Mexicans as he was leaving the fort. Bleeding from serious wounds in the back and neck and collapsed on the ground, Malone cried out for help. A file of soldiers from the fort came to Malone's assistance and captured the assailants, taking them into custody.

117. *American Flag*, November 25, 1846. Heitman does not list a "Major Lloyd Bell" as having served in the United States Army, but he is described in the *Flag* as having assumed the duties of paymaster at the post at Matamoros. "Major B. brings with him a large amount of specie, and his coming will be hailed with joy by the troops, who were beginning to think that Uncle Sam had forgotten them entirely."

118. Heitman, *Register*, vol. 2, pp. 51, 101. Colonel Ferris Foreman, was the commander of the 3rd Illinois Infantry. During the Civil war, Foreman served as colonel of the 4th California Infantry.

119. Ibid., vol. 2, p. 61. Colonel Jonas E. Thomas commanded the Tennessee Mounted Volunteers.

120. Ibid., vol. 1, p. 395. Captain Amos B. Eaton graduated from West Point in 1822. He was promoted to brevet major for gallantry displayed at the battle of Buena Vista on February 23, 1847, and retired at the rank of brigadier general on May 1, 1874.

121. Lieutenant Simmons cannot be located in Heitman or other sources.

122. Kearney, *Boom and Bust*, p. 33; Ronald V. Jackson, et al, *Texas 1850 Census Index* (Bountiful, Utah: Accelerated Indexing Systems, Inc., 1976), p. 94. The widow Stryker was probably the wife of John Stryker, who was listed as a resident of Matamoros in 1834. He had been given title to a part of the north bank of the Rio Grande formed by a change in the course of the river by flooding. This parcel of land was known as "Banco de Santa Rita." The 1850 Census of Texas for Cameron County lists a Jane Stryker Wryman, probably remarried, as thirty-six years of age with a daughter, Sarah Stryker, fourteen.

123. Heitman, *Register*, vol. 2, p. 62. Alexander M. Mitchell served as colonel of 1st Ohio.

124. Ibid., vol. 2, p. 44. Lieutenant Andrew W. Armstrong served in the 1st Ohio.

125. Kelley, *River of Lost Dreams*, p. 107. The *Aid* was a sidewheeler steamboat of 137 tons built in Cincinnati in 1843. The boat was owned by Charles Stillman, but no doubt under charter to the Quartermaster Corps during the war.

126. Ibid., p. 108; Way, *Packet Directory*, p. 53. The *Big Hatchee* was a sternwheeler of 195 tons built in 1844 in Pittsburgh, Pennsylvania, and owned by the Quartermaster Corps during the war. Way reports that "in the Protestant Cemetery at Hermann, Mo., is a three foot column surmounted by a sundial. Inscribed thereon: 'In memory of the early pioneers who perished in the explosion of of the steamboat *Big Hatchie* at the wharf at Hermann in 1842, the thirty-five dead that lie buried here in unidentified graves and the many whose bodies were never recovered from the Mississippi River.'" Way claims that the explosion actually occurred on July 25, 1845, but apparently the boat survived and was sold to the U.S. War Department in 1846.

127. Heitman, *Register*, vol. 2, p. 53. Lieutenant Colonel William R. Haddon served in 2nd Indiana Infantry.

128. Ibid., vol. 1, p. 492; Malone, *DAB*, 169–70. Brigadier General Thomas L. Hamer was commissioned leader of the Ohio brigade on July, 1846, and died December 2, 1846. A sword was voted to his nearest male relative by resolution of Congress on March 2, 1847, to "communicate the deep regret which Congress feels for the loss of a gallant man whose name ought to live in the recollection and affection of a grateful country." Hamer was a supporter of James K. Polk and the Mexican War, raising the 1st Ohio Regiment at the outbreak of hostilities. President Polk commissioned Hamer brigadier general of the Ohio Brigade, and he served with distinction at the battle of Monterrey. While in Mexico he was elected to the Thirtieth Congress, but died before he could accept the office. On his death, General Taylor commented, "His loss to the army at this time cannot be supplied." Hamer, while serving in Congress, had appointed U. S. Grant to the United States Military Academy and Grant would write in later years: "I have said before that Hamer was one of the ablest men Ohio every produced. At that time [1846] he was in the prime of life, being less than fifty years of age, and possessing an admirable physique, promising long life. But he was taken sick before Monterey, and died within a few days. I have always believed that had his life been spared, he would have been President of the United States during the term filled by President Pierce. See, E. B. Long (ed.), *Personal Memoirs of U. S. Grant* (Cleveland: The World Publishing Co., 1894), p. 48.

129. Heitman, *Register*, vol 2. p. 54. Major Thomas L. Harris served in the 4th Illinois Infantry.

130. *American Flag*, December 16, 1846. The 3rd Ohio Regiment was moved from their camp grounds on the river to the row of buildings on the northeast corner of Chapel Square (Plaza Capillia).

131. Malone *DAB*, vol. 14, p. 603. Gideon Johnson Pillow was born

in Tennessee on June 8, 1806. He practiced law with James Knox Polk, later president of the United States, and was appointed by Polk as a brigadier general of volunteers in 1846. He served under General Taylor, who left Pillow's Brigade behind in Camargo to guard supply lines when the army advanced on Monterrey in August, 1846. Pillow was transferred to Scott's Army and fought in central Mexico, where he was twice wounded. For his services to the country, Pillow was promoted to the rank of major general. Pillow served as major general in the Confederate Army and suffered disastrous defeats at Belmont and Fort Donelson. He was relieved from duty and held no important command thereafter. He practiced law after the war in Memphis, and died on October 8, 1878.

132. *American Flag*, January 30, February 3, February 13, 1847; United States Consular Dispatches, "To the Honorable James Buchannan," July 18, 1846. Captain James Henry Clay, commanding the schooner *Susannah*, left New Orleans on November 13, 1845, for Corpus Christi, Texas, bearing an assortment of merchandise. The schooner encountered heavy weather and was forced to make port at Matamoros for repairs. The ship and cargo were confiscated and Captain Clay was placed in prison at Matamoros. On April 15, 1846, with the approach of hostilities, General Ampudia ordered Clay taken under heavy guard to San Fernando, about ninety miles south of Matamoros. Clay remained there in confinement until May 23, 1846, when he was set at liberty by demand of General Taylor, who now occupied Matamoros. United States Consul J. P. Schatzell wrote that "Capt. Clay was repeatedly beaten severely and other wise abused while imprisoned in this city [Matamoros]." Clay seemed bent on revenge for his harsh treatment. On January 30, 1847, he published in the *Flag* a note "To THE PUBLIC," relating to his arrest for assault by Lieutenant Colonel McCook of the 3rd Ohio. "It is pretty well known that in December 1845 I was made a prisoner by the Mexican authorities at Matamoros, and in attempting to effect my escape, was cruelly and savagely beaten by a couple of Mexican officers. In pursuance of a determination I formed at the time of receiving those injuries, I proceeded yesterday to inflict chastisement, with a cowskin, on the last of these officers, whom I accidentaly met at the store of Mr. Peter Hale on Commercial street having some months before, went through a like pleasant exercise on the body of his compeer. While luxuriating in the bliss of satisfied revenge, the aforesaid George Washington McCook arrested and sent me to the guard house. . . ." Clay was a property holder and Matamoros business man. He published this advertisement in the February 13 issue of the *Flag*: TRANSPORTATION OF GOODS Capt. J. H. Clay would re-

spectfully inform merchants and others, that he is prepared to transport merchandize of every description from Point Isabel to this city; and as he has some forty carts employed; and is well acquainted with this region of country, he can attend to all orders and execute them with safety and despatch."

133. Ibid., December 19, 1846. Don Agapito Longoria was the 3rd Alcade of Matamoros.

134. Ibid., December 19, 1846. Sergeant Gurdon A. Babcock, Company I, 8th Infantry, had just arrived from Monterrey to visit his wife and children in Matamoros. He was evidently murdered for two watches that he was attempting to sell. His body was found completely stripped of clothing a short distance from the main plaza. He had been stabbed some fifteen times. Babcock had participated in the battles of Palo Alto, Resaca de la Palma, and the siege of Monterrey, only to return to Matamoros to fall prey to assassins.

135. Malone, *DAB*, p. 49. Jacob Brinkerhoff was an Ohio legislator. A Democrat, he served two terms in the House of Representatives from 1843 to 1847.

136. *American Flag*, December 23, 1846. The two "strolling actors," "Yankee Bill" (William Haynes) a dancer, and "the delectable Dr. McDonald" (Charles McDonald) were caught carrying a purloined trunk down the streets of Matamoros late at night. Both men claimed to have saved the trunk from a gang of Mexican thieves and were transporting it to safety when apprehended.

137. Heitman, *Register*, vol. 1, p. 573. Major General Thomas Sidney Jesup joined the service in 1808. He was promoted to brevet lieutenant colonel for distinguished service at the battle of Chippewa U C on July 5, 1814, and colonel on July 25 for his actions in the battle of Niagara.

138. Erna Risch, *Quartermaster Support of the Army: A History of the Corps, 1775–1939* (Washington: QM Historian's Office, 1962), p. 273. In response to the harsh and constant criticism of the Quartermaster Corps by Taylor, General Thomas Jesup traveled from New Orleans to Brazos Santiago to inspect the supply process personally. Taylor had complained about lack of pontoon bridges, steamboats, wagons and mules. But Jesup and his men had responded quite efficiently to the various crises that arose in the northern campaign.

139. Malone, *DAB*, pp. 457–58. The name emblazoned on the wagon sheet evidentally referred to Thomas Corwin, whose distinguished public career included the governorship of Ohio, United States Senator, and secretary of the treasury in the administration of Millard Fillmore. The Whigs had just lost their bid to place Henry Clay in the White

House, but had regained control of the Ohio Legislature, sending Corwin to the United States Senate.

140. *Dicconario Porrúa*, p. 2206. José de Urrea (1797–1849) was a general in the Mexican army during the invasion of Texas in 1836. Urrea served in the northern states of Mexico and principally fought the Comanche Indians that raided Mexico. Urrea aligned himself with Santa Anna during the many political intrigues that swept Mexico between 1838 and and 1848. In the early part of 1847, Urrea led a division of Mexican cavalry into northern Mexico through Tula Pass to interdict Taylor's line of supply and communication from the Rio Grande and to threaten the towns along that river. His forces were able to burn a major supply train and to isolate Taylor's forces at Saltillo for more than two months. After Santa Anna's army retreated from the Saltillo area, Taylor mounted an expedition that drove Urrea's division from northern Mexico and reestablished communications and opened supply routes.

141. *Monumentos Historicós Inmuebles*, vol. 1, p. 519. The main cathedral in Matamoros, Catedral de Nuestra Señora del Refugio, is still standing. Construction began in 1825 and was completed six years later. The church was damaged by a hurricane in 1844 which explains why the building was not finished when Curtis reported on it. The church has been altered from its original design by changes in the cupolas.

142. *Dicconario Porrúa*, p. 345. Antonio Canales (1800?–1852?) was a lawyer born in Monterrey. Canales was one of the men who plotted to free northern Mexico from the central government and to establish the Republic of the Rio Grande. His forces, which had enlisted the services of many Texans, were defeated at Saltillo in 1839. The Texans under Canales felt they had been betrayed by him and swore a blood oath against him. Canales and his force of irregulars helped capture the Texans that attacked Mier on December 26, 1842, in the incident that came to be known as the Mier Expedition. During the Mexican War Canales sided with Mexico and established a large force of rancheros who fought a guerrilla campaign against the United States forces in northern Mexico from 1846 until 1848. His hit-and-run methods of attack earned him the name of "Chapperal [sic] Fox" by his American adversaries. With the help of General José Urrea's men, Canales and other guerrilla leaders were able to interdict all supply and communication lines to Taylor's forces in Saltillo for more than two months during the early part of 1847. This unwritten part of the Mexican War was marked by atrocities committed by both sides on the helpless Mexican civilian population. By late 1847, a wide path of

destruction — dotted by the charred remnants of haciendas and villages — was visible along the principal roads in northern Mexico. In 1851 following the war, Canales became governor of the State of Tamaulipas. Gustav Dreisel gave this eyewitness description of the man: "Canales, a little man of brown complexion, had eyes as false as those of a mustang." See, Max Freund, *Gustav Dresel's Houston Journal* (Austin: University of Texas Press, 1954), p. 101.

143. Anna Dominga Garza de Chapa (Mrs. Menchaca) was listed as one of thirty-eight women who signed a petition directed to Don Antonio Lopez de Santa Anna, then President of the Republic of Mexico. "The petitioners beg your excellency to grant them the favor they have solicited for the prisoners, which is the commutation of the sentence of death to any other punishment which the well accredited humanity of your Excellency may think proper." The prisoners were Texans being held in Matamoros, captured during the 1836 Mexican expedition into Texas, and sentenced to death for taking up arms in rebellion against Mexico. The petition met with favor for a letter addressed to Miss [sic] Dona Loreto Allende de Loyero, the first signatory reads: "Matamoros, February 8, 1837 Madame — The prisoners of war who have been lately released by his Excellency, Major General D. Nicholas Bravo, beg leave to tender through you, to the ladies of Matamoros, their warmest gratitude for their interference in behalf of our lives and liberty. To you, Madame, particularly, do we feel that we are indebted for this great boon, and for all the happiness we shall ever enjoy. It but furnishes another proof of the great truth that the females of all countries are the best friends of humanity — and that without their moral influence, the world would, indeed, become a vast wilderness. That you, Madame, our preserver, in common with your sisters of Matamoros, may enjoy all the happiness our natures are capable of, we shall never cease to pray. Most respectfully, P. Jenks Mahan S. S. Curtis Nelson Jones L. H. Kerr W. B. Benson R. W. Pittman J. W. Bryan [Ms torn] Francis." See, *American Flag*, January 13, 1847.

144. Chance, *Mexican War Journal*, pp. 104–05, 159. General Winfield Scott arrived at Camargo on January 3, 1847, aboard the steamboat *Corvette* hoping to meet with General Taylor. Scott had ordered about 9,000 of Taylor's regular army troops, including General Worth's division, to the mouth of the Rio Grande. These troops were to form the backbone of the invasion force that was to attack Vera Cruz. Scott thought that the forces remaining with Taylor would stay on the defensive, only securing territory thus far captured in northern Mexico. But General Taylor had previously committed American troops for the capture of Victoria, capitol of Tamaulipas, and was far away. Scott

scribbled out orders for the troop movements and left Camargo the same day. The actions of Scott and the Polk administration to strip Taylor of his regular forces placed the 4,800 volunteers with Taylor in grave peril. From captured dispatches, Santa Anna soon found out about the weakened condition of Taylor's troops at Saltillo and quickly prepared his army for an attack.

145. Heitman, *Register*, vol. 2, p. 54. Captain Milton A. Haynes was a member of the Tennessee Mounted Volunteers.

146. Malone, *DAB*, vols. 15–16, pp. 315–16. John Anthony Quitman was born on September 1, 1798, in Rhinebeck, New York. He studied for the law and moved to Natchez, Mississippi, where in 1827 he was elected to the state legislature. In 1836 he organized a company of volunteer militia to aid Texans in their revolt against Mexico, but the company arrived in Texas too late to participate in the armed conflict. At the declaration of war against Mexico in 1846, Quitman was commissioned brigadier general of volunteers by President Polk. Quitman led a brigade of volunteers at the battle of Monterrey and was later transferred to Scott's army and led the attack on Mexico City. He was promoted to the rank of major general and served as military governor of Mexico City. In 1849, Quitman was elected governor of Mississippi, but resigned that position in 1850 when he was indicted by a federal grand jury in New Orleans for violation of the neutrality laws. He had been associated with Narcisso Lopez, a revolutionary who attempted to overthrow Spanish rule in Cuba. The case against Quitman was later dismissed. Quitman died at his home near Natchez on July 17, 1858.

147. Linares is a Mexican town in the state of Nuevo Leon about eighty miles southeast of Monterrey.

148. Bauer, *The Mexican War*, pp. 204–05. General Worth's garrison at Saltillo, probably numbering no more than 1,000 troops, had been threatened by Santa Anna's forces at San Luis Potosi. The Mexican force included 9,000 infantry, 4,000 cavalry, and twelve guns. Worth sent word for reinforcements from the other forces in the area, which quickly assembled at Saltillo, so quickly, in fact, that Santa Anna despaired of victory and recalled his columns, some of whom had reached as far north as Matehuala. American soldiers were irritated by the forced marches to Saltillo, and referred to this episode as "Worth's Stampede."

149. Ibid., p. 205. General John Ellis Wool's column had been garrisoned at Parras when it received an express on December 17, 1846, from General Worth at Saltillo requesting aid. Wool put his command

on the road the same day and by a forced march of 120 miles reached Agua Nueva, south of Saltillo, on December 21, 1846.

150. *American Flag*, January 4, 1847. The *Flag* reported that, "Col Curtis' boys have received and donned their new toggery, and greatly are they improved in personal appearance. Their new uniform is dark blue — fits as if each man had been measured for it, and will stand service." Two daguerreotypes at the Amon Carter Museum in Fort Worth, Texas, show soldiers in the Saltillo streets. These men may be the the 3rd Ohio dressed in their new uniforms. One image shows the unit in precise formation, a matter of much pride to Colonel Curtis. See, Martha A. Sandweiss, Rick Stewart, Ben W. Huseman, *Eyewitness to War: Prints and Daguerreotypes of the Mexican War, 1846–1848* (Washington: Smithsonian Institution Press, 1989), pp. 212–13.

151. *American Flag*, July 19, 1846, April 18, 1847. Corporal Michael O'Sullivan, of Company E, 3rd Infantry Regiment, U.S.A., was apparently a favorite in Matamoros and the *Flag* of July 19, reported that "The subscribers to the fund for presenting Corporals O'Sullivan, and Farrell, and Sergeants Maloney and McCabe with some token of public approbation, met at Banks' Arcade on the 10th and appointed an executive committee to carry out the designs of the subscribers. Corporal O'Sullivan, on the 24th of June, 1847, received his commission as lieutenant of the 3rd Infantry Regiment. Corporal O'Sullivan was reported to have . . . on the memorable 9th of May captured Marengo [Captain Mejia], General La Vega's aid-de-camp, receiving six sabre cuts in the face with his victory."

152. Heitman, *Register*, vol. 2, p. 50. Colonel James P. Drake led the 1st Indiana Infantry.

153. Claude M. Fuess, *The Life of Caleb Cushing* (Hamden, Connecticut: Archon Books, 1965), vol. 2, p. 45. The Spanish consul at Matamoros, Don Juan Lopez, did not have the best reputation with Caleb Cushing, one of the later military governors of Matamoros. Cushing confiscated a large quantity of embargoed "spiritous liquors" in Lopez' possession.

154. Heitman, *Register*, vol. 1, pg 532. Lieutenant Colonel Ethan Allen Hitchcock graduated from West Point in 1814. He was promoted to brevet colonel for gallantry at the battles of Contreras and Churubusco and to brigadier general for his services at the battle of Molino del Rey. He was mustered out of the service on October 1, 1867, at the rank of major general.

155. Ibid., vol. 1, p. 900. Major John Lind Smith entered the service in 1813. He was promoted to brevet lieutenant colonel for his conduct

during the battle of Cerro Gordo and to colonel for his bravery at the battles of Contreras and Churubusco. He died on December 18, 1858.

156. *American Flag*, January 8, 13, 1847; Chance, *Mexican War Journal*, pp. 188–89. On January 8, the *Flag* reported that, "A young Mexican, well known in the city and very respectably connected, was found dead yesterday just without the town, a musket ball having passed entirely through his body. Colonel Clarke is using every endeavor to discover the murderer and bring him to punishment." Apparently, the assassins were never discovered. Colonel Curtis, however, through his adjutant did issue the following: "Head Quarters, Matamoros, January 8, 1847. Orders No. 73 No non-commissioned officer or soldier will be allowed, hereafter, to leave the quarters, camps, or hospitals, with arms, unless ordered to do so on duty. Commanders of troops and the senior officers of hospitals will see this order fulfilled. All officers and soldiers, as they value the honor and reputation of their corps, will be vigilant and aiding in the detection and arrest of the person or persons concerned in the murder yesterday, after robbing him of his blanket, of an unoffending Mexican. By order of Colonel Clarke: Wm. D. Tidball, Lt. 3d O. Vols., Act. Adj."

157. Heitman, *Register*, vol. 2, p. 57. Captain John M. Wilson commanded Company B of the 1st Indiana Volunteers.

158. *American Flag*, July 24, 1846. "FRENCH RESTAURAT. — The undersigned have just opened on the Calle Teran a splendid EATING HOUSE, where at all times can be found every delicacy that the market affords. Active waiters are secured and prompt attention will be paid to patrons, Wines furnished at moderate charges. SIMON & Co."

159. Ibid., August 14, 1846. The establishment run by this intriguing French woman was quite likely the Coffee House, housed in the Customs House building on Commercial Street, "a few doors from the Square."

160. Ibid., July 31, October 7, 14, November 7, December 13, 1846, March 24, 1847. Darius Bacon, with a partner, ran a store on Commerical Street that sold wholesale and retail dry goods, groceries, and hardware. The partnership was terminated after October 31, 1846. Bacon later became involved with J. R. Everitt in a commission house at Mier. Bertrand Combe was the owner of the Exchange Hotel on Commercial Street near the main square. By December 10, 1846, partnerships involving O'Blenis, Combe, and Giroud, and O'Blenis and Combe were also dissolved. It may be a disputed claim from this partnership that Alcalde Menchaca had to decide. By March 24, 1847, Combe ran a billiard hall in which a fatal affray occurred. A Mr.

Mulligan shot H. C. D. La Rose through the head as a result of a "difficulty."

161. Kelley, *River of Lost Dreams*, p. 38; *American Flag*, January 20, 1847. Two of the merchants referred to were Sewell T. Taylor and Samuel A. Belden. The others remain unknown.

162. Colonel Fitzpatrick is something of a mystery. The 1850 Census for Cameron County lists a resident of Brownsville named Richard Fitzpatrick, fifty years old, born in South Carolina. Fitzpatrick lists his occupation as "gentleman."

163. Chance, *Mexican War Journal*, p. 164. As Worth's division was loading onto steamboats to proceed downriver, an observer reported that he "got a look at Genl. Worth — I expected to see a young looking man — and he is as to carriage and deportment but his hair is gray." But the general still had fire in his heart according to a "rough informant." Shortly after the *Corvette* cast off, she stuck fast on a sand bank. The informant reported: "the Genl. is tearing out his hair . . . he has cursed the bow off the boat d__ning quartermasters steam boat captains and all creation."

164. Malone, *DAB*, pp. 619–20. In April, 1837, Samuel Curtis became chief engineer on the Muskingum River (in eastern Ohio) improvement project and served in that capacity until May, 1839.

165. Heitman, *Register*, vol. 2, p. 56; Michael, "Ohio and the Mexican War," p. 77. Captain Sanders W. Johnston of the 1st Ohio Volunteers escorted the body of General Thomas Hamer to Ohio. Hamer died of disease on December 2, 1846, in camp near Monterrey. The Ohio legislature sent a delegation to Mexico to bring the remains home for a proper burial. Hamer was laid to rest in Georgetown, Ohio, at a funeral conducted by the Masons. A crowd estimated at between 7,000 and 10,000 people attended to pay their last respects to this popular politican.

166. Ibid., vol. 1, p. 299. Lieutenant Colonel Thomas Childs graduated from West Point in 1813. He was promoted to colonel for gallantry exhibited at the battles of Palo Alto and Resaca de la Palma and to brigadier general for his actions in the defense of Pueblo on October 12, 1847.

167. Ibid., vol. 1, p. 502. Colonel William Selby Harney entered the service in 1818. He was promoted to brigadier general for gallantry at the battle of Cerro Gordo. Harney retired in 1863 at the rank of major general.

168. Ibid., vol. 1, p. 387. Captain James Duncan graduated from West Point on 1831. He was promoted to the rank of brevet major for actions at Palo Alto, to lieutenant colonel for bravery at Resaca de la

Palma, and to colonel for gallantry at Monterrey. Duncan died on July 3, 1849.

169. Malone, *DAB*, vol. 20, pp. 536–37. William Jenkins Worth was born in Hudson, Columbia County, New York, on March 1, 1794. He received a common school education and was in the mercantile business when the War of 1812 began. He was appointed first lieutenant in the Twenty-third Infantry and was selected by General Winfield Scott as Scott's aid-de-camp. Worth fought with great valor at Chippewa and Lundy's Lane, receiving a serious wound in the latter battle. The wound, at first thought to be fatal, kept him confined to his bed for a year and left him lame for the remainder of his life. At the rank of brevet major, Worth became commandant of the United States Military Academy, a post he held from 1820 to 1828. He was promoted to colonel in 1838 and assumed command of the Eighth Infantry, which fought with valor in the Seminole War. He led the American division that captured the heights on the western side of Monterrey and was promoted to brevet major general on September 23, 1846, for this action. Worth was awarded a sword by Congress on March 2, 1847, for gallantry at Monterrey. He was transferred to Scott's army and fought in all the battles in central Mexico from Vera Cruz to Mexico City, always exhibiting great skill and personal initiative. After the war, he was placed in command of the Department of Texas. He died of cholera on May 7, 1849.

170. Heitman, *Register*, vol. 1, p. 616. Captain Charles H. Larnard graduated from West Point in 1827. He was promoted to brevet major for his actions at Palo Alto and Resaca de la Palma. He drowned on March 27, 1854.

171. The village of Mier, about eighteen miles west of Camargo, is the site attacked by Texian forces on December 25, 1842. The Texians, under the leadership of Colonel William S. Fisher were captured the next day by forces under Antonio Canales and General Pedro Ampudia. The walls of several buildings in this quaint and interesting village still bear the scars of that battle.

172. *American Flag*, January 30, February 3, 1847. The *Flag* reported that "outrages of a very aggravated character have recently been committed by some of the regulars in General Worth's Division upon the persons and property of Mexicans on the ranchos below the city." Within a week, Lieutenant George Deas wrote the editor requesting a "correction." Deas blamed "a few discharged soldiers and a negro boy, who were, at the time, intoxicated. All concerned were promptly arrested and tried by a court martial — the Mexicans testifying. But one

was convicted of any grevious misconduct, and he will be satisfactorily punished." If Lieutenant Deas' letter is interpreted correctly, it appears that civilians were tried and punished in a military court.

173. Heitman, *Register*, vol. 1, pg 363. Lieutenant George Deas entered the service in 1838. He was promoted to brevet major for gallantry at the battles of Contreras and Churubusco. He resigned on February 25, 1861, and served as lieutenant colonel in the Confederate Army from 1861 to 1865.

174. Ibid., vol. 1, p. 296. Captain William Chapman graduated from West Point in 1827. He was promoted to the rank of brevet major for gallantry at the battles of Contreras and Churubusco, to the rank of lieutenant colonel for his services at Molino del Rey, and to the rank of colonel for bravery at the Battle of Bull Run. Chapman retired from the service in 1863 and died in 1887.

Chapter 3: Suspense in Camargo

1. 30th Congress, 1st Session. House Executive Document No. 60. Mexican War Correspondence, N. S. Clarke to Major George A. McCall, p. 850.

2. Chance, *Mexican War Journal*, p. 208.

3. Ibid., p. 209.

4. Smith, *The War With Mexico*, vol. 2, p. 161.

5. Quaife, *The Diary of James K. Polk*, vol. 2, pp. 436–39. According to Polk's diary entry for March 23, 1847 ". . . Dr. J. [Jarvis] was direct from the army in Mexico, and was the bearer of despatches from Col. Curtis of the Ohio Volunteers, commanding at Camargo, dated on the 2nd Instant. . . . Col. Curtis must have been greatly and unnecessarily alarmed, for he called for reinforcements of fifty thousand men. . . . I [President Polk] had a long conversation with Dr. Jarvis, and became fully satisfied that the rumours of the perilous condition of the army on the line of the Rio Grande were greatly exaggerated. If Gen'l Taylor has met with any disaster, it is certain that it has proceeded from his own imprudence & want of military forecast & skill, in advancing beyond Monterey where it was expected he would have taken his position. Had he taken that position, his rear could not have been occupied by the enemy & his supplies cut off, as they have been."

6. Henderson Family Papers, "Curtis to Gov. Henderson, March 2, 1847." Center for American History, University of Texas, Austin.

7. W. P. Lane, *The Adventures and Recollections of General Walter P. Lane. . . .* (Austin: Jenkins Publishing Co., 1970), pp. 57–59. Glanton's murderous activities finally caused General Taylor to order his

arrest in Monterrey. While Walter P. Lane stalled for him, Glanton mounted his faithful steed "Old Charley," speeding away to make good his escape.

8. *American Flag*, July 4, 1846. The village of Guadaloupe on the Rio Grande was about three leagues (nine miles) from Matamoros and contained a population of "about 200 souls; herdsmen and farmers, grazing and water abundant."

9. *Forest Trees of Texas*, p. 124. The Texas Porlieria (Porlieria augustifolia [Engelm. A. Gray]) is an evergreen growing in south Texas with the common name of "Guayacan," and is sometimes referred to as "guaiacum." The wood is heavy, hard, and durable — the hardest wood in Texas and in the United States. "The lignum-vitae of commerce is produced from another species."

10. *Forest Trees of Texas*, p. 63. The cedar elm (Ulmus crassifolia Nutt.) is a native tree commonly seen along the banks of the Rio Grande.

11. Heitman, *Register*, vol. 2, pp. 55, 111. Lieutenant Arthur Higgins served in 3rd Ohio. During the Civil War, he served as lieutenant colonel of 170th Ohio Infantry.

12. Tula Pass is about fifty miles southwest of Ciudad Victoria. It is a sheer mountain pass through the Sierra Madre connecting central and northern Mexico. In the time of the Mexican War, the pass could only be traversed by light cavalry without wagons or artillery.

13. *American Flag*, July 4, 1846. Reynosa Viejo (Old Reynosa), was the original site for the city but the area was low and prone to flooding. This rancho is six leagues (eighteen miles) upstream from Reynosa on the Rio Grande and consisted of corn and stock farms populated by 500 people.

14. *American Flag*, July 4, 1846. Rancho Tepehuaje was five leagues southeast of Camargo. The rancho was probably named for the tree native to this area known locally as "tepehuaje" (Leucaena pulverulenta [Schlecht] Benth).

15. *Monumentos Históricos Inmuebles*, vol. 2, p. 135. The beautiful church at Camargo, Parroquia Señora Santa Ana, was built by Franciscans around 1750. It remains today, fronting on Plaza Hidalgo and appearing almost as it did in the time of the Mexican War when it's image was captured by several lithographs appearing in newspapers and books of that time. The distinctive cupola can still be seen from several miles in any direction.

16. Chance, *Mexican War Journal*, p. 228. The village referred to by Curtis as "New Camargo" is known locally as "Villa Nueva." This

deserted village of stone and adobe buildings is located about two miles southwest of Camargo on a hill above the Rio San Juan floodplain.

17. Heitman, *Register*, vol. 1, p. 246. Captain Forbes Britton graduated from West Point in 1830. He was promoted to the rank of captain in February 16, 1847, and resigned his commission on July 16, 1850. He died on February 14, 1861.

18. Ibid., vol. 2, p. 57. Lieutenant Charles O. Joline was a soldier in 2nd Ohio Volunteers.

19. Ibid., vol. 2, p. 71. Major William Wall served in 2nd Ohio Volunteers.

20. Captain R. M. Sutton cannot be located in Heitman or other sources.

21. Chance, *Mexican War Journal*, pp. 181–85. The fort was built to guard the extensive supply depot located across the Rio San Juan from Camargo.

22. Heitman, *Register*, vol. 1, p. 691. Thomas Marshall was commissioned a brigadier general of volunteers in July, 1846, and honorably discharged on July 20, 1848.

23. Chance, *Mexican War Journal*, pp. 191–210. Colonel Morgan's expedition into northern Mexico is described in some detail by the accounts of Franklin Smith, one of its' members.

24. John J. Delaney, *Dictionary of Saints* (Garden City: Doubleday and Company, 1980) p. 136; Chance, *Mexican War Journal*, p. 251. China is a little village about seventy-five miles southwest of Camargo on the Rio San Juan. The city derives its name in a curious way from one of the saints, Phillip de las Casas, a Franciscan born in Mexico City, on May 1, 1571. On a return trip from the Phillipines to Mexico in 1596, his ship was driven off course by a storm and onto the coast of Japan. He was arrested there and crucified at Nagasaki on February 5, 1597, with twenty-five other Christians. Around 1776, the China villagers built a church to honor the man, now beatified as Saint Felipe de Jesus. The church was named Saint Felipe de Jesus de China, since the generic name "China" was applied to all oriental locations. The village that grew up around this church was referred to simply as "China," and to this day celebrates February 5th with a fiesta in honor of their patron saint.

25. Papers of Samuel Ryan Curtis, letter from Samuel R. Curtis to "Dear Brother, Feby 17th 1847" (Huntington Library). Curtis describes Camargo to his brother: "As a military post it [Camargo] is important, perhaps more so that any other point on the river because immense quantities of stores are placed here and here everything is transshipped from steam boats to wagons and mules. — The materials of war are

crowded into every corner. The plaza in front of my quarters, is one great store house of pork, beans, hard bread, soap and candles. Long trains of wagons, and multitudes of mules and muleteers are picketed on the opposite side."

26. Heitman, *Register*, vol. 2, p. 59. Captain James M. Love served in 3rd Ohio Volunteers.

27. Captain Sanforth Kidder of Matamoros was struck by tragedy while away. "Ventura Kidder, aged 11 years, son of Captain Senforth Kidder, jr., of this city was instantly killed by the accidental discharge of a gun in the hands of a Mexican servant attached to the family. Captain Kidder, acting as interpreter to Colonel Belknap — was absent from his family at the time. . . ." *American Flag*, May 22, 1847. See also the entry for September 3, 1846.

28. Chance, *Mexican War Journal*, pp. 167, 199; Ernesto Garza Sáenz, *Crónicas de Camargo*, "El Castillo del General Carvajal" (Victoria, Tamaulipas: Universidad Autónoma de Tamaulipas, 1980), pp. 19–22. Felipe Perez, one of Canales' men, was reported to have visited Camargo on the night of January 7, 1847. The noted guerrilla leader José María Carbajal had a palacial home in New Camargo known as "Carbajal's Castle." Only three columns of this castle currently remain, the building having been destroyed in 1856 by Mexican soldiers. Garza Sáenz includes a sketch of the structure.

29. Great clouds of caliche dust enveloped the headquarters of General Robert Patterson in Camargo during the fall of 1846. Franklin Smith, not an admirer of Patterson, records that: "The General issued an order that no wagons or horsemen should pass the street facing his palace door. — It is the prinicpal street leading to the landing and one side at least very inconvenient to go round. — Twenty times a day he and his orderly and the sentry on his pavement have been thrown into spasms at ignorant teamsters and horsemen endeavouring to pass. — He has consequently lost a great deal of sleep, had to swallow much unmilitary dust, and he's doubtless had a fit of indigestion. . . . Col. [Charles] May and Lieutentant [Forbes] Britton affecting not to understand the order or to forget it gallop past the palace door a dozen times a day with lightning speed and raising a devil of a dust lost in the clouds of their own creation before the sentinel has time to call a halt. Now to send Britton to the guard house would be an easy matter but to imprison the gallant May now the darling son of America and dear to all the hearts for galloping down in a public street in a town which he helped to conquer must give the Comdg. Genl pause. . . ." See, Chance, *Mexican War Journal*, pp. 70–71.

30. Heitman, *Register*, vol. 1, p. 340. Captain George Hampton

Crosman graduated from West Point in 1819. He received a promotion to brevet major for his services at Palo Alto and Resaca de la Palma. He retired on July 29, 1866, at the rank of major general.

31. Ibid., vol. 1, p. 954. Lorenzo Thomas graduated from West Point in 1819 and was assigned to the 4th Infantry. He was promoted to brevet major as assistant adjutant general of the same regiment in 1838. He was promoted to brevet lieutenant colonel in 1846 for gallantry and meritorious conduct in the "several conflicts at Monterey, Mexico" on September 23, 1846. Thomas rose to the rank of major general in the Union army and retired from the service in 1869. He died on March 2, 1875.

32. Ibid., vol. 2, p. 61; *American Flag*, March 6, May 15, 1847; Chance, *Mexican War Journal*, pp. 133, 142, 155; *The National Cyclopedia of American Biography*, vol. 8, p. 251–52. Captain Thomas F. Marshall served in the Kentucky Cavalry. A former member of Congress from Kentucky, he was considered one of the foremost public speakers of his day. Marshall delivered an oratorical first, as reported by the *Flag*: "WASHINGTON'S BIRTH-DAY. — This ever memorable day was celebrated by the Americans of all classes at and about Camargo. Thomas F. Marshall, of the Kentucky Cavalry, pronounced an oration in his usual eloquent style, and the day passed off in harmonious order." Marshall was, by all accounts, rather hot tempered and rash when angry, and loved to partake of spiritous liquids. The *Flag* printed this denial of one of Marshall's duels: "It has been rumored here for several days that a duel has taken place in Monterrey, between Capt. Montgomery, Quartermaster at that post and Capt. Thomas F. Marshall of the Ky. Cavalry, in which the former was killed. We are happy to contradict this rumor. . . ." Not all of his duels were settled without bloodshed. He was disabled by one opponent and wounded J. Watson Webb, editor of the New York *Courier and Enquirer* who had written an article about Marshall that displeased him. Marshall was one of those individuals who could coin the phrases often quoted by others. When informed of the death of the noted horseman and famous artillerist Randolph Ridgely, Marshall exclaimed, "As well might one expect to hear of an eagle dying from the fall of his own wings as to hear of Randolph Ridgely's dying from the fall of his horse."

33. Samuel Chamberlain, *Recollections of a Rogue* (London: Museum Press Limited, 1957) pp. 106–13. Agua Nueva is a small village about fifteen miles south of Saltillo. General Taylor had encamped his army on a broad tableland as late as February 20, 1847. On receiving reports of the size of Santa Anna's army which was advancing upon Saltillo, however, Taylor abandoned the village and retreated towards

Angostura Pass, a more secure defensive site. The village was burned by retreating American forces and that event is captured by one of Samuel Chamberlain's watercolors. The little church now standing at Agua Nueva bears a strong resemblence to the earlier one pictured by Chamberlain.

34. Chance, *Mexican War Journal*, p. 174. Troops of the 2nd Ohio Regiment, under the command of Major William Wall built an earthen fort on the west side of the Rio San Juan opposite Camargo. No traces of this fort can be found today.

35. Way, *Packet Directory*, pp. 144, 194, 196, 258. The Captain Pratt mentioned could be either Captain Oscar H. Pratt, later master of the *Elephant* in 1854; Captain C. H. Pratt, master prior to the Mexican War of the *Governor Briggs*; Captain Julius A. Pratt, later master of the *Grand Bay*; or Captain P. D. Pratt, later master of the *Joseph Pierce*.

36. Peterson, *Birds of Texas*, p. 75. According to Curtis' description of a "small bluish top knot on head," he must have seen Gambel's quail (Lophortyx gambelii), not generally found so far east in the Trans-Pecos.

37. This particular quotation is not found in the Book of Psalms and may be a paraphrase.

38. The city of Montemorelos is about fifty miles southeast of Monterrey in the heart of the citrus and sugar cane growing region of northern Mexico.

39. Fulton, *Josiah Gregg*, vol. 1, p. 359; *American Flag*, July 7, 1846. The village of Marin (San Carlos de Marin) is about twenty miles northeast of Monterrey. At the time of the Mexican War Marin had a population of more than 3,000 persons.

40. Spurlin, *Texas Veterans*, p. 167. The Texans then crossing the river were members of Captain John H. Connor's Company of Thomas J. Smith's Battalion of Mounted Volunteers. The company was mustered into service September 2, 1846, and was composed of men recruited from around the vicinity of Castroville. The company was mustered out on September 25, 1847.

41. Heitman, *Register*, vol. 1, p. 556. Captain Henry Jackson Hunt graduated from West Point in 1835. He was promoted to the rank of brevet captain for his services in the battles of Contreras and Churubusco and to the rank of major for his actions at Chapultepec. He retired from the service at the rank of colonel on September 14, 1883.

42. Ibid., vol. 1, p. 993. Lieutenant Robert A. Waynewright graduated from West Point in 1831, reaching the rank of brevet colonel before his death on December 22, 1866.

43. Ibid., vol. 1, p. 213. James Gilchrist Benton graduated from

West Point in 1838 and served in the Ordnance Department throughout his career. He retired at the rank of colonel in 1879 and died on August 23, 1881.

44. Ibid., vol. 2, p. 66. Captain Hobby Reynolds served in 2nd Ohio.

45. The rancho Ramos is about twenty-eight miles northeast of Monterrey and had a population of about 100 persons during the Mexican War. The traveler of that time could acquire "meat and corn, wood and water," according to the *American Flag* for July 7, 1846.

46. J. Frank Dobie, "Mustang Gray: Fact, Tradition, and Song," *Tone the Bell Easy* (Publications of the Texas Folk-lore Society, No. 10, 1932); John J. Linn, *Reminiscences of Fifty Years in Texas* (New York: privately published, 1883), pp. 322–24; Spurlin, *Texas Volunteers*, pp. 151, 190; Smith, *Chile Con Carne*, p. 294; *American Flag*, March 13, 20, July 3, 1847, March 4, 1848; Chamberlain, *Recollections of a Rogue*; Walter P. Lane, *The Adventures and Recollections of General Walter P. Lane* (Austin: Pemberton Press, 1970), pp. 49–74. Colonel Curtis' appeal for reinforcements was answered by two companies of Texas Mounted Volunteers, among them some of the most desperate and lawless men on the entire frontier. The first company, from Corpus Christi, was led by the infamous Mabry B. (Mustang) Gray. Gray came to Texas from South Carolina in January, 1835, and fought in the Battle of San Jacinto. He migrated to south Texas, and there became one of Ewen Cameron's "Cow-Boys" who were prominent in the violent border wars that took place south of the Nueces River in the decade between San Jacinto and Palo Alto. John Linn, a resident of Victoria, Texas, during those stormy times remembered the "Cow-Boys" as a "company of organized bandits and cut-throats," and Mabry Gray as an "assassin" and a "moral monstrosity." Linn described in detail the murder by the cowboys of seven Mexicans from Camargo visiting Victoria on a trading mission. Even Compton Smith, an admitted ranger partisan, referred to this company as a "gang of miscreants under the leadership of 'Mustang Gray.'" Smith reported that "This party, in cold blood, murdered almost the entire male population of the rancho of Guadalupe, — where not a single weapon, offensive or defensive could be found! Their only object being plunder." Gray's company was disbanded by July 17, 1847, but Gray remained on the border in some unknown capacity. The *Flag* reports his death in Camargo on February 26, 1848, after an illness of several weeks. According to his wishes his body was brought to the Texas side and buried in Rio Grande City. The unmarked grave could be found as late as the 1860s but has now been lost. Mustang Gray was the type of man of which

legends are made, and in his case a romantic novel was written of his life (*Mustang Gray*, by Jere Clemens), a special rope knot used by cowhands (the Mustang Gray loop), and of course his skills as a rider (he once rode his horse up a flight of stairs and into a saloon). A famous ballad about him was written, according to Dobie, by James T. Lytle, a Texas Ranger. Dobie claims the ballad has been sung to uneasy herds of longhorns by waddys and brushpoppers on night duty all the way from south Texas to the Canadian border.

The three ranger companies that came from San Antonio to aid Curtis were led by Captain Walter P. Lane, another San Jacinto veteran, Captain Bob Taylor from Bonham, and Captain G. W. Adams from Victoria. Lane's company contained among its members such unsavory characters as John Glanton, who can only be characterized as a pathological murderer. Glanton's murder of a card player in a San Antonio saloon and his organization of a band of "scalp hunters," as found in Chamberlain's book, paint a very dark picture. Lane mentioned in his autobiography his success in stemming guerrilla activity in northern Mexico by methods left to the imagination of the reader. He soon found himself at odds with General Taylor, however, who accused his company of acting "in a manner unbecoming United States soldiers."

47. J. Lee and Lillian J. Stambaugh, *The Lower Rio Grande Valley of Texas* (Austin: The Jenkins Publishing Co., 1974), p. 89. Henry Clay Davis was born in Kentucky and came to Texas in 1833. After the Texas Revolution he lived in Camargo, Mexico. While there he married María Hilaria de la Garza, granddaughter of Francisco de la Garza Martínez. As a wedding present he was given Porcion 80, a land grant north of the Rio Grande that came to be known as Rancho Davis. Davis built a two-story brick home on this site. The settlement would later become Rio Grande City.

48. *American Flag*, April 18, 1847. That "irishman" from Mier was John Hayes.

49. Chance, *Mexican War Journal*, p. 241 n. 13. Puntiagudo, now known as "General Trevino," is a small village about fifty miles southwest of Camargo along the main road from Camargo to Monterrey.

50. Spurlin, *Texas Veterans*, p. 167. Lieutenant William G. Jett.

51. Chance, *Mexican War Journal*, p. 240 n. 6. Guardado Abajo is a small Mexican village about nine miles up the Rio Grande from Camargo on the route to Monterrey taken by the American army.

52. Webb, *Handbook of Texas*, vol. 2, pp. 13–14. Mirabeau B. Lamar was born near Louisville, Georgia, on August 16, 1789. He served as secretary to Governor George M. Troup, edited the *Enquirer*, a Co-

lumbus, Georgia, newspaper and was elected to one term as a state senator in Georgia. After a brief trip to Texas in 1835, he returned to Georgia to settle his affairs and moved to Texas. He joined the Texas army as a private. As a result of his gallantry and heroism he rose to the rank of colonel and commanded the cavalry. Lamar was elected the first vice-president and the second president of the Republic of Texas. Lamar's term of office as president is probably best remembered for his proposal to establish a system of public education endowed by public lands which became law on January 26, 1839. In the Mexican War, he served as inspector and adjutant for James Pinckney Henderson's Texas Division and commanded a company of Texans stationed at Laredo. Lamar served with gallantry at Monterrey. His service was remembered fondly by Jefferson Davis in a speech delivered some three decades later: "At Monterrey, with a bright red vest, heedless of danger, [Lamar] rushed into the thickest of the fray, and, with the cry of 'Brave boys, Americans are never afraid!', at the head of the gallant Second regiment, charged home to victory. He was an ideal Texan — a man of rare genius and tender affection." See, Monroe and McIntosh, *The Papers of Jefferson Davis*, vol. 3, p. 66.

53. Chance, *Mexican War Journal*, pp. 207–08; Benham, "Recollections of Mexico," p. 647. Mexicans caught spying on their countrymen were often put to death by torture. Benham noted that, "The usual penalty of these Mexicans detected as our spies or couriers, was hanging alive by the heels to a tree by the road-side. . . . The withered remains of one of these couriers (sent up by Colonel Morgan of Ohio from Comargo) were discovered, so suspended, with the appearance of death in great agony, the despatches having been detected in their place of deposit, sewed up between the inner and outer sole of the shoe."

54. Heitman, *Register*, vol. 1, p. 415. Lieutenant Colonel Thomas Turner Fauntleroy entered the service in 1836 and served in the 1st Dragoons. He resigned his commission on May 13, 1861, and served as brigadier general in the Virginia Volunteers of the Confederate Army.

55. Ibid., vol. 1, p. 815. Lieutenant Colonel Thomas Beverly Randolph graduated from West Point in 1808. He resigned his commission in 1815 and was elected lieutenant colonel of the Virginia Volunteers on January 7, 1847, and honorably mustered out of service on July 20, 1848.

56. Ibid., vol. 1, p. 571. Major Nathan Sturges Jarvis was a regular army surgeon.

57. Ibid., vol. 1, p. 974. Major George F. Turner was a regular army surgeon.

58. Ibid., vol. 2, p. 70. Lieutenant William D. Tidball served in the 3rd Ohio.

59. Joseph E. Chance, *Jefferson Davis's Mexican War Regiment* (Jackson: University Press of Mississippi, 1991), pp. 46, 50 61, 74, 126. Lieutenant William Henry Harrison Patterson served in the 1st Mississippi Regiment and was awarded a sword for bravery at the battle of Monterrey by the citizens of Charlottesville, Virginia.

60. Luther Giddings, *Sketches of the Campaign in Northern Mexico by an Officer of the First Regiment of Ohio Volunteers* (New York: George P. Putnam & Co., 1853), pp. 304, 324–25; Chamberlain, *Recollections of a Rogue*, pp. 175–78.

61. The village of Los Aldamas is about forty-five miles south of Camargo.

62. Chance, *Mexican War Regiment*, p. 195 n. 6. Rinconada Pass was one of the only routes through the Sierra Madre Oriental large enough to accommodate wagons. At this "corner," the intersection of two mountain ranges, is the infamous "Paso de la Muerto" where highwaymen laid in wait for merchants and travelers. At the time of the Mexican War travelers reported that the pass was lined with crosses commemorating the many murdered pilgrims. A modern two lane highway has been constructed through the pass and crosses still line the road, now commemorating victims of automobile accidents.

63. Fulton, *Josiah Gregg*, vol. 1, p. 359. The village of Salinas (El Valle de Salinas) is about twenty miles north of Monterrey where the Salinas river crossed the road from Monterrey to Monclova. Gregg estimated the population during the Mexican War at about 5,000.

64. Chance, *Mexican War Journal*, p. 252. The village of Paso del Zacate is about forty-five miles southwest of Camargo on the Rio San Juan. This village, now on the railroad line from Matamoros to Monterrey, is known currently as Estatión Zacate.

65. The Captain Hunter referred to cannot be identified with certainty but may be Captain Edward Hunter of the Arkansas Mounted Regiment, then on detached duty for a special mission.

Chapter 4: Victory at Saltillo

1. Heitman, *Register*, vol. 2, p. 52. Major Luther Giddings was a member of the 1st Ohio Regiment.

2. Scribner, *Camp Life*, p. 48. Canales Run, or Chicharonnes (fried pork rinds), is nineteen miles south of Mier on the Rio Alamo near "a beautiful cascade, constructed of stone and cement, in order to turn the channel through the town."

3. The Rio Alcantro is a stream running through the village of Mier. Farther south this stream is known as the Rio Alamo.

4. Chance, *Mexican War Regiment*, pp. 49, 93. The lancers were an elite unit of cavalry whose riders carried as their principal weapon a distinctive lance, usually nine feet in length and tipped with a long metal point. These weapons were not particularly effective against seasoned troops, but were greatly feared by the young American volunteers. Rumors abounded that the lance points were poisoned and that any wound from them resulted in a fatality. At Monterrey, they were used to commit excesses; one observer reported that the lancers "murdered indiscriminantly all the wounded Americans in that part of the field. The surgeons and their assistants, flying from the fate of their patients, were hotly pursued by the enemy. . . ."

5. Agua Leguas is a village about sixty miles west of Camargo with a population of about 1,500 persons at the time of the war. To the traveler, the *Flag* reported that "Agua Lejos" had an "abundance of all things necessary." *American Flag*, July 7, 1846.

6. Smith, *Chile Con Carne*, p. 315. Compton Smith, a surgeon serving in northern Mexico, blamed Curtis for the burning of Puntiaguda. "A few months after, on the passage of Col. Curtiss, of the 3rd Ohioans, this pretty village [Puntiaguda] was laid in ashes, in retaliation for some depredations which had been committed upon some of our trains, while on the road; and of which, there is no doubt, these people were entirely innocent."

7. Giddings, *Sketches*, pp. 289–327; *American Flag*, April 3, 1847. General Urrea's combined force of cavalry and guerrillas had driven off the tiny garrisons of American troops at Marin, Cerralvo, and Puntiaguda by March 1, 1847. These villages lay on the main wagon route between Monterrey and Camargo. Thus supplies and communication between Taylor's forces and the Rio Grande had been severed. To reopen communications, 250 men, three companies from the 1st Ohio and two from the 1st Kentucky with two pieces of field artillery set out from Monterrey. This force was to escort dispatch bearers from Saltillo with official reports of the victory at Buena Vista and a large train of 160 empty wagons to Camargo. The route between Pappagallos and Cerralvo passed through country that was covered with thick chaparral; only a narrow trail was cleared for the roadway. Consequently the line of wagons was strung out for several miles. Just before the passage of the head of this column into Cerralvo, the Mexican forces attacked. The Mexicans were able to burn forty wagons and detonate the ammunition wagon in a spectacular fireball. The American forces rallied,

however, and brought the remainder of the wagons to a park in Cerralvo, then occupied the city.

8. Heitman, *Register*, vol. 1, p. 172. Major Ripley Allen Arnold
graduated from West Point at some unknown date. He was promoted to
brevet major for his actions at Palo Alto and Resaca de la Palma. He
was murdered on September 6, 1853.

9. *Official Roster*, p. 440. Arthur Higgins was a 2nd Lieutenant in
Company D of the 3rd Ohio Regiment.

10. Smith, *Chile Con Carne*, pp. 359–61. The Colonel Romero
referred to by Curtis was Don Jesus Romero, a respected, wealthy ranchero from around Cerralvo. Before the war he had served as alcalde of
Cerralvo. Romero had on occasion been friendly to Americans, but
became a fearless guerrilla leader. He once captured part of an American mule train just as it entered Cerralvo and made off with the
supplies, even though three companies of Rangers and a battalion of the
16th Infantry were then stationed in the town.

11. The villagers of Ramos were thought by many to be implicated
in the wagon train massacre that occurred near there on February 24,
1846. In retaliation, an armed mob of teamsters, Texas volunteers, and
camp followers eager for loot burned the town and murdered many of
the citizens.

12. Heitman, *Register*, vol. 2, p. 44; Smith, *Chile Con Carne*, pp.
160–63; Giddings, *Sketches*, pp. 291, 303, 320; Benham, "Recollections
of Mexico," p. 647. Lieutenant William T. Barbour served in the 1st
Kentucky Regiment. A company of thirty soldiers under his command
escorted the enormous wagon train of 121 wagons and 137 pack mules
that was massacred on February 24, 1847, near Ramos. The wagon train
was ambushed and Barbour "found himself suddenly hemmed in on all
sides, when to resist, he well knew would insure the immediate massacre
of his little party." Barbour reportedly surrendered his command without firing a shot; that party stood by on a hillside idly watching the
Mexicans massacre the teamsters. The massacre may have been pro-
voked, though, by the previous behavior of some of their fellow drivers.
Benham reported that in January, 1847, while accompanying a wagon
train from Camargo to Monterrey, he observed teamsters committing
outrages on Mexican villagers. "Our train-masters were, some of them,
the most accomplished of the villains that are always found among the
camp-followers of an army in the field — the chief wagon-master being
afterwards, as I heard, the head of a gang of robbers on that very route;
and the teamsters, with arms in their hands for their own defence, not
being restrained by these wagon-masters (as they could not be by the
small volunteer escort), committed such outrages upon the inhabitants

along the route, especially near the half-way village of Cerralvo, that I declined to retain control of the train for the last day or two." On March 8, 1847, after recapturing Cerralvo, Major Giddings sent a message to General Urrea, offering to trade Lieutenant Barbour and his command for Mexican prisoners, but the despatch rider could not overtake General Urrea's rapidly fleeing cavalry, which was now retreating back to Tula Pass. Barbour and his command spent the remainder of the conflict as prisoners of war.

13. The village of Cadereyta is about twenty miles east of Monterrey and yet retains the quaint beauty reported on by Curtis.

14. Heitman, *Register*, vol. 1, p. 225. Major William Wallace Smith Bliss was a graduate of West Point. Bliss served as General Taylor's adjutant, and efficiently deleted many of Taylors "hells" and "damns" from his dispatches, shaping many of the "Old Ranchero's" written words into marvels of smooth diplomacy. Bliss was promoted to brevet major for his actions at Palo Alto and Resaca de la Palma and brevet lieutenant colonel for services at Buena Vista. Bliss married one of Taylor's daughters after the war. He died on August 5, 1853.

15. Guadeloupe was a large hacienda northeast of Monterrey and within sight of that city.

16. Smith, *The War With Mexico,* vol. 1, p. 239. The Bishop's Castle (La Obispada) is a massive stone building south of Monterrey perched atop Loma de Independencia. This deserted building had been fortified by the Mexicans to protect the southern entrances to Monterrey from the Saltillo road. In a daring flanking movement, General William J. Worth's division split from the main body of the American army and circled Monterrey to attack the weaker western defenses. The castle was captured by storm on September 22, 1846, by Worth and his men. It was on the slopes leading to the walls of this battlement that Richard Addison Gillespie, noted Texan, was felled by a Mexican shot. The Obispada still stands, now housing a museum. The older parts of this ornate building are literally dissolving from the effects of acid rain in this highly industrialized city.

17. The Black Fort (La Citadela) — an extremely strong work with quadrangular bastioned earthworks and a high parapet eleven and a half feet thick — was north of Monterrey and situated on a small eminence. Constructed from an unfinished stone cathedral on the site that was blackened with age, La Citadela was protected by a twelve-foot deep, partially completed ditch along the front. A garrison of 400 men defended the stronghold with eight guns and adequate supplies to last for more than a month. The elevation and strategic location allowed the defenders a crossfire to the other northeastern defenses of the city. The

fort was too strong to capture during the attack on Monterrey. From it accurate artillery fire was directed on the Americans throughout the battle. According to Wallace, at present a library and art gallery have been constructed on the site and a tablet "commemorates the historical significance of the location." See, Lee A. Wallace, Jr., "The First Regiment of Virginia Volunteers," *Virginia Magazine of History and Biography*, vol. 77, January 1969, p. 63; Smith, *The War With Mexico*, vol. 1, p. 233.

18. Heitman, *Register*, vol. 2, p. 63. Colonel Stephen Ormsbey was commander of the 1st Kentucky Infantry.

19. Ibid., vol. 2, p. 65. Captain William H. Ramsey served in the 1st Ohio.

20. Ibid., vol. 2, p. 53. Lieutenant Andrew Grubb served in 3rd Ohio Volunteers.

21. Smith, *War With Mexico*, vol. 1, p. 238. At the time of the war, Walnut Grove (Bosque de San Domingo) was a park of pecan and walnut trees watered by several springs. It was about three miles northwest of Monterrey. Taylor personally selected this site as the camp for the American army before the battle of Monterrey. The general continued to live on the site throughout his tour of duty in northern Mexico. A visitor there noted that, "a crowd of officers and men was collected about a simply dressed and plain looking individual, covered with a straw hat, that could not belong to any other person than to the 'Old Ranchero' himself, as the Mexicans used to call him. — I found him as plain and easy in his conversation as in his appearance. General Taylor seems to be very partial to his camping ground, on the Walnut Springs; and the fresh spring water and fine timber are sufficient reasons for it." See, Wislizenus, *A Tour to Northern Mexico*, p. 77.

22. Fulton, *Josiah Gregg*, vol. 1, p. 360. The Ojo Caliente was reported by Gregg to be a warm sulphur spring about four miles north of Monterrey. Gregg reported the water temperature at 106 degrees "with atmosphere in the sun nearly the same. . . . The spring is celebrated among natives for its laxative qualities, as a bath, but water is not used by them internally, I believe."

23. John S. D. Eisenhower, *So Far From God* (New York: Random House, 1989), p. 134. The spring (ojo de agua) that rose in the middle of the city and flowed north to join the Santa Catarina River was bridged in several locations. One of these bridges, La Purisima, was adorned in the center by a statue of the Virgin Mary. This bridge was defended stoutly by the Mexicans from a position on the west side. American forces were unable take the bridge during their attack of September 21, 1846.

24. Heitman, *Register*, vol. 2, p. 54. Captain Edward Hamilton was a member of the 1st Ohio.

25. Chance, *Mexican War Regiment*, pp. 65–68. The people who had viewed the defenses of Monterrey were almost in unanimous agreement with the opinions expressed by Curtis. One Mississippi Volunteer wrote, "And when I saw the place [Monterrey], every house of which is a perfect fort of itself and was fortified; when I saw every street barricaded and ditched . . . and that they had in addition to the private fortifications, some twenty or thirty forts and forty pieces of artillery, I cannot for the life of me see how we made such progress into the town as we did, without losing more men. . . ." See, *Vicksburg Whig*, October 27, 1846. General Taylor was criticized by many for the favorable terms of surrender granted to the Mexicans, but the most vociferous critics were in Washington, out of the range of bombs and balls. Most critics failed to understand or appreciate the perilous position of the American army on September 24, 1846.

26. Heitman, *Register*, vol. 1, p. 688. Major Joseph King F. Mansfield graduated from West Point in 1818. He was promoted to brevet major for his services in defense of Fort Brown, to lieutenant colonel for gallantry at Monterrey, and colonel for his actions in the battle of Buena Vista. He died of wounds received at the battle of Antietam on September 17, 1862, while serving at the rank of brigadier general.

27. Ibid., vol. 1, p. 333. Major Henry Knox Craig joined the service in 1813. He was promoted to lieutenant colonel for gallantry at Monterrey.

28. Santa Catarina was about fifteen miles south of Monterrey and just off the east side of the Saltillo road. This village was about one days travel by foot from Monterrey, so most infantry regiments traveling to Saltillo camped near this site. By December 17, 1846, Josiah Gregg reported his stay in Santa Catarina: "I reached camp late (long after most of the corps). . . . I walked out in search of supper, in the border of the town. Yet I was astonished that all the doors were barred against me; and the children within sometimes screamed with fright when I knocked. . . . Again next morning, on riding through town, women and children fled at the sight of me. I never learned (for I did not then suspect the cause) what outrages might have been committed the evening before by the volunteers, upon these poor ignorant villageois [sic], to inspire them with such horror at the sound or sight of an American." See, Fulton, *Josiah Gregg*, vol. 1, pp. 313–15.

29. Heitman, *Register*, vol. 1, p. 375. Major Roger Sherman Dix was an 1827 graduate of West Point. He was promoted to brevet lieutenant colonel for his bravery at Buena Vista. Samuel Chamberlain remem-

bered that Major Dix was instrumental in rallying the 2nd Illinois Regiment at Buena Vista when it faltered. "Dix seized the national colors from the Illinois regimental colorbearer, and waved the flag aloft from his huge bay horse, a most prominent target for Mexican gunners." See, Chamberlain, *Recollections of a Rogue*, p. 121. Chamberlain was so impressed by this act of bravery that he included a watercolor of the event in his diary. Dix was promoted to brevet colonel for gallantry at the battle of Buena Vista, February 23, 1847. He died on January 7, 1849.

30. Scribner, *Camp Life*, p. 53–54; Fulton, *Josiah Gregg*, vol. 1, pp. 316–17. The Rinconada Ranch (La Rinconada) was located halfway between Monterrey and Saltillo in the famous Rinconada Pass. Scribner described the town as being "built of mud . . . Tending to and from the town is a beautiful grove of trees, forming a shady archway above, and is interspersed with enormous century plants, the stalks of which rise from fifteen to twenty feet." Josiah Gregg, who passed through La Rinconada on December 18, 1846, was mortified to report that he could "see the volunteers tearing down houses for fuel — carrying away, not only rib-poles, etc. and fencing, but planks, benches, and even doors and tables and other furniture for fuel!" The next day Gregg visited the nearby little rancho of San Gregorio and reported that, "In the poor family, who resided there, there were two or three girls, for whom I could not but feel a compassion, when I went to leave, — as they timorously solicited me, for god's sake, not to go away, as when I was gone, they feared the volunteers would ill-treat them!" By January 5, 1847, Gregg returned to Rancho San Gregorio to find it depopulated, "the doors, door and window frames, etc. abstracted for fuel — two or three small houses torn down and burned, — palm-trees burned, etc."

31. Fulton, *Josiah Gregg*, vol. 1, p. 326. Gregg visited Ojo Caliente on January 5, 1847, and found it occupied, but the servants there "gave dreadful account of the depredations of the two regiments (Kentucky & Ohio) who had encamped there on the night of the first inst."

32. Ibid., vol. 1, p. 339. The Rancho Santa María was fifteen miles from Saltillo on the Monterrey road.

33. *American Flag*, February 17, 1847; Chamberlain, *Recollections of a Rogue*, pp. 133–35; Henry, *Campaign Sketches*, p. 246; Scott, *Encarnacion Prisoners*, p. 34. One of the surprises that greeted General Worth's column as it advanced to accept the surrender of Saltillo in November, 1846, was the sight of "four young women, habited in American dress" standing by the roadside three miles from the city. When queried as to why they were so far from home the ladies explained that they "were from New Jersey, and engaged in superintend-

ing the female operatives in a cotton and woolen factory hard by. . . ." Chamberlain described the factory as white-walled and surrounded by a garden of roses and other choice flowers "far diffent from the ugly piles that make our New England factories"; his diary includes a watercolor of the building. Chamberlain, the perpetual ladies man knew that the female in charge of the workers was a certain "freckled, snubbed nosed and red haired" Miss Caroline Porter, formerly of Lowell, Massachusetts, "who had come to Mexico three years before the war to teach the senoritas how to weave cotton cloth." All sources seem at variance as to who owned the cotton mill. Chamberlain states that the factory was owned by General Arista, Henry claims ownership for an Englishman, and Scott contends that the mill was "owned and operated by Irishmen." Perhaps several of these parties owned the mill as a joint venture.

Chapter 5: The War in Northern Mexico after Buena Vista

1. Justin Smith Transcripts, Latin American Collection, The University of Texas, Austin, Texas. "The Citizen Mariano Salas to my fellow citizens," April 21, 1847.

2. Executive Document No. 60, #41, p. 1138.

3. Ibid., pp. 1142–43.

4. Smith, The War With Mexico, vol. 2, p. 422.

5. Executive Document No. 60, #41, p. 1138; Giddings, Sketches, pp. 324–25. Giddings points an accusing finger at the Ranger Company of Captain Mabry "Mustang" Gray as the men who committed the massacre at Rancho Guadaloupe.

6. Chamberlain, Recollections of a Rogue, pp. 176–77.

7. Charles Adams Gulick, Jr., and Katherine Elliot, The Papers of Mirabeau Buonaparte Lamar (Austin: A. C. Baldwin & Sons, 1922), vol. 4, No. 2326, pp. 167–68, "1847, Apr. 4, A Canales to."

8. Executive Document No. 60, #53, p. 1178.

9. Giddings, Sketches, p. 335.

10. At the date of Curtis' arrival to Saltillo, the military force consisted of 1st and 2nd Illinois Infantry, 2nd and 3rd Indiana Infantry, 2nd Kentucky Infantry, several companies of the 2nd Kentucky Cavalry, several companies of the Arkansas Mounted Regiment, several companies of the 1st and 2nd Dragoons, and three batteries of artillery. The volunteer regiments had all been mustered for one year's service and their time was due to expire by May-June, 1847.

11. K. Jack Bauer (ed.), "General John E. Wool's Memoranda of the Battle of Buena Vista," Southwestern Historical Quarterly, vol. 77, July, 1973, pp. 111–23.

12. Herman J. Viola, "Zachary Taylor and the Indiana Volun-

teers," *Southwestern Historical Quarterly*, vol. 72, no. 3, pp. 335–46. Brigadier General Joseph Lane, commander of the Indiana Brigade, was angry over charges that the 2nd Indiana Regiment was guilty of cowardice and had run from the enemy at Buena Vista. General Lane blamed the commander of the 2nd Indiana, Colonel William A. Bowles, for the misconduct of the regiment and petitioned General Taylor to have Bowles court-martialed for cowardice. Taylor refused to do so; Lane then demanded that a court of inquiry be convened to investigate Lane's actions during the battle, hoping at least to clear himself from any hint of wrongdoing. The court cleared Lane of any charges on April 26, 1847. Colonel Bowles by this time, had also requested a court of inquiry to investigate his actions. This court convened on April 12, 1847, and concluded on April 27, 1847, that "throughout the engagement and during the whole day Colonel Bowles evinced no want of personal courage or bravery, but that he did manifest want of capacity and judgement as its commander." See, Perry, *Indiana in the Mexican War*, p. 311

13. Perry, *Indiana in the Mexican War*, p. 311. Colonel William A. Bowles, a physician from Orange County, Indiana, led the 2nd Indiana Volunteer Regiment. Bowles, as prescribed by the tradition of the volunteer militia, was popularly elected by vote of his troops to the rank of colonel. Bowles was "ignorant of company, battalion, and brigade drills," as brought out in a court of inquiry after the Battle of Buena Vista. He much preferred, as an amateur botanist, to take field trips to collect specimens rather than drill his men. Bowles was no coward, however, and after his men deserted their posts during the battle, he picked up a musket from the field and joined the Mississippi Regiment to fight as a private.

14. Sandweiss, et al, *Eyewitness to War*, p. 195. An excellent daguerreotype of John M. Washington, taken at Saltillo in 1847, is found therein.

15. Heitman, *Register*, vol. 1, p. 409. Captain William Eustice graduated from West Point in 1826. He was promoted to the rank of captain in 1845 and resigned his commission on August 4, 1849.

16. Ibid., vol. 2, p. 52. Major Cary H. Fry was a member of the 2nd Kentucky Volunteer Infantry.

17. Ibid., vol. 1, p. 301. Colonel Sylvester Churchill entered the army on March 12, 1812, at the rank of first lieutenant in the 3rd Regiment of Artillery. He was promoted to the rank of brevet brigadier general on February 23, 1847, for gallantry and meritorious conduct in the battle of Buena Vista. Churchill resigned his commission on September 25, 1861, and died on December 7, 1862.

18. Ibid., vol. 2, p. 72. Lieutenant Colonel William Weatherford was a member of the 1st Illinois Regiment.

19. Ibid., vol. 2, p. 71. Lieutenant Colonel William B. Warren served in the 1st Illinois Regiment.

20. Eisenhower, *So Far From God*, pp. 241–47. Colonel Alexander Doniphan led the 1st Missouri Mounted Infantry against the Mexicans in the Battle of Sacramento, fought on February 28, 1847. With unconventional tactics, Doniphan defeated a superior force and triumphantly entered the city of Chihuahua, on March 1, 1847.

21. Heitman, *Register*, vol. 1, p. 755. Lieutenant John Paul Jones O'Brien was a graduate of West Point promoted to brevet major for his bravery at the Battle of Buena Vista. O'Brien had lost two pieces of field artillery under his command to the attacking Mexicans on February 23, 1847, as he struggled to hold his position on the central plateau. His testimony concerned the events leading up to the capture of the guns. Both pieces were later recaptured by American forces at Churubusco in central Mexico. O'Brien died on March 31, 1850.

22. Brian Sandwich, *The Great Western, Legendary Lady of the Southwest* (El Paso: Texas Western Press, 1991), pp. 29–31; Tom Owen the Beehunter [Thomas Bangs Thorpe], *Anecdotes of Zachary Taylor and the Mexican War* (New York: D. Appleton & Company, 1848), pp. 96–98; Russell A. Buchanan, "George Washington Trahern: Texan Cowboy Soldier From Mier to Buena Vista," *The Southwestern Historical Quarterly*, vol. 58, no. 1, pp. 84–85. This six-foot-two-inch, red-headed giantess was the darling of the army. She had survived the siege of Fort Brown, making camp kettles of coffee for the men while the cannon balls whizzed overhead and many a soldier was hiding in the bombproofs. The Great Western was mother to the troops. She washed their dirty clothes, cooked for them, and nursed them when they were sick and dying. She could also be tough. Wash Trahern swore that she "would whip most anybody in a rough and tumble fight." Captain George Lincoln had enlisted her into the army at Jefferson Barracks, Missouri, as a washerwoman and she kept house for this bachelor officer for several years and had a fond spot in her heart for him. When Lincoln was killed at Buena Vista, she laid his body out, washing and wrapping it in a burial shroud. A few months later at an auction of Lincoln's personal effects, she bought his milk-white horse: "[She] said that a man who offered seventy five dollars for a horse like that could not want it — that she would give two hundred and fifty dollars for the animal, and at that price it was knocked off to her. When asked what occasion she had for the horse, she declared her intention to keep it till an opportunity offered for forwarding it to Lincoln's mother, for whom she designed it as a present.

The soldiers of the 2nd Kentucky Volunteers wanted to return this horse to Capt. Lincoln's father, living in the United States, and she relented possession of the animal to them."

23. *The Vedette*, vol. 2, no. 4, January, 1881, "Letter from H. W. Benham, 'A Little More Grape.'" In later years, Henry Benham, an Engineer on General Taylor's staff, wrote these words about the death of George Lincoln: "[I] saw at the feet of the horses of one of his pieces all that was left of the gallant Lincoln, so recently in full and joyous life. My first impulse was to save his sword, as of priceless value to those that loved him; and I carried it with his pistol to our field-hospital under the edge of the plain for safety. Upon retiring some short time after, and finding his body still left where he fell I had that also taken off the field. He had pressed forward as I passed him to the front of Bissell's regiment, then forming to support a section of artillery under Thomas, and to meet the charge of the advancing columns. Riding along their front, he turned back to their left and rear to cheer them on with the words, 'Come on, my brave Illinoisians, and save this battery.' In the storm of musketry that then rained down upon them, one ball struck him in the waist, another entered the back of his head; and drooping slowly forward . . . he was laid upon the ground, without a moan or a whimper. After waiting several weeks, I sent a long letter to his friends, giving them every detail, and with it flowers which had blossomed on the spot where he fell. Long may flowers bloom over this gallant son of a noble race of Massachusetts. . . ."

24. DeWitt H. Clinton served two terms as governor of New York, the first, 1817–1822, the second, 1825–1828.

25. *Picket Guard*, Saltillo, Coahuila, Mexico, April 19, 1847, May 10, 1847, Barker Texas History Center, University of Texas at Austin; Lota M. Spell, *Pioneer Printer* (Austin: University of Texas Press, 1963), pp. 49–57; Thomas William Reilly, "American Reporters and the Mexican War, 1846–1848," Ph.D. Dissertation, University of Minnesota, 1975; Dayton W. Canady, "Voice of the Volunteer of 1847," *Journal of the Illinois State Historical Society*, vol. 44, 1951, pp. 199–209. The *Picket Guard* was published by William and Moses Osman, two professional printers who served as volunteer soldiers in the 2nd Illinois Regiment. For the price of one bit Americans at Saltillo could catch up on the news of the army in northern Mexico, official and unofficial. The press used to print the newspaper had been captured from the state government of Coahuila and was probably the same one employed by pioneer printer Samuel Bangs in 1822 when he worked in Saltillo printing Mexican governmental decrees. Publication ceased on May 21, 1847,

with the return of the 2nd Illinois to the United States in June, 1847. Only seven issues of the the *Picket Guard* were ever released; copies of six survive.

26. Bauer, *The Mexican War*, pp. 208–09; Chance, *Mexican War Regiment*, pp. 115–16; Chamberlain, *Recollections of a Rogue*, pp. 89–92; Captain Albert Pike, "Sketch of the Battle of Buena Vista," *Arkansas State Gazette* (Little Rock), April 24, 1847; Jonathan W. Buhoup, *Narrative of the Central Division* (Pittsburgh: M. P. Morse, 1847), p. 137. The Arkansas Mounted Regiment was composed of men "quite famous in their own locality as fighting men, but possessing an independence of character and self-confidence fatal to their efficiency as soldiers." This regiment entered Mexico as a part of General Wool's column and quickly developed a reputation for insubordination. They were led by Colonel Archibald Yell, who seemed to understand little of the military. General Wool reported that "Col. Yell's Regiment is composed of very good materials but without any instruction. They do not appear to be under the control of their officers." On February 10, 1847, units of the Arkansas Regiment attacked a party of Mexican civilians in a cave near the little village of Catana, and killed twenty or thirty, according to eyewitness accounts. Wool appointed a military commission to identify the guilty parties and companies B and G of the regiment were singled out for punishment. Taylor ordered these individuals to be moved to the mouth of the Rio Grande but the order was never carried out. The majority of the regiment ran from the enemy at the Battle of Buena Vista, though small units and certain individuals did remain on the field and fight valiantly. Colonel Archibald Yell was killed by a Mexican lancer while defending against a cavalry attack. As reported in the *Arkansas State Gazette*, Captain Albert Pike of the regiment boldly spoke the truth: "It is a sad thing that brave men, for they were brave, should be so destroyed for want of discipline. . . . Poor Yell! He atoned for his error with his life: but other brave men died with him, who were not at fault. . . . It will not answer to take undisciplined troops, especially undisciplined cavalry into the field. It is murderous. Men must not only be drilled but disciplined. They must not only like, but respect their officers for their superior knowledge. . . ." Before the Arkansas Mounted Regiment returned home from Saltillo, Lieutenant Colonel Gaston Meares raised a cavalry company of volunteers from the regiment who enrolled to serve "for the duration of the war." The volunteers were to receive an additional 160 acres of land as an enlistment bonus. Mears was elected captain of the company, not James F. Preston.

27. Heitman, *Register*, vol. 1, p. 890. Lieutenant Lorenzo Sitgreaves

graduated from West Point in 1827. He was promoted to brevet captain for his services at the battle of Buena Vista.

28. Malone, *DAB*, pp. 457–58; Smith, *The War With Mexico*, vol. 2, p. 278; Bauer, *The Mexican War*, p. 363. Thomas "Black Tom" Corwin, Whig Senator from Ohio, delivered a shocking speech on the floor of the Senate on February 11, 1847, denouncing the war as a means for the acquisition of new lands. Bauer recorded: "If I were a Mexican, I would tell you, 'Have you not room in your country to bury your dead men? If you come into mine we will greet you with bloody hands, and welcome you to hospitable graves.'" The speech, coming just prior to news of the Battle of Buena Vista and the long casualty lists that appeared in newspapers, struck many Americans as an act of treason. According to Justin Smith, this speech "sounded the knell of its author's great political hopes." The effigy of Corwin, dressed in a Mexican uniform, reportedly burned by the Ohio troops near Buena Vista had these few lines of verse posted nearby: "Old Tom Corwin is dead and here he lies; Nobody's sorry and nobody cries; Where he's gone and how he fares, Nobody knows and nobody cares."

29. Heitman, *Register*, vol. 1, p. 357. Captain Charles W. Davis entered the service on August 8, 1846, as a quartermaster and was honorably discharged on February 23, 1849.

30. The famous American House at Saltillo, kept by Sarah, was described by one veteran as "a sort of headquarters for everybody," and was immortalized in a Samuel Chamberlain watercolor. Sarah was reported to be an excellent monte player, who once won eighteen dollars from the famous scout Ben McCulloch. Free and open activities at the American House were greatly restricted when General John Ellis Wool assumed command of American forces at Saltillo. Special Order No. 517 specified that "Mrs. Bouget, having by permission of the General established a Boarding House in the vicinity of Camp for the accomodation of the officers — it is to be well understood that this permission is to be continued on condition that there shall not be a drop of liquor of any kind sold or kept at the establishment. A sentinel will be posted at the Rancho occupied as above, and will be instructed not to permit, under any pretense whatever, soldiers, Teamsters, citizens, or women (other than the servants of Mrs. Bouget) to come near the buildings. After sundown the Building will be closed to all whatever." See, Sandwich, *The Great Western*, pp. 18–19.

31. Lieutenant Tidball had been sent by Curtis to deliver a message of warning to General Scott, then at Tampico, on the grave situation on the northern lines. See the entry for March 2, 1847.

32. Although small skirmishes had been fought at the National

Bridge a few days before, the battle of Cerro Gordo actually began on April 18, 1847.

33. Heitman, *Register*, vol. 2, p. 60. Captain John McCougall served in the 1st Indiana Regiment.

34. Ibid., vol. 2, p. 73. Captain Louis D. Wilson served in the North Carolina Volunteer Regiment.

35. Lee A. Wallace, Jr., "Raising a Volunteer Regiment For Mexico, 1846–1847," *North Carolina Historical Review*, vol.35, January, 1958, p. 27; Lee A. Wallace, Jr., "The First Regiment of Virginia Volunteers, 1846–1848," *Virginia Magazine of History and Biography*, vol. 77, January, 1969, pp. 46–77. As an enticement to volunteers, congressmen proposed a bill granting a bounty of a 160 acres of western land to men who served in Mexico. States such as North Carolina sweetened the ante by offering a bounty of $10 for each man who enlisted. Companies of the North Carolina regiment began to be seen on the streets of Saltillo by early May, 1847. The unit was to garrison Saltillo for the remainder of the war and see no active fighting. Bored soldiers had little to do with their spare time in Saltillo except dream of home and get into trouble. In August, 1847, the regiment and members of the Virginia and Mississippi regiments became involved in a mutiny against Colonel Robert Treat Paine. Paine, who commanded the Tar Heel Regiment, was an unpopular officer who believed in strict discipline. The incident was initiated by a wooden horse, built by Paine for punishment. An unruly mob of soldiers assembled around the horse one evening and destroyed it. Later that night stones were thrown at Colonel Paine's tent and another mob assembled. Paine advanced on the men and ordered them to disburse or he would open fire. "Fire God damn you," was the response. Paine fired a single shot that wounded one Virginia volunteer and mortally wounded a North Carolinian. None of the soldiers involved in the mutiny could be identified, but officers felt that an example should be made of insubordinate troops. Excessive punishments were meted out to several errant soldiers. Samuel Chamberlain described one such case in the execution of Private Victor Galbraith. See, Chamberlain, *Recollections of a Rogue*, pp. 224–25.

36. Heitman, *Register*, vol. 2, p. 73. Colonel Isaac H. Wright led the Massachusetts Volunteer Regiment.

37. Bauer, *Mexican War*, p. 268. Outside the city of Perote in Vera Cruz state lies the famed Fort San Carlos de Perote, referred to by its Texian prisoners captured at Mier as Perote Castle. The castle served as a prison and a storehouse for munitions. The famous Big Foot Wallace, an unfortunate shut-in there in 1843, is said to have buried a dime near

the flag pole in the courtyard and promised to his fellow Texian prisoners that he would return some day in triumph to recover the coin.

38. Eisenhower, *So Far From God*, p. 272. General Valentin Canalizo, a recent interim president and Santa Anna loyalist, led a brigade of cavalry and 2,000 national guard troops from Perote. This force was ordered to seize the National Bridge on the highway between Cerro Gordo and Vera Cruz and to hold it against an American advance.

39. Major Edgar Erskine Hume, Southern Sketches Number 6, First Series, *Colonel Theodore O'Hara, Author of The Bivouac of the Dead* (Charlottesville, Virginia: The Historical Publishing Co., 1936), pp. 18–19. Word of the American victory at Buena Vista was received in a somber mood in Kentucky when the long list of Kentucky dead was published. The citizens of Frankfort, Kentucky, gathered in the streets on April 17, 1847, to urge their legislature to arrange for the return of the bodies of Kentuckians killed at Buena Vista so that they might be reburied in the "State Burying Ground." On July 20, 1847, some 20,000 attended a great public funeral in Frankfort presided over by John C. Breckenridge. The bodies of William R. McKee and Henry Clay, Jr., were among those buried. On February 5, 1848, the Kentucky Legislature appropriated funds for a military monument to honor its Mexican War dead. At the formal dedication on July 25, 1850, Theodore O'Hara read for the first time his famous poem, "Bivouac of the Dead." The first and probably the most famous verse of this martial poem is: "The muffled drum's sad roll has beat The soldiers last tattoo; No more on life's parade ground shall meet That brave and fallen few. On Fame's eternal camping-ground Their silent tents are spread, And glory guards, with solemn round, The bivouac of the dead."

40. *American Flag*, July 16, 1846. Curtis attempted to obtain vaccine for immunization against small pox, which was sweeping through the American army camps of northern Mexico. The *Flag* reports efforts to immunize the general population at a much earlier date: "Dr. P. H. Craig, of the U.S. Army, offers his services to the inhabitants of Matamoros, and would inform them that he is prepared with vaccine matter to operate for the prevention of Small Pox. He can be found at his tent, near the head quarters of General Taylor. Matamoros, June 12, 1846."

41. Heitman, *Register*, vol. 2, p. 62. Lieutenant Colonel David D. Mitchell served in the 2nd Missouri Volunteers.

42. Buhoup, *Central Division*, pp. 137–38. While on picket duty, members of the Arkansas Mounted Regiment intercepted Mexican messengers. "About this time, the 17th of May, we had a visit paid us by two Mexican officers. They came to one of our piquets and requested

to be conducted in. They were accordingly taken to the Arkansas camp first, and I have no doubt they thought they were a used up community, for the Rackensackers made a perfect charge to get a good look at them. Not having had much time for an examination at the charge on the rancho on the 23rd of February, they were anxious to know how they looked on closer inspection. We noticed one fellow examining every thing minutely, at the conclusion of which he scared the Mexican almost out of his saddle by looking at him, grinning like an ourang outang [sic] and saluting him with that emphatic Spanish word, which every volunteer has learned, 'carrajo!'"

The message to General Taylor was from General Mora y Villamil, commanding at San Luis Potosi. The Mexican officer protested American brutality to Mexican civilians: "that the towns and their inoffensive inhabitants suffer devastation, ruin, conflagration, death, and other depredations of similar character, which have been permitted on their occupation, by some of the troops under your command, whose conduct, at the present time, is not only opposed to the law of nations, in view of its unhappy effects, but is contrary to the usages and practices established by common consent among all civilized nations." For the entire text see, Executive Document No. 60, #41, pp. 1139–41.

43. Heitman, *Register*, vol. 1, p. 434. Lieutenant William Buel Franklin graduated from West Point in 1839. He was promoted to brevet first lieutenant for gallantry as the battle of Buena Vista and to brigadier general for his services in the battles before Richmond, Virgina, on June 30, 1862. He resigned his commission on March 15, 1866, at the rank of major general.

44. *Official Roster*, p. 448. Private A. D. Lewis of Company H was reported to have been murdered by Mexicans on May 20, 1847, at Santa Catarina, Mexico.

45. The Curtis letter requesting 50,000 troops had now been circulated to the press and was being ridiculed by newspapers in Ohio and the American Midwest.

46. *American Flag*, March 17, April 18, May 5, 1847; Rowland, *Mississippi*, vol. 2, pp. 231–32; *The Saltillo Picket Guard*, April 19, 1847. The 2nd Mississippi Regiment had been charged with crimes even while camped at New Orleans waiting transportation to south Texas. The men had been bivouaked at New Orleans in tents during severe weather; the exposure brought on bouts of illness. The men were then packed into transports and brought to Texas, "not suffered to plant their feet upon land for thirty-one days." The regiment suffered high rates of sickness and death. By March 17, 1847, 135 men had died from disease and other non-combat causes, and sixty-five had been dis-

charged. A regiment of 850 now could show only 600 effective men with more than fifty still on the sick list. By May 5, 1847, it is reported that small pox had broken out in the ranks of the Mississippi Regiment with more than eighty cases diagnosed. The officers of the regiment were Reuben Davis, colonel, Captain Fitzpatrick, lieutenant colonel, and Ezra R. Price, major. The regiment was moved to Saltillo, spending a short time there, then moved to "Calderito" outside of Monterrey where it spent the remainder of the war. The editors of the *Picket Guard* wrote that "The 2nd Mississippi Regiment, now at Monterey, has the reputation of being a 'wild set of b'hoys.' A Matamoros correspondent of the Delta speaking [sic] of them, says — 'Their drill is peculiar to themselves, and in performing their evolutions they are thrown into all sorts of postures and attitudes throwing themselves on their backs, crawling on their bellies, and dodging and cavorting about in a manner perfectly original. As to their fighting, there can be no doubt but that they would run a tilt against the devil, backed by a [whole] legion of his imps."

47. Reilly, *American Reporters*, p. 301. *The New Orleans Picayune*, in an undated article from their war correspondent John E. Drivage, reported the murder of this Arkansas volunteer. Drivage described the interrogation of forty Mexicans arrested on suspicion of the crime as a "circus." He noted that "Mexicans certainly can lie with the best face of any people in the world. . . . When we [begin] to civilize the people of this country, the precepts of the venerable and excellent matron, Mother Goose, should be inculcated in every juvenile mind, and the familiar verse which holds up the terrible fate in store for liars painted up in every domocil throughout . . . the land."

48. *Arkansas State Gazette* (Little Rock), April 24, 1847; Robert Lipscomb Duncan, *Reluctant General: The Life and Times of Albert Pike* (New York: E. P. Dutton & Co., 1961), pp. 129–31. Captain Albert Pike was a member of the Arkansas Mounted Regiment and fought at the Battle of Buena Vista. He was mortified at the poor performance of the regiment and wrote a letter back home to Arkansas describing the regiment's erratic behavior. John Seldon Roane, another officer of the regiment, was so angered by Captain Pike's letter that he challenged Pike to a duel. On July 29, 1847, the two men met on a sandbar in the Arkansas River near Fort Smith and exchanged shots. Neither man was injured and both agreed that honor had been satisfied. Pike was a poet, and wrote an epic poem about the battle: "Buena Vista," which appeared in newspapers throughout the country. Pike served in the Confederate army at the rank of brigadier general.

49. Wallace, "Virginia Volunteers." The Virginia Regiment began

arriving in Saltillo by late April, 1847. This regiment was a part of the second call for volunteers, and the men had enlisted to serve "for the war." The regiment garrisoned Saltillo and did not participate in active duty. But life in Saltillo could be interesting. One soldier wrote on February 12, 1848, that he "had witnessed the execution of five men at ten o'clock; attended church at eleven o'clock; visited the cockpit at three o'clock, where the priest who had conducted the service was acting as judge; and at five o'clock was at the race course." The regiment eventually included fourteen companies as the Virginia governor continued to enlist and send men for duty to Mexico. Two officers of the regiment fought a duel that resulted in both of their deaths. On the late afternoon of May 20, 1847, at the foot of a small mountain outside of China on the Camargo road the two antagonists met. Washington L. Mahan, armed with a musket, a "five shooter," a pair of duelling pistols, and a large bowie knife, faced Carlton R. Munford, who was armed with a musket and a small dirk. Munford had called Mahan a "damn liar" and a coward and would not retract the statements. The men exchanged three rounds of musket shots, with the third round, at a distance of about twenty-five paces mortally wounding both parties.

50. Henry Benham, "Recollections of Mexico and Buena Vista by an Engineer Officer," *Old and New*, vol. 3, no. 6, p. 649; Fulton, *Josiah Gregg*, vol. 1, pp. 270–71. Benham described Sanchez and his wealth, "The owner of Agua Nueva, and of the larger portion of these ranches and villages for some two hundred miles or more to the north-west, was one Don Jacobo (or Jacob) Sanchez, a gentleman of education and breeding, though nearly a black Indian in appearance. He was the son, by an Indian woman, of a shrewd and unscrupulous Spanish-Mexican lawyer, who acquired, often unjustly it was thought, these immense properties in the troublous times of the first revolts from Spain. Don Jacobo we sometimes saw in Saltillo, where he had his town mansion; though he generally resided at his hacienda, some thirty miles southwest, where he lived in princely style, with his own private band of musicians for his own amusement." Josiah Gregg, in his travels with General Wool's column through the country southwest of Saltillo, notes that, "The Hacienda de las Hermanas is a large plantation — sugar and corn chiefly cultivated — with some 120 work-hands . . . total population, at least 300 souls. The residences are embraced in an extensive building divided into three squares . . . This estate is owned by one Don Jacobo Sanchez, who resides in Saltillo."

51. Fulton, *Josiah Gregg*, vol. 1, pp. 290–91. The Riddle referred to here is probably the same one discussed by Gregg who made a daring

escape from the Mexicans at Presidio del Rio Grande by floating downriver on a log to Laredo.

52. Bauer, *Mexican War*, p. 284. Nicholas P. Trist had been sent to
Mexico by the state department in April, 1847, with a draft of a peace
treaty for signature by the Mexican government.

53. Manuel Balbontin, "The Battle of Angostura Pass (Buena
Vista)," *Journal of the Military Institution of the United States*, vol. 8,
1887. Early in 1847, General Gabriel Valencia commanded Mexican
forces occupying Victoria. When Taylor's forces advanced toward that
city in December, 1846, the firebrand Mexican general begged Santa
Anna for permission to attack the strung-out columns of untried American volunteers. But Santa Anna, then at San Luis Potosi, realized that
he could not reinforce Valencia's small force and denied his request.
Taylor's forces were permitted to occupy Ciudad Victoria unopposed. A
young officer on this expedition, Lieutenant Benjamin S. Roberts,
noted that, "[Taylor] has a strong desire to get hold of Valencia, who is
said to be the best officer in the Mexican service."

54. Heitman, *Register*, vol. 2, p. 54. Colonel John F. Hamtramack
was elected as colonel of the Virginia Volunteers.

55. Ibid., vol. 2, p. 64. Colonel Robert T. Paine led the North
Carolina Volunteers.

56. Ibid., vol. 1, p. 393. Major Jubal A. Early graduated from West
Point in 1833 and resigned his commission in 1838. He served as major
in the Virginia Volunteers from January 7, 1847, until August 3, 1848.
He served in the Confederate army as lieutenant general from 1861 to
1865. He died March 2, 1894.

57. Ibid., vol. 2, p. 69. Major Monfort S. Stokes served in the North
Carolina Volunteer Regiment.

58. Ibid., vol. 1, p. 719. Captain Alexander Montgomery graduated
from West Point in 1830. He retired on January 15, 1874, at the rank
of major.

59. David Nevin, *The Mexican War* (Alexandria, Virginia: Time-
Life Books, 1978), pp. 88–89. The artist was William Garl Brown, Jr.,
and this painting is the property of Library of Congress.

60. The little village of Papagallos, about halfway between Cerralvo and Monterrey, was on the main road between Camargo and
Monterrey. It has since been bypassed by the modern highway. Today,
the town appears much as it must have looked in 1846 and 1847. The
old road passing through the center of the village is still rutted by the
wheels of Taylor's supply wagons.

61. Heitman, *Register*, vol. 1, p. 1037. Lieutenant Joab Wilkinson

was appointed to the infantry, April 19, 1847, and resigned on May 13, 1848.

62. Ibid., vol. 1, p. 172. Major John T. Arthur, quartermaster for the 1st Ohio Regiment, was discharged on June 30, 1847. He remained with the service after this date as quartermaster and was honorably discharged on October 15, 1848.

63. *Official Roster*, p. 433. The 3rd Ohio Regiment lost sixty-four men during the year's service.

64. Heitman, *Register*, vol. 1, p. 242. Lieutenant Thomas Jefferson Brereton graduated from West Point in 1839. He was promoted to brevet first lieutenant for distinguished service at Palo Alto and Resaca de la Palma. He resigned his commission on December 20, 1858, at the rank of captain.

65. Ibid., vol. 1, p. 542; *American Flag*, June 30, 1847; Albert G. Brackett, *General Lane's Brigade in Central Mexico* (Cincinnati: H. W. Derby & Co., 1854), pp. 24–32; Florence Johnson Scott, "George Washington Clutter in the Mexican War," *Texas Military History*, vol. 4, 1964, pp. 127–30. Enos D. Hopping was appointed brigadier general of volunteers on March 3, 1847. He was stationed at Mier, commanding a camp of instruction to train the new volunteers and regular soldiers that were replacing troops taken by Scott for the central Mexico campaign. The troops were exercised in their studies by Colonel Belknap to prepare soldiers for General Taylor's column. Units initially assigned to the camp were the 16th Regiment, two companies of the 13th Regiment, a battalion of the 3rd Dragoons, one regiment each of infantry from Ohio and Indiana, one battalion each from Delaware, Maryland, Alabama, one company from Florida, four companies of horse from each of Illinois, Arkansas, Ohio and Alabama, two companies from Virginia, and one company from North Carolina. These units and others were incorporated into the 10th, 13th, and 16th regiments. By August 24, 1847, they were broken up: the 10th Regiment was sent to garrison towns along the Rio Grande, the 13th Regiment became a part of Caleb Cushing's brigade and was sent to the mouth of the Rio Grande to be transported to central Mexico, and the 16th Regiment was sent to garrison Monterrey. General Hopping, an elderly man, was sick most of the time the camp was in operation and died September 1, 1847. His body was buried in a plot between the camp and the Rio Grande in company with the many volunteers who died of various illnesses.

66. Way, *Packet Directory*. p. 123; Kelley, *River of Lost Dreams*, pp. 38, 51, 108. The *Del Norte* was a sternwheel wooden hull packet of 114 tons. The hull was built in Elizabeth, Pennsylvania, in 1846 and taken

to Zanesville, Ohio, to be fitted out. Her first captain was Charles Bowen, who operated her on the Zanesville to Pittsburgh run. She was sold to the firm of Ellmaker and Viosca of New Orleans with William F. Bowen retaining interest. Bowen delivered her for private operation on the Rio Grande. After she was snagged in 1849, the ship was purchased by the firm of Bodman and Clark of Brownsville, Texas, and retained for use on the Rio Grande.

67. Scott, "George Washington Clutter," p. 124. Lieutenant Clutter, a recruit being sent to the Mier camp of instruction, reports to his wife that, "In my letters written on Sunday last . . . I stated that we were detained at Reynosa, there being an attack expected from Urrea at that point; but it all turned out to be a 'stampede,' for nothing — we therefore, had not the good luck to meet the great Lancer and his party. . . ."

68. Heitman, *Register*, vol. 1, p. 757. Edmund Agustus Ogden graduated from West Point on July 1, 1827. He was promoted to captain on July 7, 1839, as assistant quartermaster and was elevated to the rank of brevet major on May 30, 1848, for meritorious conduct. He died on August 3, 1855.

69. Samuel French, *Two Wars, An Autobiography of Gen. Samuel G. French* (Nashville: Confederate Veteran, 1901), p. 87; Lytle, *Merchant Steam Vessels*. General French remembered his April, 1847, passage on the *James L. Day* from Brazos Santiago to New Orleans as a rather hazardous voyage. "On arrival at Port Isabel there were a brig and a steamer ready to sail for New Orleans. I was put on board the brig, but it was so dirty that I could not remain, preferring to risk my life on the old sidewheel steamer *James L. Day*. . . . The steamer was unfit for a voyage on the ocean, although the weather was calm and the sea smooth. I amused myself watching from my cot the partition boards slide up and down, caused by the gentle rolling of the vessel." The *James L. Day* was a sidewheel steamer of 414 tons, built in New York, New York, in 1843. This vessel was transferred to Confederate service in 1861, becoming the C.S.S. *James L. Day*.

70. Heitman, *Register*, vol. 1, p. 394. Major Thomas B. Eastland was a quartermaster of volunteers, appointed on June 26, 1846, and honorably discharged on March 3, 1849.

71. Rowland, *Mississippi*, vol. 1, pp. 632–36. Reuben Davis was born near Winchester, Tennessee, on January 18, 1813. He was trained as a physician but changed to law. Davis served as brigadier general of Mississippi militia after about 1840. In January, 1847, he was elected colonel of the 2nd Regiment of Mississippi Volunteers, an act that he frankly admitted was the "most fatal step of my life." Throughout the remainder of his life he blamed his stint of duty in Mexico for most of

his bad luck and troubles. Davis suffered from chronic diahrrea and — at the point of death — resigned his commission to return home. He was a Union Democrat and worked in Congress to preserve the Union. When Mississippi seceded, however, he accepted an appointment as brigadier general and finally major general in the Confederate army. After the war he practiced law. He died at Huntsville, Tennessee, on October 14, 1890.

Bibliography

Books

_____. *Catálogo Nacional: Monumentos Históricos Inmuebles, Tamaulipas.* Secretario de Educación Pública, 1987.

_____. *Diccionario Porrúa de Historia, Biografía, y Geografía de México.* 2d ed. Mexico City: Editorial Porrúa, 1965.

_____. *Forest Trees of Texas.* College Station, Texas: Texas Forest Service, 1963.

_____. *National Cyclopedia of American Biography.* New York: James T. White and Co., 1906.

_____. *Official Roster of the of the Soldiers of the State of Ohio in the War of the Rebellion, 1861-1866, and in the War With Mexico, 1846–1848.* vol. 12. Norwalk, Ohio: The Laning Company, 1895.

[Alcarez, Ramón, et al.] *The Other Side or Notes for the History of the War Between Mexico and the United States.* Translated and edited by Albert C. Ramsey. New York: John Wiley, 1850.

Archer, Sellers G. and Bunch, Clarence E. *The American Grass Book: A Manual of Pasture and Range Practices.* Norman: University of Oklahoma Press, 1953.

Bauer, K. Jack. *The Mexican War 1846–1848.* New York: Macmillan Publishing Co., 1974.

Brackett, Albert G. *General Lane's Brigade in Central Mexico.* Cincinnati: H. W. Derby and Co., 1854.

Brooks, Nathan. *A Complete History of the Mexican War 1846–1848.* Chicago: The Rio Grande Press, 1965.

Buhoup, Jonathan W. *Narrative of the Central Division, or, Army of Chihuahua, Commanded by Brigadier General Wool. . . .* Pittsburgh: M. P. Morse, 1847.

Calcott, Wilfrid H. *Santa Anna, the Story of an Enigma Who Was Once Mexico.* Norman: University of Oklahoma Press, 1936.

Carleton, James Henry. *The Battle of Buena Vista, with the Operations of* the "Army of Occupation" for One Month. New York: Harper and Brothers, 1848.

Chamberlain, Samuel E. Recollections of a Rogue. London: Museum Press Limited, 1957.

Chance, Joseph E. Jefferson Davis's Mexican War Regiment. Jackson: University Press of Mississippi, 1991.

Chance, Joseph E. (ed.). The Mexican War Journal of Captain Franklin Smith. Jackson: University Press of Mississippi, 1991.

Clemens, Jeremiah. Mustang Gray: A Romance. Philadelphia: J. B. Lippincott, 1858.

Crawford, Ann Fears (ed.). The Eagle: The Autobiography of Santa Anna. Austin: The Pemberton Press, 1967.

Cutrer, Thomas W. Ben McCulloch and the Frontier Military Tradition. Chapel Hill: University of North Carolina Press, 1993.

Davis, Reuben. Recollections of Mississippi and Mississippians. Oxford: University and College Press of Mississippi, 1972.

Delaney, John J. Dictionary of Saints. Garden City: Doubleday and Co., 1980.

Dillon, Lester R. American Artillery in the Mexican War, 1846–1847. Austin: Presidial Press, 1975.

Ditmars, Raymond L. The Reptiles of North America. Garden City: Doubleday and Co., 1953.

Eisenhower, John S. D. So Far From God: The U.S. War With Mexico, 1846–1848. New York: Random House, 1989.

Ferrell, Robert H. (ed.). Monterrey Is Ours! The Mexican War Letters of Lieutenant Dana, 1845–1847. Lexington: University Press of Kentucky, 1990.

French, Samuel G. Two Wars: An Autobiography of Gen. Samuel G. French. Nashville: Confederate Veteran, 1901.

Freund, Max (ed.). Gustav Dresel's Houston Journal. Austin: University of Texas Press, 1954.

Frost, John. Pictorial History of Mexico and the Mexican War. Philadelphia: Thomas, Copperwait and Co., for James A. Bill, 1848.

Fuess, Claude M. The Life of Caleb Cushing. 2 vols., New York: Harcourt Brace and Co., 1923.

Fulton, Maurice G. (ed.). Diary and Letters of Josiah Gregg. 2 vols., Norman: University of Oklahoma Press, 1944.

Furber, George C. The Twelve Months Volunteer: Or, Journal of a Private in the Tennessee Regiment of Cavalry, in the Campaign in Mexico, 1846–7. . . . Cincinnati: J. P. Jones, 1857.

Garza Sáenz, Ernesto. Crónicas de Camargo. Victoria, Tamaulipas: Universidad Autónoma de Tamaulipas, 1980.

BIBLIOGRAPHY

[Giddings, Luther]. *Sketches of the Campaign in Northern Mexico in Eighteen Hundred Forty-Six and Seven.* New York: George P. Putnam, 1853.

Grant, Ulysses S. *Personal Memoirs of U. S. Grant.* New York: Charles L. Webster and Co., 1894.

Greer, James K. *Colonel Jack Hays.* New York: E. P. Dutton and Co., 1952.

Gulick, Charles Adams, Jr., and Elliot, Katherine (eds.). *The Papers of Mirabeau Buonaparte Lamar.* vol. 4. Austin: A. C. Baldwin and Sons, 1922.

Heitman, Francis B. *Historical Register and Dictionary of the United States Army, From Its Organization September 29, 1789, to March 2, 1903.* 2 vols. Reprint. Urbana: University of Illinois Press, 1965.

Henry, Robert S. *The Story of the Mexican War.* New York: The Bobbs-Merrill Company, 1950.

Henry, William S. *Campaign Sketches of the War in Mexico.* New York: Harper and Brothers, 1847.

Horgan, Paul. *Great River: The Rio Grande in North American History.* 2 vols. New York: Holt, Rinehart and Winston, 1968.

Howe, Henry (ed.). *The Historical Collections of Ohio in Two Volumes.* Cincinnati: C. J. Krehbiel and Co., 1902.

Hume, Edgar Erskine. *Colonel Theodore O'Hara: Author of The Bivouac of the Dead.* Charlottesville, Virginia: The Historical Publishing Co., Inc., 1936.

Jackson, Ronald Vern, Teeples, Gary Ronald, and Schaefermeyer, David. *Texas 1850 Census Index.* Bountiful, Utah: Accelerated Indexing Systems, Inc., 1976.

Johannsen, Robert W. *To The Halls of the Montezumas.* New York: Oxford University Press, 1985.

Johnson, Florence Scott. *Old Rough and Ready on the Rio Grande.* Waco, Texas: Texian Press, 1969.

Johnston, William Preston. *The Life of Albert Sidney Johnston.* New York: D. Appleton and Company, 1878.

Kane, Harnett T. *Queen City New Orleans: City by the River.* New York: Bonanza Books, 1949.

Kearney, Milo, and Knopp, Anthony. *Boom and Bust: The Historical Cycles of Matamoros and Brownsville.* Austin: Eakin Press, 1991.

Kelley, Pat. *River of Lost Dreams: Navigation on the Rio Grande.* Lincoln: University of Nebraska Press, 1986.

Kenley, John R. *Memoirs of a Maryland Volunteer.* Philadelphia: J. B. Lippincott and Co., 1873.

Lander, Alexander. *A Trip to Texas Comprising The History of the Galveston Riflemen, Formed April 28, 1846, at Galveston, Texas; To-*

gether With The History of The Battle of Monterey; Also Descriptions of Mexico and Its People. Monmouth, Illinois: Printed at the "Atlas Office," For the Publisher, 1847.

Lane, Walter P. *The Adventures and Recollections of General Walter P. Lane.* Austin, Texas: Pemberton Press, 1970.

Lavender, David. *Climax at Buena Vista: The American Campaign in Northeastern Mexico.* Philadelphia: J. B. Lippincott and Co., 1966.

Lea, Tom. *The King Ranch.* Boston: Little, Brown and Company, 1957.

Lentz, Andrea L. (ed.). *A Guide to Manuscripts at the Ohio Historical Society.* Columbus: Ohio Historical Society, 1972.

Leslie, James W. *Land of Cypress and Pine.* Little Rock, Arkansas: Rose Publishing Co., 1976.

Linn, John J. *Reminiscences of Fifty Years in Texas.* New York: published privately, 1883.

Livingston-Little, D. E. (ed.). *The Mexican War Diary of Thomas D. Tennery.* Norman: University of Oklahoma Press, 1970.

Lonard, Robert I., et al. *Woody Plants of the Lower Rio Grande Valley, Texas.* Austin: Texas Memorial Museum, 1991.

Lynch, James D. *The Bench and Bar of Mississippi.* New York: E. J. Hale, 1881.

Lytle, William M. *Merchant Steam Vessels of the United States, 1807–1868.* (Forrest R. Holdcamper, ed.). Mystic, Connecticut: Steamship Historical Society of America, 1952.

McCutchan, Joseph D. *Mier Expedition Diary.* (Joseph Milton Nance, ed.). Austin: University of Texas Press, 1978.

McEniry, Sister Blanche Marie. *American Catholics in the War with Mexico.* Washington: Catholic University, 1932.

McIntosh, James T. (ed.). *The Papers of Jefferson Davis, Volume 2, June 1841 – July 1846.* Baton Rouge: Louisiana State University Press, 1974.

McIntosh, James T. (ed.). *The Papers of Jefferson Davis, Volume 3, July 1846 – December 1848.* Baton Rouge: Louisiana State University Press, 1981.

McWhiney, Grady, and Jamieson, Perry. *Attack and Die — Civil War Military Tactics and the Southern Heritage.* University, Alabama: The University of Alabama Press, 1982.

McWhiney, Grady, and McWhiney, Sue. *To Mexico With Taylor and Scott, 1845–1847.* Waltham: Blaisdell Publishing Co., 1969.

Malone, Dumas. *Dictionary of American Biography.* New York: Charles Scribners' Sons, 1933.

Nance, Joseph Milton. *After San Jacinto.* Austin: University of Texas Press, 1963.

Nevins, Allan (ed.). *Polk: The Diary of a President, 1845–1849*. New York: Longmans, Green, and Co., 1952.

Nichols, Edward. *Zach Taylor's Little Army*. Garden City: Doubleday and Co., 1963.

Owen, Tom, The Bee-Hunter [Thomas Bangs Thorpe]. *Anecdotes of Zachary Taylor and The Mexican War*. New York: D. Appleton and Company, 1848.

Parker, William Harwar. *Recollections of a Naval Officer, 1841–1865*. New Work: Charles Scribner's Sons, 1883.

Perry, Oran. *Indiana in the Mexican War*. Indianapolis: Wm. B. Burford, 1908.

Peterson, Roger Torrey. *A Field Guide to the Birds of Texas*. Boston: Houghton Mifflin Company, 1963.

Popenoe, Wilson. *Manual of Tropical and Subtropical Fruits*. New York: The Macmillan Company, 1927.

Quaife, Milo Milton (ed.). *The Diary of James K. Polk During His Presidency, 1845 to 1849*. 4 vols., Chicago: A. C. McClurg and Co., 1910.

Reid, Samuel C. *The Scouting Expeditions of McCullough's Texas Rangers*. New York: Books for Libraries Press, 1847. Reprinted 1970.

Risch, Erna. *Quartermaster Support of the Army: A History of the Corps, 1775–1939*. Washington: QM Historian's Office, Office of the QM General, 1962.

Robertson, Brian. *Wild Horse Desert*. Edinburg, Texas: New Santander Press, 1985.

[Robertson, John B.]. *Reminiscences of a Campaign in Mexico By A Member of the "Bloody First."* Nashville: J. York and Co., 1849.

Robinson, Fayette. *Mexico and Her Military Chieftans*. Glorieta, New Mexico: Rio Grande Press, 1970.

Robinson, Fayette. *An Account of the Organization of the Army of the United States with Biographies of Distinguished Officers of all Grades*. 2 vols. Philadelphia: E. H. Butler and Co., 1848.

Rose, Victor M. *The Life and Services of Gen. Ben McCulloch*. Philadelphia: Pictorial Bureau of the Press, 1888.

Rowland, Dunbar. *Mississippi*. Atlanta: Southern Historical Association, 1907.

Sandweiss, Martha A., Stewart, Rick, and Huseman, Ben W. *Eyewitness to War: Prints and Daguerreotypes of the Mexican War, 1846–1848*. Washington: Smithsonian Institution Press, 1989.

Sandwich, Brian. *The Great Western Legendary Lady of the Southwest*. El Paso: Texas Western Press, 1991.

[Scott, John A.]. *Encarnacion Prisoners, Comprising an Account of the*

March of the Kentucky Cavalry. . . . Louisville: Prentice and Weis-sanger, 1848.

Scott, Winfield. *Memoirs of Lieut.-General Scott, LL.D., Written by Himself.* New York: Sheldon and Co., 1864.

Scribner, Benjamin Franklin. *Camp Life of a Volunteer: A Campaign in Mexico or A Glimpse at Life in Camp by "One Who Has Seen the Elephant."* Philadelphia: Grigg, Elliot and Co., 1847.

Silver, James W. *Edmund Pendleton Gaines, Frontier General.* Baton Rouge: Louisiana State University Press, 1949.

Simon, John Y. *The Papers of Ulysses S. Grant, Volume 1, 1837–1861.* Carbondale: Southern Illinois University Press, 1967.

Smith, Compton. *Chile con Carne, or The Camp and The Field.* New York: Miller and Curtis, 1857.

Smith, Justin. *The War With Mexico.* 2 vols. New York: The Macmillan Company, 1919.

Spell, Lotta M. *Pioneer Printer: Samuel Bangs in Mexico and Texas.* Austin: University of Texas Press, 1963.

Spurlin, Charles D. *Texas Veterans in the Mexican War.* Nacogdoches: Erickson Books, 1984.

Thorpe, Thomas B. *Our Army at Monterey.* Philadelphia: Carey and Hart, 1848.

Thorpe, Thomas B. *Our Army on the Rio Grande.* Philadelphia: Carey and Hart, 1846.

Wallace, Lew. *An Autobiography.* 2 vols., New York: Harper and Brothers, 1906.

Way, Fredrick, Jr. *Way's Packet Directory 1848–1983.* Athens: Ohio University Press, 1983.

Webb, Walter P. *The Handbook of Texas.* 2 vols. Austin: Texas State Historical Association, 1952.

Wills, Mary M., and Irwin, Howard S. *Roadside Flowers of Texas.* Austin: University of Texas Press, 1961.

Wislizenus, Adolphus. *Memoir of a Tour to Northern Mexico.* Glorieta, New Mexico: Rio Grande Press, Inc., 1969.

Yater, George H. *Two Hundred Years at the Falls of the Ohio: A History of Louisville and Jefferson County.* Louisville: Pinaire Lithographing Corporation, 1979.

Government Documents

Executive Document No. 13, 31st Congress. "Letter from The Secretary of War, transmitting a report on the route of General Patterson's division from Matamoras to Victoria," December 19, 1850.

Executive Document No. 17, 30th Congress, 1st Session. "Correspondence with General Taylor," January 4, 1848.

Executive Document No. 60, 30th Congress, 1st Session. "Mexican War Correspondence," undated.

Executive Document No. 65, 31st Congress. "Message from The President of the United States communicating the report of Lieutenant Webster of a survey of the gulf coast at the mouth of the Rio Grande," July 27, 1850.

Hughes, George W. (Captain, Corps Topographical Engineers, Chief of the Topographical Staff). Memoir Descriptive of the March of A Division of the United States Army, Under the Command of Brigadier General John E. Wool, San Antonio De Bexar, in Texas, to Saltillo, in Mexico. 31st Congress, 1st Session, Senate Executive Document 32.

Manuscripts and Collections

Bloom, John Porter. "With the American Army into Mexico, 1846–1848." Dissertation, Emory University, Atlanta, 1956.

Curtis, Samuel Ryan, "Diary," Bancroft Library, University of California at Berkeley.

Curtis, Samuel Ryan, "The Letters of," The Huntington Library, Department of Manuscripts, San Marino, California.

Henderson Family Papers, University of Texas Archives.

McDonald, Laurier B., undated letters to Joseph E. Chance.

Michael, Steven Bruce. "Ohio and the Mexican War: Public Response to the 1846–1848 Crisis." Dissertation, Ohio State University, Columbus, 1985.

Mississippi Department of Archives and History, Tax Records and Wills of Jane Edwards and Edwards family of Wilkinson County, Mississippi.

Reilly, Thomas William. "American Reporters and the Mexican War, 1846–1848." Dissertation, University of Minnesota, Minneapolis, 1984.

Spurlin, Charles D., Manuscript on the Mexican War, unpublished.

The Justin Smith Transcripts, Latin American Collection, University of Texas at Austin.

Newspapers

American Flag, Matamoros, Mexico, July, 1846 – July 1848.

Arkansas State Gazette, Little Rock, April 24, 1847.

The Picket Guard, Saltillo, Mexico, April 19, May 10, 1847.
The Vicksburg Whig, Vicksburg, Mississippi, 1846–1847.

Articles

Balboutin, Manuel. "The Battle of Angostura Pass (Buena Vista)." Journal of the Military Service Institution of the United States, vol. 8, 1887.
Balboutin, Manuel. "The Siege of Monterey." Journal of the Military Service Institution of the United States. vol. 8, 1887.
Barringer, Graham A. (ed.). "The Mexican War Journal of Henry S. Lane," Indiana Magazine of History, vol. 53, December 1957.
Bauer, K. Jack. "General John E. Wool's Memoranda of the Battle of Buena Vista." Southwestern Historical Quarterly, vol. 77, no. 1, 1973.
Benham, Henry. "Recollections of Mexico and Buena Vista." Old and New, vol. 3, no. 6, 1871, vol. 4, no. 1, 1872.
Benham, H. W. "A Little More Grape." The Vedette. vol. 2, no. 4, January 1881.
Brown, Walter Lee. "The Mexican War Experiences of Albert Pike and the 'Mounted Devils' of Arkansas," Arkansas Historical Quarterly, vol. 12, Winter, 1953.
Buchanan, A. Russell. "George Washington Trahern: Texan Cowboy Soldier from Mier to Buena Vista." The Southwestern Historical Quarterly, vol. 58, no. 1, July, 1954.
Buley, R. C. "Indiana in the Mexican War," Indiana Magazine of History, vol. 15, September-December, 1919, vol. 16, March, 1920.
Canady, Dayton W. "Voice of the Volunteer of 1847," Journal of the Illinois State Historical Society, vol. 44, Autumn, 1951.
Deas, George. "Reminiscences of the Campaign on the Rio Grande," Dawson's Historical Magazine, vol. 7, no. 1, January, 1870; no. 2, February, 1870; no. 4, April, 1870; no. 5, May, 1870.
Dobie, J. Frank. "Mustang Gray: Fact, Tradition, and Song." Tone the Bell Easy, Publications of the Texas Folk-lore Society, no. 10, 1932.
Engelmann, Otto B. (trans. and ed.). "The Second Illinois in the Mexican War: Mexican War Letters of Adolph Engelmann, 1846–1847," Journal of the Illinois State Historical Society, vol. 26, January, 1934.
Fakes, Turner J., Jr. "Memphis and the Mexican War." West Tennessee Historical Society Papers, vol. 2, 1948.
Kailbourn, Thomas R. "The View from the Ojo de Agua: A Daguerreian Relic of Saltillo, Mexico." Southwestern Historical Quarterly, vol. 95, October, 1991.
Kurtz, Wilbur G., Jr. "The First Regiment of Georgia Volunteers in the

BIBLIOGRAPHY

Mexican War," *Georgia Historical Quarterly*, vol. 27, December, 1943.

Morrison, George S. "Letters from Mexico by George S. Morrison, A Member of Capt. Albert Pike's Squadron," *Arkansas Historical Quarterly*, vol. 16, Winter, 1957.

Pace, Eleanor D. "The Diary and Letters of William P. Rogers, 1846–1862," *Southwestern Historical Quarterly*, vol. 32, 1929.

Pike, Albert. "A Sketch of the Battle of Buena Vista," *Arkansas State Gazette*, Little Rock, Arkansas, April 24, 1847.

Ryan, Daniel J. "Ohio in the Mexican War." *Ohio Archaeological and Historical Quarterly*, vol. 21, April-July, 1912.

Scott, Florence Johnson. "George Washington Clutter in the Mexican War." *Texas Military History*, vol. 4, 1964.

Smith, Justin. "American Rule in Mexico." *American Historical Review*, vol. 23, 1917–1918.

Spurlin, Charles. "Camp Life of Texas Volunteers in the Mexican War." *Military History of Texas and the Southwest*. vol. 15, no. 4, 1967.

Spurlin, Charles. "Mobilization of the Texas Militia for the Mexican War." *Military History of Texas and the Southwest*. vol. 15, no. 3, 1967.

Viola, Herman J. "Zachary Taylor and the Indiana Volunteers." *Southwestern Historical Quarterly*, vol. 72, January, 1969.

Wallace, Lee A., Jr. "The First Regiment of Virginia Volunteers, 1846–1848." *Virginia Magazine of History and Biography*, vol. 77, January, 1969.

Wallace, Lee A., Jr. "Raising a Volunteer Regiment for Mexico, 1846–1847." *North Carolina Historical Review*, vol. 35, January, 1958.

INDEX